STUDIES OF THE INSTITUTE OF WORLD AFFAIRS

THIS STUDY IS PRESENTED IN COLLABORATION WITH
THE CARNEGIE ENDOWMENT FOR INTERNATIONAL PEACE

Military Occupation and the Rule of Law

OCCUPATION GOVERNMENT IN THE RHINELAND, 1918-1923

ERNST FRAENKEL

OXFORD UNIVERSITY PRESS

LONDON   NEW YORK   TORONTO

1944

A WARTIME BOOK

THIS COMPLETE EDITION IS PRODUCED
IN FULL COMPLIANCE WITH THE GOVERN-
MENT'S REGULATIONS FOR CONSERVING
PAPER AND OTHER ESSENTIAL MATERIALS

20329

Printed in the United States of America

Preface

IN the fall of 1942 the Graduate Faculty of Political and Social Science of the New School for Social Research submitted to the Rockefeller Foundation a proposal for a study of the Rhineland occupation after the last war. From such a study, placed in the wider framework of a research project on 'Germany's Position in European Postwar Reconstruction,' significant conclusions could be expected for the tasks of occupation, relief, and reconstruction in Central Europe after this war.

The Rockefeller Foundation acknowledged the importance of the project by granting the financial means for its execution. But before the investigations of the Graduate Faculty had advanced to the particular issue of the Rhineland occupation, the Division of Economics and History of the Carnegie Endowment for International Peace had invited Dr. Ernst Fraenkel to undertake a similar study in the course of disarmament inquiries that it was conducting under the direction of Dr. Sanford Schwarz. In the fall of 1943 the Institute of World Affairs—which carries on the research projects on international problems formerly conducted by the Graduate Faculty—and the Carnegie Endowment for International Peace agreed jointly to sponsor Dr. Fraenkel's work. In December 1943 a preliminary draft was submitted as a confidential memorandum to the government agencies concerned. The present publication contains the results of the investigation in their final form.

It is hardly necessary to state that neither of the sponsoring institutions identifies itself with the views expressed in this book. They are glad, however, to present to a wider public what, in their opinion, is a serious attempt to demonstrate in a scientific manner the many ramifications of a problem that is as complex as it is topical.

Both institutions wish to express their gratitude and appreciation to Miss Elizabeth Todd, Editor of the Institute of World Affairs, to whose critical penetration, sympathetic understanding, and selfless devotion the book owes its present form.

JAMES T. SHOTWELL

Director, Division of Economics and History, Carnegie Endowment for International Peace

ADOLPH LOWE

Executive Director of Research, Institute of World Affairs

Contents

PREFACE BY JAMES T. SHOTWELL AND ADOLPH LOWE, v

INTRODUCTION, ix

PART I. THE ARMISTICE PERIOD

I. INSTITUTIONS OF THE OCCUPYING POWERS, 3

The Occupied Territory, 6
General Administration, 8
Commercial Activities, 15
Judicial System, 21

II. RELATIONS WITH THE OCCUPIED COUNTRY, 25

General Administration, 25
Commercial Activities, 37
Labor, 41
Judicial System, 42

III. PROSECUTION OF WAR CRIMINALS, 47

Legal Background, 49
Allied Prosecutions of Rhineland Residents, 54
A Possibility for the Future, 63

PART II. THE PEACE PERIOD

IV. THE RHINELAND AGREEMENT, 71

V. INSTITUTIONS OF THE OCCUPYING POWERS, 81

The High Commission, 81
Local Representatives of the High Commission, 91
Commercial Activities, 97
Interallied Comparisons, 105

VI. RELATIONS WITH THE OCCUPIED COUNTRY, 111

The Reichskommissar, 111
General Administration, 116

Public Utility Administration, 131
Labor, 135
Social and Economic Organizations, 141
The Collaborationists, 142

VII. ADMINISTRATION OF JUSTICE, 149

Jurisdiction of Military Tribunals and German Courts, 149
Court Procedures and Practices, 162
Civil Cases, 167
Public Law Cases, 171
Powers of Military and German Police, 175

VIII. JURISDICTION OF THE OCCUPYING POWERS, 183

Armistice Period, 183
Peace Period, 189

IX. JUDICIAL REVIEW BY COURTS OF THE OCCUPIED COUNTRY, 207

X. CONCLUSIONS, 225

APPENDIXES

I. TEXT OF THE RHINELAND AGREEMENT, 233

II. SELECTED ORDINANCES OF THE HIGH COMMISSION, 237
Ordinance 1, 237
Ordinance 2, 238
Ordinance 3, 245
Ordinance 5, 246
Ordinance 90, 248

BIBLIOGRAPHY, 249

TABLE OF CASES, 259

INDEX, 261

Introduction

LEOPOLD VON RANKE once remarked that it cannot be the task of a historian to provide statesmen with practical solutions for urgent political problems. He added, however, that history may teach future generations to grasp the deeper significance of their own period.

A study of the Rhineland occupation cannot provide answers directly applicable to the future occupation of Germany, for the problems that will arise at the end of the present war are unique in character. The absence of a responsible German government, the necessity to purge both the German bureaucracy and the leading economic and social groups, the fact that Germany as a whole is likely to be occupied, and not merely a small part of the country—these circumstances, and many others as well, are basically at variance with those that prevailed at the end of the last war.

Nevertheless, an analysis of the Rhineland occupation may prove of some value for understanding the problems that will confront a future occupation regime. Once the isolated facts of that occupation have been reduced to the discussion of a few basic problems, it becomes apparent that the overthrowing of an arbitrary regime by the military force of democratic powers raises issues that cannot be solved by reference to considerations of military expediency alone. The liquidation of a war that is waged as a struggle of law against lawlessness automatically raises the problem of the restoration of law under the peculiar conditions of military occupation.

It is scarcely necessary to emphasize that 'rule of law,' as the term is used in the present study, means that the bearers of public power respect definite rules of jurisdiction and procedure in their governmental and administrative activities—that they recognize those formal principles that are indispensable for the protection of the individual from arbitrary interference with his personal integrity. Attempts have been made to discredit the rule of law as a merely 'formal' concept, but the history of the last twenty-five years provides ample evidence of the short-sightedness of this interpretation. It is rather from its strictly formal character that the rule of law derives its unique dignity and its specific significance as one of the chief safeguards of individual freedom. Attempts have been made, too, to transform the idea of rule of law from a general principle of procedure into specific rules of substantive law, which in practice would be applicable almost exclusively to the protection of vested interests. This abuse of the rule of law for onesided group interests serves only to distort the principle and to obscure its function as one of the basic elements of western civilization.

The rule of law is primarily a principle of constitutional government, intended to protect citizens from despotic measures of their own sovereign. But the question arises whether the basic ideas to which it gives expression are subject to national delimitation. The main concern of the present study is whether a principle that is applicable to national governments, exercising their powers by virtue of national laws, is not also applicable to the regimes of foreign governments that exercise their powers by virtue of international law.

The book deals primarily with the armistice period of occupation after the last war, and the first years of the peacetime regime. When the American troops left the Rhineland, and the French and Belgian armies marched into the Ruhr, early in 1923, the situation changed so basically that the occupation of Germany became a quite different chapter of history.

The circumstances in which this book originated have been briefly described in the Preface. To both sponsoring institutions, the Carnegie Endowment for International Peace and the Institute of World Affairs, the author is deeply indebted for the support and encouragement he has received. In particular he gratefully acknowledges the friendly guidance given him by Dr. Sanford Schwarz, of the Carnegie Endowment, through all stages of the project. The close contact with him opened new insights into general problems of international law and specific problems of military occupation. And to Dr. Adolph Lowe, of the Institute of World Affairs, the author is especially indebted for his encouragement and counsel in the writing of the book and for his efforts in arranging for its publication. He took upon himself the chore of reading the first rough draft of the manuscript, and his constructive criticisms led to a revision of many parts of the book. The stimulating discussions with him are an unforgettable experience for the author. In addition, the manuscript has been read by Professor James T. Shotwell, Professor Walton Hamilton, and Mr. Pierrepont Noyes, the first American High Commissioner in the occupied Rhineland; and they have offered numerous suggestions of great value.

Miss Elizabeth Todd contributed to the book far more than the usual editorial aid. In her untiring efforts she not only corrected and improved the language, but also revised the organization of the book and made numerous suggestions concerning the substance. Her logical mind, her deep interest in the problems discussed in the study, and her infallible sense of language made the discussions with her an intellectual pleasure as well as a continuous source of mental stimulation.

Miss Hedwig Wachenheim relieved the author of the ungrateful task of rectifying all citations.

In the text, bibliographical references have been abbreviated as far as possible; full citations are presented in the bibliography at the end of the book.

ERNST FRAENKEL

Washington, 6 June 1944

PART I

THE ARMISTICE PERIOD

11 November 1918–10 January 1920

I

Institutions of the Occupying Powers

ON 30 June 1930, the last French soldier of the Rhineland occupation army left German soil; on 30 June 1940, the German armies had occupied half of France. Not only the Rhineland occupation itself, which was intended to guarantee France's security, but also the termination of the regime before schedule, which was to encourage the reconciliation of Germany, had failed in its purpose. As a whole, the post-1918 occupation of the Rhineland represents a chapter of modern history in which 'the greatness and misery of a victory' found one of its most tragic expressions.

A future historian will probably not lay much emphasis on the Rhineland occupation as a positive factor contributing to the present war. He is likely to find the historical significance of that episode merely in the negative fact that it did not accomplish its purpose of preventing the Second World War. But if he is interested in historical 'tendencies' as well as in 'facts,' he can find in the Rhineland of the early 1920's the microcosm of most of those forces which during the 1930's were to break through as eruptive powers and ultimately bring about the collapse of the Versailles system. In 1933 an English writer published his memoirs on the Rhineland occupation under the title, *Prelude to Hitler;* with the same accuracy, and on the basis of the same reasoning, the occupation could be called a prelude to the Second World War. In our efforts to prevent a disarmed Germany from once again endangering the security and peace of the world, after another twenty years, we shall do well to view the Rhineland occupation as a symptomatic link in the

3

chain that connects the two great catastrophes of our period.

In its final form that regime was a symbolic mixture of 'realism' and 'idealism.' It represented the exercise of power politics against a conquered enemy, and at the same time, in applying Wilsonian principles to the field of military occupation, it reflected an almost unlimited belief in the force of law. The contradictions between these two tendencies foreshadowed the conflicts that were to undermine, a few years later, the League of Nations and the whole system of international security.

But the conflict between political cynicism and legal idealism is not sufficient to explain the collapse of the Versailles system. The experiment of 1919 was undertaken in the course of a social revolution which the framers of the new order misinterpreted as a merely transitory phenomenon. They honestly believed that the social unrest of the postwar period could easily be overcome by military force and the collaboration of all 'respectable' elements. What became world-famous as appeasement policy, twenty years later, was actually begun early in 1919, when the occupying powers in the Rhineland took the part of the German reactionaries, bureaucrats, and militarists in their fight against the progressive forces of the German democratic revolution.

In a world full of economic conflicts the exercise of military power cannot be isolated from its surrounding social forces. One of the crucial questions of the post-1918 period was whether those who were in control of the power positions, in internal and international business life, would be allowed to abuse the political and military influence of their countries for their own benefit. The Rhineland occupation provides ample evidence of the dangers involved in a military occupation in which the holders of military power consider the furtherance of private business interests a part of their patriotic duty. Business activities based on military power led to a reaction by the victims of these transactions—a reaction in which the social resentment of the underprivileged was inseparably intermingled with the nationalistic aspirations of the vanquished. The occupied Rhenish territory was one of the first regions in western Europe to produce an amalgamation of socialist and nationalist tendencies.

The Rhineland occupation, which was planned as a model of legally restricted exercise of military power, was used by the Germans as one of their most efficient propaganda weapons against the Versailles treaty. By contrasting the procedures that were actually followed in the occupied territory with the principles that had found expression in the programmatic Rhineland Agreement, the Germans tried to convince public opinion in the western democracies that they had fallen victim to an unprecedented deception. Their propaganda against the Rhineland occupation represents a rehearsal of their attacks against the validity of the Versailles treaty and the binding force of the disarmament program. In their campaign against the methods applied by the occupants in the Rhenish territory the Germans realized how strong a propaganda weapon they had at their disposal if they compared the realities accompanying the enforcement of the Versailles treaty with the vague general principles that were supposed to be the moral and legal justifications of those acts.

The astonishing success of the German propaganda campaign was primarily due to the disunity of the nations that participated in the Rhineland occupation. Since France and Belgium, on the one hand, and the United States and Britain, on the other hand, aimed at basically different purposes in the occupied Rhineland, it was relatively easy for Germany to play off one group of occupants against the other. On her own soil Germany learned how to split the 'United Nations' of the First World War. After the ratification of the peace treaty ended the immediate military purposes of the armistice period, France and Belgium desired the Rhineland occupation because they regarded German control of the Rhenish provinces as dangerous to their security; the United States and England participated in the occupation because they considered French control of the Rhineland incompatible with world security. France occupied the Rhineland with a view to separating it from the Reich; the Anglo-American powers occupied the Rhineland with a view to keeping it within the framework of the Reich. As E. H. Carr has pointed out (p. 49), that joint occupation, for mutually incompatible purposes, first brought to the surface the underlying divergence between the French and British attitudes toward Germany, a divergence that played so decisive a role in the twenty years' armistice between Compiègne and Munich.

The Occupied Territory

The area entered by the soldiers of the Allied and Associated Powers, early in December 1918, consisted of all German territory on the left bank of the Rhine, and three bridgeheads of about a 20-mile radius—opposite Cologne, Coblenz, and Mainz—on the right bank. In 1921 an additional 200 square miles or so, the cities of Düsseldorf and Duisburg in the Ruhr basin, was also subjected to occupation. All together this territory amounted to about 12,000 square miles, and contained, according to the last prewar census, nearly 7 million inhabitants—approximately 7 per cent of the post-Versailles area of Germany, and over 11 per cent of its population. The occupied parts of Germany were roughly equivalent to the area of Belgium, though their population was slightly less than that of Belgium.

Two-thirds of the inhabitants of the occupied zones lived in Prussian territory, about 90 per cent of these in the Prussian Rheinland province and the remainder in the Prussian province of Hesse-Nassau. Prussia had an even greater proportion—nearly three-fourths—of the area that was under occupation. The greater part of the remaining fourth was in the Palatinate, a province of Bavaria which was completely occupied. Three other states of the German Reich were affected: Hesse (about half occupied); Baden (the city of Kehl); and Oldenburg (the enclave of Birkenfeld in the Rheinland province).

The occupied territory was divided into four zones. Belgian forces controlled the highly industrialized northwestern zone, which had important mining, textile, and metal centers (Aachen, München-Gladbach, Krefeld, Neuss). The British army occupied Cologne, by far the most important city of the occupied territory, and also the area surrounding that city, with important chemical (Leverkusen) and metal industries (Solingen). There was almost no industry in the American zone, which was primarily agricultural and constituted one of the most famous wine regions of Germany; the city occupied by the American troops was Coblenz, capital of the Rheinland province and significant primarily as an administrative center. The French zone, partly industrial, partly agricultural in character, contained two giant chemical works (in Ludwigshafen and Höchst), one of the leading German automobile factories (Opel), and important machine factories. The Bavarian and Hesse parts of the occupied territory were exclusively under French control, but the Prussian part was divided among all four occupying powers. The Saar Valley district (about 750 square miles), with its vital mining and heavy-industry establishments, was also under French control during the armistice period.

When the soldiers of the occupying armies entered this region they arrived as instruments of government. Henceforth, for a period not yet determined, its administration was to be the responsibility of the victorious nations, under the conditions already laid down for the armistice and subsequently to be determined for the period of peace. In a basic order of 15 November 1918 (562 CR, reprinted in Boyer, p. 239) Marshal Foch declared that the conditions of normal life were to be re-established within the occupied area, and he promised assistance in restoring the usual functioning of schools, churches, courts, hospitals, chambers of commerce, municipal councils, and the other institutions of community organization. Nevertheless, at the moment the armistice was signed, ultimate authority in the Rhineland was transferred to the victorious powers and their agents.

This region, however, composed of parts of five different German states, had of course its own extensive system of local administration, consisting not only of high regional and municipal officials but also of a vast network of offices and agencies concerned with the routine problems of government. And in the process of re-establishing and continuing the customary routines of community life it would have been practically impossible to replace all the existing German agencies and officials and transfer their tasks to representatives of the occupying governments, strangers in the land and unfamiliar with its needs and customs. The only practicable procedure was to retain the German agencies, and to make use of them as organs of administration, under the supervision of the occupation authorities.

This crucial question was settled in the armistice agreement, which declared (Article 5) that the occupied territory should be 'administered by the local authorities under the control of the . . . armies of occupation.' The agreement expressly provided for the retention of 'all civil and military personnel at present employed' on railroads, roads, bridges, telegraph and telephone systems (Article 7), and in his basic order Marshal Foch extended this principle to all officials of the Reich, the states, and the municipalities.

Thus the German bureaucracy was taken over *en bloc* by the occupation authorities. But before its functioning can be understood it is necessary to describe the administrative structure that the occupying powers created to supervise it.

General Administration

In his basic order concerning the armistice period of occupation (Boyer, p. 239), Marshal Foch, supreme commander of the Allied and Associated Powers, referred to the Hague Convention as basis of the supervision to be exercised over the German administrative structure. And he asserted—also in conformance with the Hague Convention—that the existing German laws and regulations would be respected unless they contravened the rights and security of the occupying armies.

The significance of this expression of intention to conform

with the Hague Convention should not be underestimated. During the war the German military machine, in occupation of French and Belgian territory, had flagrantly violated the principles of international law and of common humanity; and there was a substantial body of opinion to the effect that Germany had forfeited her right to enjoy the benefits of the Hague Convention by ignoring the obligations that it entailed (Boyer, pp. 67-71). In these circumstances, a professed adherence to the principles of international law, proclaimed by the French commander in chief, represented a triumph of law over the temptations of revenge. Many critics of the Rhineland occupation, and especially of the French part in it, have failed to recognize that Marshal Foch's attitude on this vital question represented a spirit of generosity and law consciousness which reflected the best traditions of French history. It is true that the occupation did not always conform with the principles laid down at the beginning. But the very fact that they were proclaimed, in the embittered mood of 1918, is of considerable significance.

During the first weeks of the armistice occupation, the Rhineland was under a purely military government. This was at the beginning a necessary expedient, as the armistice of 11 November was concluded for a period of only five weeks, and at that time no one could foresee with certainty whether the war might be renewed after a short period. The first step taken by the commanders of the individual armies was the proclamation of a state of martial law. Thereby the military forces took the responsibility for preserving public order, and the civil liberties of the population were drastically restricted.

From the beginning, the commanding generals of the four armies of occupation possessed a considerable degree of independence. Only those measures requiring action which in ordinary circumstances would derive from a legislature were reserved for the highest command, represented by Marshal Foch. Otherwise the commanders of the individual armies were autonomous in their own territories. The Supreme Command (located in Luxemburg) issued a model ordinance for basic police regulations, and the commanding generals issued their own decrees on the basis of the model draft, making any changes that were necessitated by conditions in their own zones (Nast, 'L'occupation . . .' p. 146; Hunt, pp. 40-41).

As early as 14 November a special co-ordinating agency, for the administration of the whole occupied territory, was created in the general staff of Marshal Foch. This agency had special sections for administrative, diplomatic, economic, financial, judicial, and legislative questions. Its actual head was Paul Tirard, a French civilian who later played a decisive role in the peacetime phases of the Rhineland occupation. On 22 December he was entrusted by Marshal Foch with the power of *contrôleur-général*, and in that capacity he began to appoint to his staff not only officers but also civilian officials—a development that became increasingly evident during the armistice period. In the words of Jean Rousseau, a legal adviser and staff member of the French occupation authorities (*La Haute Commission* . . . p. 25), 'This development was characterized by a progressive substitution of military control by the control of civil agencies, whose dependence on military authorities became less and less marked and tended to be replaced by direct subordination to the Allied governments.'

At the beginning the commanding generals met once a month in order to co-ordinate the measures that had been taken in the various zones, and the contrôleur général soon began to arrange meetings of the officials entrusted by the commanding generals with the handling of civilian affairs. But in spite of such attempts at co-operation there were difficulties and tensions between the Supreme Command and the individual commands that were never completely overcome. 'The regulations, so exactly laid down by the Marshal, were not always followed . . . In some cases, no attempt was ever made to enforce the regulations of the High Command, when they lay counter to the national policy of the army in question' (Hunt, p. 43; see also Allen, *Occupation*, p. 34).

The organization of the military and administrative agencies that executed the orders of the general staffs was entrusted to the individual armies. Consequently, rather different systems of administration existed during the armistice period in the various zones of the occupied territory.[1]

The French army of occupation created a special bureau of civil affairs, which was entrusted with practically all matters of military government. The chief of that bureau was the immediate superior of four 'district' administrators, and those in turn supervised the activities of the administrators in the urban and rural 'circles,'[2] all these officials forming the 'Corps des Affaires Civiles.' The French system, like the British and the Belgian, was from the beginning based on the territorial units of the country, not on the structure of the military organization.

The British somewhat decentralized their administration by entrusting authority to the commanders of the individual British armies rather than to the British army headquarters. In the general staff of each army a special section was created and staffed with persons trained in civil affairs, and this method was followed throughout the administrative structure, down to the lowest unit.

In the Belgian army three new sections were created in the chief general staff, and were put under the immediate supervision of the highest military commander in the Belgian zone. The first was concerned with administrative control, the second with military court problems, the third with economic questions. The Belgians appointed civil administrators for the two 'districts' and each of the 'circles' in the area under their super-

[1] General Allen of the United States Army has devoted to this subject a special chapter of his book on *The Rhineland Occupation;* pp. 90-101.

[2] In this study the German term *Kreis* is literally translated as 'circle,' because that was the practice of the occupation authorities in their official publications; the word could be roughly translated as 'county.'

vision, and, in addition, special contrôleurs for civil affairs were attached to the staff of each army division.

In contrast to their allies, the Americans first organized their administration on the basis of tactical military units rather than according to the administrative districts of the occupied country. This system was found to be inefficient, however, and was abandoned in June 1919, in favor of the other method. Each army commander had a special staff section for civil affairs, and within these sections departments were created for public works and utilities, fiscal affairs, sanitation and public health, schools and charitable institutions, and legal questions.

In his basic order 562 CR, Marshal Foch declared that these military agencies had the power to direct and control the German administration. But the distinction between 'direction' and 'control' remained unexplained. In the 10th French Army the officials of these agencies were called *contrôleurs*, in the 8th they were called *administrateurs*, though their functions were almost identical. Theoretically the German officials were no more than agents of the occupation authorities; actually both administrators and controllers confined themselves to supervising the German bureaucracy.

The administrative structure thus far discussed was merely the conventional machinery of postwar military occupation. This distribution of functions corresponded to what had existed after the Franco-Prussian war and even earlier conflicts, and the problems had been analyzed in a classic study (by Raymond Robin) shortly before the outbreak of war in 1914. The occupying armies were well prepared to handle such tasks, which had primarily the character of police functions.

It soon became evident, however, that the magnitude of the task in the Rhineland had been underestimated. New and unforeseen difficulties arose, caused by the fact that war had changed its character. The armistice of Fontainebleau in 1871 had ended a military duel; the armistice of Compiègne in 1918 brought to an end the first total war. An occupation regime after a total war must confront the effects produced by such a war—the strains and dislocations that have appeared in every area of living.

The military agencies responsible for the drafting of the armistice of November 1918, and for the first steps taken in the occupied Rhineland, had not wholly realized that the semi-starved people of that territory, whose lives up to that moment had been wholly formed by the demands of war, could not be left alone to work out their own salvation in regard to economic, social, and financial problems. So far as these were concerned, the armistice agreement merely declared that 'No measure of a general or official character shall be taken which would have as a consequence the depreciation of industrial establishments or a reduction of their personnel' (Article 6). This clause was negative in character, and merely assured protection from arbitrary interference with the economic life of the population. It did not touch upon the problems of mass unemployment, social unrest, and hunger, or upon the economic and financial collapse that threatened the population of that highly industrialized territory, especially after it had been administratively separated from the remainder of Germany.

During the first weeks of the occupation no systematic attempt was made to solve such problems. At the beginning, particularly urgent economic matters were handled by the military authorities; thus several French generals, on their own initiative, distributed large quantities of food to the population, and their example was soon followed by the commanders of the other armies (Tirard, p. 280). In the early months of 1919, however, many Inter-Allied committees (listed in Bane and Lutz, p. 354) were set up outside the Rhineland to deal with economic questions. Separate committees were created for food problems; for the financial problems arising out of commercial relations between Germany and the Allies; for blockade questions; for dealing with the commercial aspects of the food deliveries; and for various other similar functions.

It soon became evident that the economic problems of the Rhineland could not be effectively dealt with by such a variety of authorities. Not only were there too many of them but their functions overlapped and they were guided by no common policy. A further handicap to smooth operation was the fact that they were made up partly of military officers and partly of civilian administrators, with the United States and England represented by civilians and France by army officers.

The Supreme Economic Council of the victorious powers took this matter in its own hands and recommended to the Supreme War Council that an Inter-Allied commission be set up in the Rhineland as co-ordinating agency for food, economic, and industrial questions. The Supreme War Council accepted this suggestion, and decided that the new agency should be civilian in character. Tirard, contrôleur général of the occupied territories, was appointed chairman, and it was explicitly provided that he should hold both positions. The new body, called the Inter-Allied Rhineland Commission, held its first meeting on 29 April 1919, and in the next months it became the most important element in the administrative structure of the occupied territory. Though it was at first restricted to economic matters it was soon entrusted also with administrative functions that had hitherto belonged to the military agencies. Between 28 June 1919, the day the peace treaty was signed, and 10 January 1920, the day of its ratification, the Inter-Allied Rhineland Commission —although it still acted in the name of the chief commander, Marshal Foch—actually gave directions to the occupying armies, both in economic and in administrative matters ('La France sur le Rhin,' 1929, p. 125). Thus in the course of a few months the center of administrative activities and responsibilities shifted from military to civilian agencies—from agencies concerned primarily with military control to those whose jurisdiction extended throughout the economic field. Purely military occupation had proved inadequate as a means of liquidating total war.

After peace had been restored the Inter-Allied Rhineland Commission became the highest administrative authority in the occupied Rhineland. There was an important difference, however, between the armistice body and the Inter-Allied Rhineland High Commission of the peace period. The former, though it was the highest governing agency, derived its power from the military, whereas the peacetime High Commission was the sovereign power in the Rhineland, superior even to the occupying armies.

COMMERCIAL ACTIVITIES

The provisioning of the Rhineland during the armistice period represented a mixture of charity, business, and high politics, and, as a result, commercial relations between the victorious nations and the occupied territory constituted an extremely complicated situation. The population was in desperate need of food and other provisions; the factories had to have raw materials; and even finished goods were required in an economy that had been stripped to the bone by wartime requirements. On the other hand, all combatants in the war had enacted Trading with the Enemy acts, and had subjected the economic life of their citizens to strict rules of supervision, restriction, and direction. Moreover, the armistice agreement declared, as a matter of principle, that 'the existing blockade conditions . . . shall remain unchanged' (Article 26); the blockade, which crippled economic life in the occupied country, was desired as a means of pressure for the coming peace negotiations.

But the armistice provided for a relaxation of the blockade in regard to food shipments to Germany, such deliveries to be left to the discretion of the victorious powers. In pursuit of this provision the Brussels Food Conference, which was a meeting of several Inter-Allied committees, decided on 14 March 1919 to send Germany 270,000 tons of foodstuffs, and in addition to allow her to import, monthly, 70,000 tons of edible fats and 300,000 tons of bread grain during the period May through August of that year (*Der Waffenstillstand*, vol. 2, p. 83). The conference declared that the governments of the Allied and Associated nations should have the final decision on how these foodstuffs should be divided between the occupied and unoccupied territories, and provided that in the occupied territory the military officials should distribute the food immediately to the local authorities.

In addition, it was possible, of course, for Allied businessmen to export goods to Germany, if they were licensed to do so by their own government. German firms and individuals that wished to do business with foreign countries also had to have a license for that purpose, but, as will be discussed in the next chapter, the German foreign-trade agencies that would have supervised such matters were rendered virtually ineffective in the Rhineland. The licensing of German businessmen was entrusted to economic boards of the various military commands, and a special committee of the administrative section of Marshal Foch's staff served as co-ordinating agency. This agency, known from its seat of operations as the Luxemburg Commission, existed until May 1919, when it was incorporated into the Inter-Allied Rhineland Commission. It was charged with the distribution of raw materials for the factories in the Rhineland, with the sale of German products to nationals of the Allied and Associated countries, and with all the administrative work that arose out of the development of controlled commercial relations between nations that were legally still at war. The agencies of the different commands retained, however, a considerable degree of autonomy in these matters (Allen, *Occupation*, p. 40; Hunt, p. 47); their activities varied greatly in the different zones of occupation.

The situation had a particular political significance for France. Her peace aim was the Rhine as Germany's western frontier, and it is in the light of this consideration that a French decree of 15 January 1919 (*Journal officiel de la République Française*, 1919, p. 540) proves to be one of the most important documents for understanding the history of the Rhineland occupation in the armistice period. This decree provided that exemptions from the French Trading with the Enemy Act of 27 September 1914 could be granted for commercial relations with residents of the occupied territory, and thus France, before the blockade was lifted or the armistice was ended, took active steps toward a large-scale resumption of trade with the Rhineland.

The economic agencies that functioned in the French zone under the Luxemburg Commission were known as *sections économiques*. In addition to granting licenses to German firms for business transactions with French merchants these agencies acted as 'true commercial offices with the principal task of informing and guiding French businessmen, who were eager to trade with the Rhinelanders' (De Pange, p. 209). They required the German manufacturers to answer detailed questionnaires concerning their actual stocks, their needs, and their prices, and on the basis of these official investigations they informed French businessmen about the financial status of the German producers. Many French merchants made use of these facilities, with 'brilliant' results (Aulneau, p. 345). The *sections économiques*, in the words of another French author, gained 'a considerable reputation in the region and a perfect knowledge even of its smallest resources' (Isambert, p. 443).

The activities of these agencies and the business methods of the French merchants were subjected to severe criticism. It was said that the military authorities of a postwar occupation were using their influence and power in order to stimulate the commercial interests of their fellow nationals and the political interests of their government; and in the words of General Allen (*Occupation*, p. 93) this sort of activity 'scarcely seemed germane to a holding force.'

The Germans characterized the *sections économiques* as centers of economic espionage (Wachendorf, p. 103) and as instruments of a French attempt to blackmail German businessmen for the sake of France's power politics. German public opinion indicted the French for commercial dishonesty. The French, said the Germans, made use of the *sections économiques* in order to get rid of military stocks which they could not sell to anyone else, such as spoiled fat, wet cigarettes, rusty cans of corned beef, and the like. The French were accused of sending tremendous amounts of luxury goods to the occupied territory and at the same time, because the French manufacturers feared German competition, preventing the Germans from exporting goods of their own to France. Referring to the French trade policy as the chief reason for the 'hole in the west,' the open wound in the German economic body, the Germans made France responsible for the increasing process of German inflation.

In the German denunciations of the *sections économiques* there was a mixture of fact and exaggeration. The inflation, for example, cannot be attributed to the 'hole in the west,' even though that phenomenon played an important part. But it is noteworthy that during the first period of the occupation, German anti-French propaganda was based primarily on economic arguments.

There were French writers too, however, who criticized the activities of these agencies. Thus Georges Blondel, economist at the Sorbonne, had this to say, in 1921 (*La Rhénanie . . .* pp. 201 ff.):

A considerable number of French businessmen entered the Rhine territory along with our armies; their number has been estimated at more than 6,000. Many of these devoted themselves to activities which, though undoubtedly profitable to them personally, must be classified in reality as smuggling. They provided Germany with many things she was lacking, such as oil, fats, soap, liquor, rubber, of which the blockade had deprived her for so long a time . . . It must be admitted that the renewal of our relations with Germany did not take place in the open. It rather took the form of what the Germans call *Schleichhandel*, contraband trade, which undoubtedly gave to certain persons an opportunity to make a lot of money, but led to great disarrangements. The . . . profiteers, interested only in moneymaking, sold a considerable amount of goods of poor quality. These methods discredited the good reputation of French merchandise. Our commercial relations were not of the kind they should have been.

Blondel repeated an estimate that 'in the course of a few months business transactions of more than 3 billion [francs] were carried out.' But the State Secretary of the Reich Ministry of Trade estimated the illegal imports from spring to October 1919 at 17 billion marks, including 4 billion for cigarettes alone and 9 billion for other luxury goods (Grünfeld, p. 83, note 1).

Lebaud, a retired French colonel who had for several years commanded the French garrison in Kaiserslautern, declared in 1926, in a remarkable article on 'Why Germany is Nationalist' (p. 254): 'The occupied territory was regarded as a richly laden plum tree to be shaken for our benefit. Were we not in a conquered country? Didn't the Boche have to pay? . . . The number of soft jobs and fat pickings, especially during the inflation of the mark, seemed limitless.'

Needless to say, the flood of illegal trade that passed through the 'hole in the west' would not have been possible without the co-operation of certain German businessmen. As Kahn, columnist of the *Frankfurter Zeitung*, put it in December 1919:

It is our misfortune that the French are importing over our western frontier the most useless stuff for a consideration of paper marks. Suffering from anaemia, we are deprived by this method of our last drop of blood . . . these measures represent also a misfortune for France . . . But who compelled Germany to buy all these goods for prices that . . . are considerably overvalued? It should be admitted that frequently economic need demanded these transactions, as in the case of clothes. Also, however, an unrestricted hunger for profits and the desire of the population for luxury goods frequently stood behind these activities. [Kahn, p. 17.]

The same writer castigated the banks and the big commercial firms for having given financial backing to these irresponsible business methods, and indicted them for economic stupidity.

The other governments followed quite other methods in their handling of commercial relations. The Belgians, their own economy in a chaotic condition, appear to have conducted little trade with Germany in this period. And the Americans and British, desiring above all an orderly Rhineland that would remain a part of Germany, were far more scrupulous in their commercial relations. The Americans, for example, in deciding on the grants of licenses to German firms, delegated to local chambers of commerce the examination of the companies (Allen, *Occupation*, p. 40; Hunt, pp. 47-8). Also, they waited until 14 July 1919, the day on which the blockade was officially lifted, before granting general licenses to Americans for trade with Germany.

And the Americans and the British presented the French with formidable competition. By providing Germany with necessary goods rather than with products which in the peculiar situation of that time could not be sold to any other customers, the British and American businessmen greatly strengthened their position in the German market. Thus for example in Wiesbaden and Mainz, in the French zone itself, no fewer than 500 French firms had established themselves by the end of 1919, but they were confronted with considerable difficulty on account of the British and American competition (Malaurie, p. 103).

German countermeasures began as early as May 1919, when several German cartels proclaimed a boycott against French firms (Bane and Lutz, p. 449). This was the first step in the fight between German economic power and French military and political strength, a fight that was to play a tremendous role during the next years. Once the peace had been ratified, the French attempts to conquer the German markets through unorthodox business transactions met the resistance of the highly organized German economic system.

The *sections économiques* were not the only institutions that were indicted by the Germans for 'using their official positions to obtain trade secrets' (Allen, *Occupation*, p. 67). Similar reproaches were raised against the *sections de contrôle industriel*, which were subdivisions of the Armistice Commission, created by the Belgian and French military authorities for the purpose of examining German factories in the occupied territory and determining whether use was being made of machines and other goods that had been removed by the German armies from northern France and Belgium. These commissions were composed of very active engineers who worked under the command of an efficient officer.

French trade policy made for a tightening of control over German economic activity in the occupied territory during the armistice period. Once the Rhineland had been provided not only with fats, meat, bread, and vegetables, but also with cigarettes, soap, chocolate, liquor, wines, and silk stockings, the question arose how trade could be prevented between the occupied and unoccupied parts of the country. Eager to uphold the blockade against unoccupied Germany, the French extended their control to such fields as banks and commercial enterprises, which at the beginning of the occupation had not been subjected to supervision (Rousseau, *La Haute Commission* . . . p. 17; Aulneau, p. 298; Boyer, p. 94).

Since no proper methods for the handling of economic questions had been planned in advance, they had to be improvised. And it could scarcely be said that during the armistice period of the Rhineland occupation they were improvised either wisely or well. The 'hole in the west' is ample evidence of the unpreparedness, inability, and unwillingness to handle the most difficult problems that arose in connection with the occupation. As far as economic questions were concerned, the armistice occupation was one of lawlessness.

JUDICIAL SYSTEM

The judicial process is essentially different from other forms of administration, for it is subject to no orders from superiors. Administrative agencies of the executive branch of government can be subjected to outside supervision and control without changing their basic structure, because in any case they function on the principle of hierarchical authority. The activities of the courts, however, can be only accepted or rejected; if the independence of the judiciary is to be respected at all, the courts cannot be subjected to interference. For this reason an occupation regime must create its own courts for all litigation that it is not willing to entrust to the free functioning of the courts of the occupied country.

In the Rhineland two types of courts—military tribunals and provost courts—were created for cases of this kind occurring during the armistice period. They were provided for in an instruction of Marshal Foch of 15 November 1918 (reprinted in De Jaer, p. 72), the principles of which were approved by the commanders of the individual armies on 22 November. This instruction recognized the autonomy of each army with regard to all problems connected with the creation and functioning of such courts, and declared that procedure should be in accordance with the national laws and customs of each individual army.

The provost courts had jurisdiction in all cases arising out of violations of the police regulations enacted by the occupying armies, and could inflict punishments up to six months in jail or a 5,000 mark fine. It was up to the prosecutor to decide whether a specific case should be brought to a provost court or to a military tribunal; the latter, of course, was not restricted to such relatively mild sentences. The decisions of the American provost courts were subject to confirmation by the military commander, and could be revoked, mitigated, or commuted by him. In April 1919 this idea was adopted by Marshal Foch, who then granted to each convicted person the right of informal appeal to the highest commander of the army concerned.

The military tribunals enforced the criminal law of their respective nations. Questions of procedure and evidence were regulated by the codes of military procedure and the general legal principles of the particular nation; Inter-Allied military tribunals were unknown during the whole course of the occupation. In criminal cases the military tribunals had complete jurisdiction over the members of the occupying armies, and partial jurisdiction over the residents of the occupied territory: if such persons committed crimes against an occupying army as a whole or its individual members, they were subject to arraignment before a military tribunal. In some cases of this kind, however, the tribunal allowed jurisdiction to revert to the German courts. Thus, for example, a young German boy in the Wiesbaden area stole goods belonging to the French army. But since French statutes forbade criminal proceedings against juveniles, the boy could not be arraigned before a French military tribunal. Therefore the jurisdiction of the German courts revived, and the boy was sentenced in accordance with German law for a crime committed on German territory—a judgment that was confirmed by the German Supreme Court (Reichsgericht) on 25 November 1921 (JW 1923, vol. 52, p. 184).

In the armistice period no special tribunals existed for civil cases. Since the German courts could claim no jurisdiction over persons who belonged to the occupying forces, German plaintiffs in civil cases could sue such persons—if at all—only in courts where the defendants were domiciled (Niboyet, p. 51). No provision was made, nor does any seem to have been needed, for civil cases in which the plaintiff was a member of the armed forces.

In his basic instruction on judicial questions Marshal Foch declared explicitly that no penalty should be inflicted except by ordinary court procedure (De Jaer, p. 72). In regard to police violations, however, this provision was not followed in the French area of occupation until after 31 January 1919. Until that time the French generals, making use of their prerogatives as military commanders, reserved for themselves the right to inflict punishment when police regulations were violated by the population (Niboyet, p. 48; Schweisguth, p. 109; Cornier, p. 66; Nast, 'L'occupation . . .' p. 150). It may be mentioned that during the German wartime occupation of France and Belgium, the German generals, too, had assumed the power to inflict punishments on the inhabitants of the occupied territory without court procedures,[3] and therefore the early abandonment of this practice in the Rhineland is particularly noteworthy.

The recognition of due process was confined, however, to cases involving actual violation of law or of regulations. When residents of the occupied territory, though violating no law, engaged in conduct that was considered reprehensible, the military commanders had the right to inflict administrative sanctions—such as expulsion from the occupied territory, the closing of shops or enterprises, or the infliction of collective fines on whole units, particularly municipalities (Cornier, p. 67). In such cases no legal remedies existed. The military tribunals were not entitled to issue writs, such as mandamus or injunction, by means of which the individual could be protected from arbitrary interference with his personal liberties; nor could they exercise the functions of administrative tribunals in the sense of continental law. Thus the purely administrative acts of the military authorities were not subject to judicial review.

It is to be remembered, however, that during the armistice period a state of siege existed in the occupied Rhineland, and that authoritarian discretion is a necessary consequence of martial law. In a special instruction of 26 March 1919, Marshal Foch suggested that the commanding generals restrict the imposition of collective fines to serious cases in which the citizens of the municipality involved had either sympathized with or rendered assistance to persons responsible for hostile acts.

[3] According to a German judge, Helmuth Mende (p. 225), no less than 242,332 punishments were inflicted by the German authorities in Belgium from 1 January to 31 December 1917. Of this astonishing number, only 7,746 were inflicted by virtue of ordinary military court procedure; 4,796 were 'protective custodies,' and the remainder were inflicted outside the courts by the military commanders and officials, under the authorization of the German Governor General.

II

Relations with the Occupied Country

THE fourteen months between the signing of the armistice and the ratification of the peace treaty were for Germany a period of utmost confusion. Nerves and physical strength were exhausted. The political situation, when not in actual upheaval, was very precariously balanced. And the transformation of industry from war to peace production was seriously hampered by the lack of materials and continual interruptions of work. War weariness and hunger and the shock of defeat had disrupted the functioning of the entire nation.

It was in this situation that the armies of the victorious powers exercised their authority in the Rhineland, through the instrumentalities described in the previous chapter. And it remains now to describe how those institutions functioned during the armistice period in relation to the institutions and activities of the occupied territory.

GENERAL ADMINISTRATION

The armistice provision (Article 5) that the Rhineland should be administered by 'local authorities,' under the control of the occupation armies, raised a question of the utmost importance. Did the term 'local' mean all authorities that were located in the occupied territory, or only those that were 'local' in character? Even under the second interpretation there were serious problems, because in Germany some of the most important local units are at the same time district agencies of the central government. This is particularly true of the 'circles.' The president of a circle, who is known as the Landrat, is not only the execu-

tive officer of an important local unit but is also an agent of the
central government, appointed by it and subject to its supervision. Even the city circles, which enjoy far greater independence than the rural, are not autonomous organizations in the
Anglo-American sense. This coexistence of local and state agencies characterizes almost every level of the German administrative hierarchy, and therefore on the interpretation of the term
'local' depended the politically crucial question whether the
central governmental agencies, domiciled outside the occupying
armies' immediate sphere of influence, were to remain in control
of their local subdivisions.

The German armistice delegation immediately raised this
question, after it had been presented with the original draft of
the armistice. And its head, State Secretary Erzberger, in his
formal reply to the armistice conditions, suggested that Article 5
be supplemented by an additional section which should read as
follows: 'Notwithstanding the foregoing provisions the unified
character of the legislation as well as of the administration . . .
of the German Reich shall remain unchanged.' Marshal Foch
answered that it did not seem proper to supplement the text by
such an amendment, but he added that the wording of the armistice agreement did not entail a change of the German administrative organization (*Der Waffenstillstand*, vol. I, p. 27).

Thus not only the subordinate but also the leading administrative officials were allowed to remain in office, and even certain political representatives as well, such as the governor of
the Rheinland province and the presidents of the various districts and circles. This recognition of various governmental
agents was particularly remarkable as in Germany these representatives, unlike other officials of the bureaucracy, could be removed from office for mere political considerations.

Within a few months the French were to realize the significance of the decision not to interfere with the hierarchical, centralized German administrative system, for the German civil
servants, wholly dependent on the central governments in Berlin

and Munich, vehemently opposed all separatist movements. If only local authorities had been recognized, local patriotism might have triumphed over national interests.

Needless to say, the recognition of all officials did not at all mean that their jobs were guaranteed. The idea of vested rights for civil servants—so deeply rooted in German legal institutions and popular feeling—and the various legal protections from dismissal are contrary to the conditions of a state of martial law. During the armistice period the occupying armies recognized no legal restriction on their power to dismiss civil servants without cause, and even to expel them from the occupied territory. On the other hand, during this period the military authorities made little use of their power to appoint German civil servants, although they insisted, as a matter of principle, upon their right to do so (a decision concerning such an appointment is published in the High Commission's *Gazette*, 1920, No. XI-XII, p. 97).

One reason for the wholesale recognition of all resident German officials was the well-known character of the German bureaucracy as strictly disciplined and wholly obedient to those in power, regardless of party or creed. It may be noted incidentally—and this consideration is of the utmost importance—that it is highly doubtful that this attitude persists to any appreciable extent today; in Nazi Germany the officials are shaped by political education rather than by the quasi-military traditions of their service.

Technical considerations constituted another reason why it was decided not to touch the structure of the German administrative system. Under the conditions that then prevailed it would have been practically impossible to administer the Rhineland with only the help of local administrative units. Plans for the demobilization of the army were prepared by the central government, and the German Armistice Delegation very ably stressed the difficulties that might arise if the central authorities were prevented from supervising demobilization in the occupied territory. This argument, addressed to military leaders, underlined the military aspect of the problem, but even more convincing arguments existed in regard to the food and raw-material situation. Germany's whole economic policy was based on 'planning' and central authority, and anarchy could hardly have been avoided if the central government had not been allowed to co-ordinate the activities of administrative agencies in the occupied territory with those in the unoccupied parts of the Reich.

But there were also political reasons behind the decision to retain the old personnel of the German administrative system. Immediately before the armistice negotiations had started, the revolutionary movements which spread over Central Europe late in 1918 had led to the overthrow of the German monarchical constitution and the creation of local 'workers' and soldiers' councils' all over the country. These councils originated in the necessity, amid the general breakdown, for some kind of organization. For the most part they were influenced by the unions and the socialist parties, the only parts of the German population that had opposed the nationalistic tendencies of the imperial government. In the words of John W. Davis, American Ambassador in London, 'there seems to be clear evidence that the great majority in the Workmen's and Soldiers' Councils, under the influence mainly of the soldiers, are strongly in favor of orderly, constructive, republican constitutionalism and federalism' (*Paris Peace Conference*, vol. 2, p. 126).

During the short period of their existence, the workers' and soldiers' councils fulfilled quite different functions. Up to 17 December 1918, they regarded themselves as the sole bearers of state power, and in some communities they replaced the most extreme representatives of the old regime with new and less reactionary officials. On 17 December, however, it was decided, at a general congress of the councils (*see* Allgemeiner Kongress . . .), to substitute the sovereign power of a democratically elected National Assembly for the revolutionary situation that had prevailed during the first weeks after the collapse of the German army. While a minority of the members, under the influence of the Russian revolution, attempted to continue the councils as a political institution, the majority of the councils followed the line of the moderate Social Democratic and trade-union leaders, as expressed in the decision of 17 December. Thereafter the councils confined themselves, in the main, to watching over the activities of the regular authorities.

The situation was quite different in the various parts of the country. It was mainly in central Germany and southern Bavaria that the councils were opposed to a relinquishment of their powers; in most parts of western, southern, and northern Germany they abided by the decision of the December congress. The population of the occupied territory belonged politically to the moderate part of the Reich, and included very few supporters of the Independent Socialists and the Spartacists, forerunners of the Communist party. As a matter of principle, however, the occupying powers objected to the councils, and refused to recognize even the few changes in administrative personnel that the councils had effected before the troops had entered the Rhineland.

General Fayolle, commander of the French armies in the Palatinate and Hesse, decided that the new councils could not be recognized because they were contrary to public order (Nast, 'L'occupation . . .' p. 148; Cornier, p. 49). Posters of the councils were removed, and in many communities the councils themselves were dissolved. In Saarbruck the French punished the head of the local state railway agency because he had applied in his district the eight-hour-day statute enacted during the first days by the revolutionary government in Berlin (Nationalversammlung, vol. 326, p. 197). 'The first act of the British was to demand to see that the properly constituted civil authority and the Burgermeisters reappeared from hiding and once more took over the reins in the *Rathäuser*' (Reynolds, p. 34).

In Darmstadt, capital of Hesse, the officers of the returning German army had been expelled by the soldiers, and the soldiers' council had taken command of the troops. One of its first steps was the discharge of all men who lived in the territories that were going to be occupied by the Allies. But in the early part of December hundreds of these men suddenly appeared in Darmstadt and informed the soldiers' council that the French army did not recognize the certificates of discharge signed by the council. The French had threatened to treat as prisoners of war all former soldiers who were not in possession of a certificate of discharge signed by an officer of the old army. Under this pressure it was necessary for the local soldiers' council to negotiate with the former officers. The latter refused to sign the certificates unless they were generally recognized as officers, and the soldiers' council was compelled to capitulate.

The French General Mangin, in an interview granted to representatives of the local Socialist party in Mainz, was asked why France, the motherland of the democratic revolution, did not recognize the revolutionary and republican councils. The general is reported to have answered as follows (Schweisguth, p. 99): 'Sir, you are very young revolutionaries. You have been a republic for only a month. We French, on the other hand, had our revolution more than a century ago. When you have had a little more experience you will appreciate what we have known for a long time: in revolutions what first mounts to the surface is scum. That is exactly what your councils of workers and soldiers are. That is why we old revolutionaries will have nothing to do with you.'

By recognizing exclusively the functionaries of the old regime as the legitimate authorities to deal with, the commanding generals of the occupying armies threw their influence not only on the side of law and order but also on the side of the very elements of the population that represented the militarism and nationalism at the roots of the war itself. For the old bureaucracy, despite its 'objectivity' and 'non-political' dedication to its duties, was drawn primarily from the conservative middle classes, and constituted a privileged caste not greatly different in spirit from the officer corps of the old army. When today one looks back at these events, it is evident that the appeasement policy toward German nationalism began even before the German nationalists realized what a tremendous chance was being offered them.

The German military authorities and reactionary forces were well aware of the opportunity that was given them by the attitude of the Allied military authorities. In the middle of December 1918 the German High Command ordered the dissolution of all workers' and soldiers' councils in the neutral zone on the right bank of the Rhine, east of the occupied territory; the commanding general of the Westphalian district justified this step as a 'protective measure,' taken exclusively in the interest of the members of these councils. Wolff's news agency had spread the rumor, which was not contradicted by the German High Command, that in the neutral zone all members of the councils would be arrested by the Allied authorities. The rumor had no basis whatever, except the well-known dislike of the occupying armies for the representatives of the German revolution. It is interesting, however, that the mistrust of the Allies was so strong that in many places the members of the councils fell victim to this political manœuvre and decided on dissolution. The significance of the manœuvre is indicated by the fact that the territory affected included such cities as Düsseldorf, Duisburg, Mülheim, Gelsenkirchen, and Essen—the heart of the Ruhr basin and the center of German mining and heavy industries. It was a shrewd plan to exploit at once the Allied generals' fear of the German revolution and the German revolutionaries' fear of the Allied generals (see Allgemeiner Kongress . . . pp. 51, 124, 194-5).

In considering the attitude of the military authorities on this question it should not be overlooked that an army of occupation holding territory in the throes of revolution is faced with highly complicated political, technical, and legal problems. In an interesting study on 'The Relations of Invaders to Insurgents,' Thomas Baty has formulated very clearly the questions that arise when, under the eyes of an occupant, two or more groups engage in an open struggle for power over the occupied country. 'Is it quite adequate,' he asks (p. 978), 'to say that the decision must be postponed until the force of the invading power is withdrawn? Is "the sacred right of revolution" suspended indefinitely by invasion? . . . Must everything, save for the exigencies of the invading forces, be left in *status quo?* In short, must we say that because the test of force is inapplicable, we are left with no test?' Baty, while granting that it is easier to raise such questions than to solve them, is against permitting any change of government; otherwise, he holds, the occupant may be tempted to turn the possibility of change to his own advantage (p. 979). Nevertheless, the fact remains that a decision in favor of the traditional forces, in suppression of the opposition, may be as unneutral as open intervention in the latter's favor. As Talleyrand said, 'Nonintervention is difficult to define; it is almost the same as intervention.'

As long as it is still an open question whether the old traditional regime or the 'higher law' of the revolutionary groups represents the true law of the occupied country, the occupant is free to decide what part he will take in the internal struggle for power. Actually, in the absence of a rule of international law governing the situation, the occupying power, confronted with a revolution in the occupied country, is likely to be guided by considerations of military expediency and of its own political interest.

Late in 1918, when the military occupation authorities in Germany frowned on the workers' and soldiers' councils, technical and military considerations were important factors in their attitude. Thus Colonel Hunt (p. 248) justified the refusal to deal with the councils on the ground that billeting could be more smoothly handled through the experienced bureaucrats. The French Colonel Schweisguth (p. 99) called the councils 'soviets,' and declared that their primary purpose was 'to Bolshevize the Allied armies.' This opinion seems to have been held by many other commanding officers of the French army, and certainly French opposition to the councils was most outspoken.

American diplomats did not share Schweisguth's views, and even expressed sympathy with the Ebert Government (*Paris Peace Conference*, vol. 2, Bullitt report, pp. 99-101, and Dresel report, pp. 134-5). Also the American military authorities, in failing to recognize the councils, may have been motivated by a desire to co-ordinate their attitude with that of the Ebert Government. It was an open secret in those days that several leaders of the moderate socialists were privately opposed to the councils. Today it is impossible to say whether the American military authorities were primarily motivated by a sincere belief that non-recognition of the councils in the occupied territory corresponded to the true intentions of the leading men in the German Government; or whether they simply overlooked the political implications of their decision and treated a highly political problem as if it were a technical one; or whether their decision was affected by the anti-revolutionary trend which was so strong in those days in the United States.

The attitude of the French generals toward the representatives of the German revolution is fully understandable only in the light of France's Rhineland policy. On 29 November 1918, Jusserand, the French Ambassador in Washington, presented to the American Secretary of State a preliminary study on various peace problems which contains the interesting statement that 'even now one may notice the antagonism of the Centralist tendency, which was that of the Hohenzollern Prussian Administration, the National Liberals and the Socialists, to the Federalist tendency . . . We are interested in favoring Federalism' (*Paris Peace Conference*, vol. 1, p. 366). As a result of the demilitarization of the Rhineland the councils in the occupied territory were composed entirely of workers. Hence the influence of the socialist parties was even stronger in the Rhenish councils than in those that included soldiers. Also, the Rhenish councils, as symbols of the socialist Prussian Government, were violently opposed by large parts of the Catholic population; the latter was deeply stirred by the policy of the Prussian Minister, Adolf Hoffmann, which aimed to separate church and state and to eliminate the influence of the church in public education. In large parts of the Prussian Rheinland province anti-Prussian feeling was stronger than it had ever been before. Thus a French policy intended to promote federalist tendencies in Germany would inevitably back Catholic opposition to the workers' councils.

The failure to recognize the councils proved as unfavorable for the French effort to separate the Rhineland as the restoration of the power of the bureaucrats, for it was the workers who became the most militant opponents of the French separatist policy. The Dorten putsch of 1 June 1919 collapsed primarily because of the general strike that had been called by the unions; in the Palatinate the workers stormed the buildings that had been occupied by the separatist leaders, beat up the latter, and thus terminated the first act of that tragi-comedy.[1]

In this context there is interest in a discussion that took place in the French Chamber of Deputies on 29 August 1919, concerning the Rhineland policy of the French Government. Even Maurice Barrès, leading advocate of an active French policy, was compelled to admit that certain groups of the working class in the Rhineland had come to feel strongly about French influence in that territory. Barrès could not refute the argument of a left-wing deputy that the reactionary policy of the occupation authorities in regard to labor questions was responsible for the sudden outbreak of nationalism among groups of the German population that had hitherto proved immune to nationalist agitation. No one could foresee in that hour of victory the dangers that would ultimately arise out of a combination of nationalist instincts and socialist arguments.

Although the occupation authorities actively discouraged participation of Rhinelanders in the workers' and soldiers' councils,

---

[1] An excellent analysis of the separatist movement can be found in Gedye, *The Revolver Republic*; see also Dorten.

they did not interfere at all in the elections for the state parliaments and the National Assembly. The latter, one of the most important elections in modern German history, took place on 19 January 1919, a few weeks after the beginning of the occupation, and was wholly undisturbed by the occupying armies. The body elected on that date served as the assembly for the drafting of the Weimar Constitution, and after the adoption of the Constitution, on 11 August, it remained in office as national legislature until the first elections to the Reichstag, in June 1920. The Germans, generally very clever in collecting material against the occupation authorities, did not raise the slightest charge that the Allies had interfered with this election of representatives to the constitutional assembly.

This liberality was not apparent, however, in the attitude toward elections for the municipal councils. In Germany the latter exist not only in the municipalities in the narrower sense of the word, that is, in the cities and villages, but also in the circles and even the provinces, which are organized as municipal units of a higher order. In the first stage of the occupation, the military authorities prevented residents of the occupied territory from participating in the meetings of the municipal council of the Rheinland province, which were held in Düsseldorf (at that time still unoccupied). This measure, however, had only temporary significance.

More important was the attitude toward new elections in the Rheinland province. There the municipal councils had been elected in the prewar period, on the basis of an election statute of 1856. This old statute divided the constituency into three classes, according to income, thus giving a few wealthy people the same political power as the broad masses. As a result, the workers had not a single deputy in the municipal council of Cologne, although they had carried that district in the Reichstag election of 1912, which had taken place under a truly democratic election statute. After the revolution one of the first steps of the newly elected Prussian constitutional assembly was to substitute a modern statute for the reactionary 'three classes election law' and to order immediate elections all over Prussia. Even the most reactionary Junkers did not criticize this measure, which they considered inescapable.

But in a note of 21 February 1919, a high official on the staff of Marshal Foch informed the German Government that the Marshal objected to the elections for municipal councils. He declared that collaboration with the existing municipal councils in the occupied territory had proved satisfactory, and that it did not seem desirable to change the situation. The elections were not permitted until August of that year, and it goes without saying that labor interpreted the incident as further evidence of the reactionary sympathies of the occupying armies, the more so as the 'three classes election statute' had become a symbol of Prussian reaction.

In the Palatinate the commanding French general attempted to set up a special council for the occupied territory. A 'council of notables' was planned, as a sort of intermediary between the military authorities and the population for all economic questions (Wachendorf, p. 32); its jurisdiction was expected ultimately to include political problems as well (Jacquot, pp. 67 ff.). The council of notables had hardly started its activities, however, before its meetings were interrupted by the first separatist revolution. It was never summoned again. The collapse of that putsch of 1 June 1919 represents the end of the French attempts to conquer the Rhineland by quasi-democratic means.

Although a history of the separatist movement is outside the scope of this study, mention should be made of the part played by the American military authorities in the failure of that effort. The adherence of the American zone, which constituted a corridor between the Wiesbaden and Cologne elements of the movement, was essential to the success of any separatist coup. And General Pershing informed President Wilson that he had given General Liggett 'instructions not to permit the entry of political agitators into our sector, no matter by whose orders they might claim to be operating' (Baker, vol. 2, p. 87).

Following this order General Liggett, the American commanding officer, refused to permit the Coblenz part of the program to be carried out, and even refused to allow posters of the French-sponsored Rhenish republic to be displayed. In seeking the collaboration of the American zone, the separatists went so far as to attempt to high pressure the Americans into accepting the revolution as a *fait accompli*. On 31 May, the night before the Rhenish republic was to be proclaimed, a French staff officer awakened the American General Malin Craig, informed him that the next day fifty agents of the Rhenish republic would come to Coblenz, and requested the necessary facilities for them. General Craig declared that he would do nothing before morning, and the next morning the French demand was refused by General Liggett (Tuohy, 'France's Rhineland Adventure,' p. 31).

The American generals, unlike the French, were consistent in their refusal to collaborate with a revolutionary movement. Like the French, however, they were not entirely untouched by considerations of high politics, though in their case the political currents that they conducted were directed toward the maintenance, not the separation, of the Rhineland. Those spring days, after the treaty had been written but before it had been signed by any government, were electric with possibilities that something might wreck the whole desperately contrived balance of conflicting aims.

COMMERCIAL ACTIVITIES

Two different kinds of institutions were engaged in the German administration of foreign trade: the customs offices and the foreign-trade agencies. The customs officers in the occupied Rhineland were federal civil servants of the normal German type. In Germany the vast majority of the petty officials came from the army. After a military service of twelve years or more, non-commissioned officers had a legal right to a job in the bureaucracy; and to great numbers of the peasantry and petty bourgeoisie this was an enticing reward, carrying the perquisites of authority, prestige, and a guaranteed pension. It would have been difficult to find a group of persons more closely interested, both mentally and economically, in the survival of a unified Reich.

The situation was far different in regard to the foreign-trade agencies. While the customs officers were the exponents of a century-old bureaucratic tradition, the foreign-trade agencies had been improvised during the war in order to handle the almost wholly unforeseen economic tasks that were then developing. It is well known that Walther Rathenau, when interviewing the Prussian Minister of War in the first days of August 1914, was informed by the chief of the greatest military machine of the world that practically no preparations had been taken for coping with economic problems that might arise during the war (Rathenau, pp. 8, 9).

Entrusted with the task of organizing Germany's war economy, Rathenau made use of the elaborate system of cartels that already existed. Without loss of their original character the cartels were converted into public law institutions with a broad jurisdiction in the field of economic administration (Rathenau, pp. 28-30). In the course of the war the control and regulation of foreign trade became one of their chief tasks. This peculiar use of semi-private business organizations under the supervision of state officials was called economic 'self-administration,' and the system survived under the Weimar Republic in a few sectors, particularly in the field of foreign-trade control. It should be noted, incidentally, that the planned economy of the Nazis is based on this same system of economic self-administration. Thus in this field the occupying armies after the end of the present war will be confronted with the same type of problems that existed in the Rhineland after 1918.

It was not possible for the occupation authorities to govern either the customs offices or the foreign-trade organizations, in which the top officials were not civil servants but businessmen, with the same type of loose supervision that was exercised over other German agencies of administration. For one thing, some of the statutes that the German foreign-trade agencies and customs offices were expected to enforce were contrary to the purposes of the occupying armies. Moreover, these armies had created agencies of their own, intended to represent their own nationals in the same fields in which the German agencies were intended to represent German nationals. And finally, there was no likelihood that those who were in control of the German foreign-trade agencies might be won for the Allied point of view, because they represented their own interests as well as those of their country.

It could hardly be expected, for example, that the Allies would entrust the German cartels with the task of deciding what trade agreements should be concluded with Allied firms; or that the business activities of Allied merchants should be subjected to German statutes that had been created as weapons against the Allies. And it was equally unthinkable that Allied and German foreign-trade agencies should coexist in a territory under a state of martial law, where the Allies had the right to control all spheres of activity.

The agencies and procedures that the occupation authorities developed for handling questions of foreign trade have already been fully described. Through them the German agencies in this field were rendered ineffective as instruments of Reich economic policy. The German customs officials were either dismissed or subjected solely to the orders of the Allied economic authorities, and the Reich's foreign-trade organizations, though allowed to continue a formal existence, were deprived of any real authority; in fact, the head of the Rhineland section of the federal trade agency was expelled from the occupied territory, because of his 'continual interferences with the import and export regulations issued by the British Army Authorities' (Grünfeld, pp. 14 and 28).

As a result, Germany had virtually no control over imports and exports in the Rhineland. An order issued by Marshal Foch on 18 January 1919 seemed in accordance with the German statutes (Grünfeld, p. 28), but shortly afterward the military authorities issued a decree nullifying, in the occupied zone, all German war statutes concerning imports and exports, and forbidding the German customs officers to apply them. A prominent British official (quoted in Ireton, p. 464) has characterized the situation as follows:

We regarded the occupied territory at that time for trading purposes as if it were part of France and Belgium. We dealt with the situation as if the Rhine was the frontier of these countries, and we suspended practically all laws that restricted the free movement of goods into or out of the occupied territory. About the only German regulation that was recognized in the British zone was a sanitary provision for the sale of fish.

Germany tried to uphold her sovereignty in this field by threatening to prosecute German citizens who violated the 'Trading with the Enemy' regulations, and by ordering the customs officers to prevent such transactions (Cornier, p. 61). But these efforts remained without practical effect. On 21 July 1919, Germany enacted a statute requiring that customs duties be paid on the gold standard, but this statute, too, was disallowed by the occupation authorities, so far as it pertained to the western frontiers (De Pange, p. 204; Aulneau, p. 348; Grünfeld, p. 15).

It was only on the Holland, Belgian, and Luxemburg frontiers that German customs officers were recognized at all. The old French-German customs line had been made obsolete by the French reincorporation of Alsace-Lorraine, and it was not until 15 November 1919 that the French allowed the German customs officers to take up their duties along the new line (Allen, *Occupation*, p. 83). In the meantime the German customs agencies continued to function, but they were run partly by French soldiers, partly by officials of the *sections économiques* (Schweisguth, p. 107; Grünfeld, p. 14). In the words of Jean De Pange (p. 204):

. . . the *sections économiques* had all customs agencies on the western frontier of Germany under their control. They strictly applied the German customs statutes, but they raised the customs duties only in paper marks, whereas on all other frontiers of Germany the German Government raised the customs duties in gold marks. This practice resulted in a considerable advantage for our trade. The papers on the other side of the Rhine call this phenomenon the 'hole in the west.'

LABOR

The armies of occupation, entering the Rhineland in the midst of a political and social revolution, cast their vote in favor of the traditional forces. This decision, made during the first days after the armistice, affected the attitude of the occupying forces toward social questions during the whole armistice period.

Little information is available concerning the attitude of the occupying armies toward labor conflicts, and what there is comes mainly from American sources. During the armistice period the American occupation authorities forbade strikes of workers engaged by the occupying armies themselves (Hunt, pp. 171-3; Allen, *Occupation*, p. 105), and also, at first, strikes of workers in public enterprises; after a short while, however, as the process of inflation gathered momentum, strikes had to be permitted in public enterprises, because of the urgency of the wage problem. The occupation authorities made it clear that they were interested also in strikes of workers in private enterprises, but they were prepared to interfere with such conflicts only 'if their own interests were directly concerned' (Allen, *Occupation*, p. 105). Picketing was generally forbidden, and striking workers who refused to accept another job were expelled from the occupied territory; this regulation, 'which under other circumstances might well be construed as unfair to Labor, was necessary for the preservation of order' (Hunt, p.

169). There was a secret order that the names and addresses of all union leaders should be ascertained, but it led to no practical consequences. The American attitude toward labor questions was characterized by General Allen (*Occupation*, p. 105) with the statement that 'even in purely industrial strikes we adopted a strictly military policy.'

The position of the Americans was severely criticized by the French writer Thiallet (p. 61), who contrasted the 'sometimes excessive liberalism' of the American occupation authorities with their 'frequent application of brutal methods of repression,' and added that the 'German authorities were never able to understand the bitter irony' of these different attitudes. Thiallet's vehemence about the American attitude toward labor must be regarded primarily as a retort to the American criticism of the French methods of occupation. What he called the 'irony' of the American methods was but a reflection of the social situation in the United States during the early 1920's.

But the American policy was not confined to coercion and force. Not only did the officers in charge of civil affairs make frequent visits to the factories, but early in the armistice period the American army created special boards of conciliation before which opposing interests had to try to reconcile their differences; strikes and lockouts were permitted only if these attempts proved futile (Ireton, p. 468). As a rule, one meeting of such a board was sufficient to settle the conflict (Hunt, pp. 170-71). This idea of conciliation boards, as will be shown later, was taken over during the peace period and incorporated in the statutes of the governing body.

JUDICIAL SYSTEM

For court cases involving only residents of the occupied territory, the jurisdiction of the German courts was, in general, not disputed. There was an exception, however, in regard to German prosecutions for high treason. This raises an issue of the utmost importance, for the handling of political crimes under a state of martial law involves problems quite different from those concerning the routine work of the judges.

In the Rhineland these problems were not free from emotional overtones. A few months before Marshal Foch's armies entered the Rhineland the Belgian courts had fought a heroic struggle against the attempt of the German *Généralgouvernement* in Belgium to interfere with their activities. They had insisted upon their right to prosecute for high treason those Belgian citizens who had participated in the German-sponsored Flemish autonomous movement. Would the German courts in the Rhineland follow their example and bring to trial the adherents of the French-sponsored separatist movement? In Belgium the German occupation authorities had prohibited the Belgian courts from exercising their judicial functions in these cases, whereupon the Belgian Supreme Court had suspended its sittings in protest; and the lower courts shortly followed its example. Would the Allied and Associated armies of occupation apply to the position of the German judges in the Rhineland the practice of the *Généralgouvernement* or the theories of the Belgian courts?

In the opinion of the present writer, occupation authorities enforcing a state of martial law are entitled to restrict the jurisdiction of the occupied country's courts in high-treason cases. High-treason proceedings represent, in legal form, political measures taken by a government against those whom it considers enemies of the state. Martial law empowers a government to fight against enemies of the state with extra-legal weapons. And the right to subject enemies of the state to court proceedings cannot be separated from the right to subject them to martial law. Therefore when governmental power is split between the agencies of two countries, with one country entitled to apply martial law, that country must also have the ultimate decision whether high treason proceedings shall be initiated. An occupying power, enforcing a regime of martial law, cannot allow its friends to be treated as enemies by the authorities of the occupied territory. Once a state of siege has been declared, respect for the independence of the courts must carry the proviso that the activities of the courts do not contravene the application of martial law.

Thus the Rhineland occupation authorities, in an order of 29 January 1919, declared that German arrests in political cases were permissible only with the consent of the military authorities. And there were several instances in which the German courts were in fact restrained from high-treason proceedings.

It has already been mentioned that the occupying armies had the power to dismiss, at will, German officials and state employees whose actions or personalities they mistrusted. The authorities recognized, however, that the judiciary could not be subjected to such an arbitrary determination of tenure. For more than a hundred years the independence of the judiciary had been regarded in Germany as the cornerstone of the Rechtsstaat and the chief guarantee of the freedom of the individual—a principle that had not been altered by the November revolution. Under German law, judges were assured both 'personal' and 'functional' independence. Their personal independence was assured by the grant of life tenure and by the prohibition of dismissal or removal to another place except by virtue of a court decision. Their functional independence arose from the prohibition of any interference, by either the legislative or the executive branch of the government, with the activities of the courts in any pending case.

This tradition of independence was respected by the occupying armies to a remarkable extent. Very few cases are on record in which either the personal or the functional independence of a German judge was violated. One of these rare instances was the case of Judge Hüsgen of the Municipal Court in Rheinberg (*Dokumente* . . . vol. I, pp. 121-2). A Belgian general ordered Judge Hüsgen, who was also recording officer in Rheinberg, to file in the register of the court certain documents favoring Belgian and French stockholders. Both the judge and the clerk refused to obey this order, and were fined by the Belgian military officials. This case was introduced by Reich Minister of the Interior Koch, in his speech in the National Assembly on 17 January 1920 (Nationalversammlung, vol. 332, pp. 4464-8) as evidence of the arbitrary regime of the occupying armies in the Rhineland, but actually the incident represented an abuse of power on the part of the military which was undoubtedly contrary to the intentions of the occupation authorities.

Another instance, also mentioned in the National Assembly, concerned a high-treason case (Nationalversammlung, vol. 328, p. 1884). The defendant, a certain Hompa, had been prosecuted by Judge Frisch of the municipal court in Kehl (Baden) for participation in the Dorten putsch. The French military authorities not only released Hompa from prison but also arrested the judge and the prosecuting attorney, Werber, for having violated the order of 29 January 1919. Frisch was sentenced to three months in jail, Werber to six months, and each was fined 2,500 marks. Even among high-treason cases this was the only one in which penalties were imposed on German court officers. The Frisch-Werber case was the subject of an exchange of notes between the German Government and the Allied Armistice Commission, but it is interesting to note that both parties refrained from mentioning the Belgian precedent of 1918. Having changed their roles within a year, both were well aware that occupation law is not determined by the principles of the categorical imperative.

This recognition of the independence of the courts did not mean, however, that there was no effort to check on their activities. In the area occupied by the French armies, special rules for overseeing the courts were enacted in January and February 1919 (Cornier, p. 50). One member of the staff of each district supervising agency was entrusted with this task. He had the privilege of attending all meetings of the courts, and also had access to the files—a right necessitated by the fact that not all meetings of the courts are public in Germany. But there is no evidence that these prerogatives were abused. On the contrary, an instruction issued in the Palatinate, for the *contrôleurs* of the courts of that Bavarian district, warned that proceedings should go along as usual, and expressly forbade these officers to interfere with the activities of the courts (Niboyet, p. 51).

III

Prosecution of War Criminals

WAR crimes may be thought of as falling into two separate categories: military measures, pursued in the course of actual fighting, which are contrary to accepted rules of warfare; and 'occupation crimes,' committed in the course of belligerent occupation of enemy territory. To be sure, these types may not be mutually exclusive, but on the whole they represent different kinds of motivation and quite different problems of prosecution. During and after the last war the chief indictment of Germany concerned crimes of the first type—violations of the rules of international law regarding land and sea warfare. Those responsible for such violations were granted immunity during the armistice period, but in the peace conference provisions for bringing them to justice were attempted. The Versailles treaty (Articles 227-30) obliged Germany to extradite such persons to the Allied and Associated powers, and provided for specific procedures in these cases.

This aspect of the problem has no connection, however, with military occupation, and will not be dealt with in the present study. Moreover, in the current war such violations, committed in the course of actual warfare, are far outweighed by 'occupation crimes.' Consequently the war-criminal problem of the last war's armistice period, when occupation crimes were the reason for prosecution, is probably more meaningful for present discussions of this subject than is the much better known story of the prosecution of war criminals by virtue of the Versailles treaty, when strictly military measures were the main cause of action.

47

Occupation crimes include a broad range of criminal acts that may be roughly described as actions of individual soldiers or officers against non-belligerents—murder, assault, theft, and comparable crimes. It is of course extremely difficult to identify and obtain custody of the persons guilty of such actions. During the course of a war, either side may take prisoner individuals subsequently recognized as such culprits, but for the most part, neither identification nor arrest is likely until after the end of hostilities. And even then there are great practical difficulties, even if the identity of such criminals is known. Thus, in regard to occupation criminals, the known cases of arrest and prosecution during the last war, and afterward, in the occupied Rhineland, are far from numerous. The handling of these cases, however, and the underlying jurisdictional considerations, are of basic importance for the future.

It should be emphasized that recognition of the practical difficulties involved in obtaining custody of occupation criminals is by no means an implication that the punishment of such persons is only a matter of power and opportunity. The power to punish is admittedly an attribute of victory, except in regard to prisoners of war. But the power to punish has to be reinforced by valid legal justification of the right to punish, and by valid principles in regard to what is punishable. Without such a body of defensible doctrine, the prosecution of war criminals becomes either a matter of lawless vengeance or—as it was, in the main, after the last war—a just legal procedure that breaks down because of the weakness of its own instruments. Either eventuality is a deplorable outcome of a war waged for the supremacy of law.

Before proceeding with the discussion of this question it should be mentioned that there is no evidence whatever of extra-legal personal vengeance in the Rhineland for crimes committed during the war. Thousands of dismissed German soldiers and officers who had participated in the German occupation of Belgium and northern France resided in the territory which was now occupied by the soldiers of those nations. But not even German propaganda mentioned a single case in which members of the occupying forces took revenge for crimes committed in their own countries by German soldiers during the war. Since German propaganda against the Versailles treaty was for many years based to a considerable extent on the alleged crimes of occupation soldiers in the Rhineland, its failure to mention examples of lynch justice is ample indication that no such spontaneous revenge actions occurred.

LEGAL BACKGROUND

Before the First World War only the United States had developed a clear theory on the punishment of war criminals. The American principles, which go back to the Civil War and its aftermath, distinguish between war prisoners and other persons who come under the power of an opponent belligerent. War prisoners can be punished for criminal acts which they committed before their capture, if they have not been punished by their own sovereign. This principle, laid down in Section 59 of the famous Lieber Instructions of 1863 (Moore *Digest*, vol. 7, p. 220), makes no 'territorial' distinction; that is, it is immaterial whether the territory in which the crime was committed was under the sovereignty of the captor's or of the prisoner's state.

As far as non-prisoners are concerned, the United States Supreme Court decided in 1878, in Coleman *v.* Tennessee (97 U.S. 509), that the courts of formerly occupied territory have no jurisdiction over dismissed members of the occupying army. A soldier of the Northern army had murdered a Tennesseean, in Tennessee, and had been apprehended by Tennessee authorities, but the Supreme Court denied that a Tennessee court had jurisdiction in the case after the end of the hostilities: the defendant enjoyed immunity from proceedings in Tennessee courts for any criminal acts which he had committed in that state as a member of the occupying army. One year later, in Dow *v.* Johnson (100 U.S. 158), Mr. Justice Field applied the same princi-

ples to a case concerning a member of the Confederate army.
And twenty-five years after the end of the Civil War these
principles were again upheld in Freeland *v.* Williams (131 U.S.
405).

As recently as 1943 George Manner declared (p. 423) that
'in the absence of international agreement abrogating or modi-
fying the customary rule granting immunity to hostile forces
from the normal jurisdiction of the place, the view expressed
by the U.S. Supreme Court after the Civil War of 1861-65 to
the effect that the local civil courts of former belligerents have
no postwar jurisdiction over war crimes committed during hostilities by former enemy persons in occupied territory still
states the true rule of international law.' The only exceptions
to this rule, according to Manner, are the trials of Rhineland
residents, held during the armistice period by Belgian and French
courts. Manner's attitude is in accordance with the view of so
eminent an authority as George A. Finch, who in 1920 expressed
the opinion ('Jurisdiction of Local Courts . . .' p. 218) that
'local territorial courts have no jurisdiction to try a punishable
crime committed by members of the invading army, either during or after the enemy occupation.'

British international lawyers have tended to accept the American view on this matter. Thus they have expressed the opinion
that members of an occupying army enjoy extraterritoriality
privileges, and are subject exclusively to the jurisdiction of their
own courts, but that war prisoners may be punished by the
captor's courts for crimes committed before their capture, provided they have not been punished by their own military courts
(Oppenheim, vol. I, pp. 670-71).

At the time of the last war, and afterward, both France and
Germany tended, however, toward a 'territorial' principle of
war-criminal prosecution, which was rather different from the
position taken by American and British jurists. Early in the war,
in the Vogelgesang case, France followed the principle that
German war prisoners could be punished for criminal acts that

they had committed on French territory before their capture (*Journal du droit international*, 1915, vol. 42, p. 54). Germany applied the same principle to the case of a Russian war prisoner who had stolen a 1,000 mark note from a civilian in East Prussia before he had been taken prisoner (*Berliner Tageblatt*, 10 February 1915, no. 74; for a brief summary of the German attitude on the treatment of war prisoners see Kirchenheim). The German courts denied their jurisdiction, however, in the case of the French war prisoner Courjou, who was indicted for having kicked German prisoners of war on French territory, before his capture (Gerbaulet, pp. 184-8). Here the stumbling block was the fact that the crime had been committed in territory that was under the legal and factual control of the opponent belligerent. And this circumstance was regarded as a stumbling block also by French jurists, who rejected Professor Clunet's suggestion that French courts had jurisdiction in cases in which French prisoners of war had been maltreated inside Germany (*Revue pénitentiaire et de droit pénal*, 1916, vol. 40, p. 37).

The 'territorial' principle was given explicit recognition at a meeting of the French Prison Society in 1916, in which eminent French authorities on international law participated (*Revue pénitentiaire* . . . 1916, vol. 40, pp. 20 ff.). In 1915, after a dramatic discussion between the famous international lawyer Renault and a young attorney Helmer, the Society had rejected Helmer's theory that members of the German occupying army were protected by rights of extraterritoriality from being prosecuted by French courts after the occupation was ended (*Revue pénitentiaire* . . . 1915, vol. 39, p. 475). The principle was adopted that the courts of the occupied country are only de facto prevented from prosecuting war criminals for crimes committed in the occupied zone: since occupation does not touch upon the sovereignty of the occupied state, the courts of the occupied territory retain their virtual jurisdiction. As Professor Mérignhac (pp. 5 ff., especially p. 32) put it in 1917:

The occupying power exercises only a de facto authority, which is restricted to the period of occupation. The legal sovereign remains invested with the judicial power, and nothing prevents him from exercising this power if by any circumstances whatever—for instance by capture—he obtains custody of persons who are guilty of a punishable crime . . . If the jurisdiction of the occupying power were the only competent one, there would frequently be a denial of justice.

The German territorial theory found its most absurd expression in two military orders, issued by Ludendorff on 23 November 1916 and 24 January 1918 (quoted in Verdross, p. 19). These orders, which referred, however, to strictly 'military' measures, provided that captured pilots who had dropped leaflets over the German trenches should be indicted for sedition committed on territory under German control. It would seem that Ludendorff regarded psychological warfare as a violation of international law. War, to him, was apparently a duel between sovereigns: if one sovereign attempted to incite the subjects of the other, he violated the rules that should control war as a purely military conflict within the framework of an established society; even in the midst of a total war, the belligerents should respect each other's political and social structure. But by thus degrading the prosecution of war criminals to a terror weapon, Ludendorff not only himself committed a war crime; he implicitly recognized the principle that true war criminals should be subjected to punishment in accordance with law.

The armistice agreement left much unsaid in its treatment of the war-criminal problem. As already mentioned, it declared (Article 6) that for the duration of the armistice no person in the occupied territory should 'be prosecuted for having taken part in any military measures previous to the signing of the armistice,' but it said nothing about the prosecution of war crimes as distinguished from 'military measures.' There had been no immunity provisions at all in the conditions originally presented to the German delegates. Erzberger, head of the German delegation, suggested the inclusion of a clause providing that no criminal prosecution should be initiated against residents of the occupied territory for having participated, before the signing of the armistice, in actions connected in any way whatever with the war. And Marshal Foch accepted this suggestion in part, though he rejected almost all other proposals of the German armistice delegation. As Finch has recently remarked ('Retribution of War Crimes,' p. 84): 'The delegates who drew up and signed the armistice terms were professional men of arms. It does not seem out of place to suggest that possibly they did not view the acts of the invading armies in the same light as the civilian victims and consequently were loath to turn over men of their profession to the wrath of the victorious peoples.'

In the Rhineland a further limitation of jurisdiction in this field was established by the military authorities themselves. Even in regard to occupation crimes, the defendant may plead that he has acted on command of his superiors, and this plea is one that professional soldiers are likely to respect; failure to recognize it would imply that each individual soldier has a right to review the commands of his superiors, and to disregard all military orders that in his eyes are contrary to the law. Thus the Allied military authorities in the Rhineland declared that no one who had acted on command of his superiors should be prosecuted for having removed property in the formerly occupied parts of Belgium and northern France (Hunt, p. 231). This decision, though it referred only to pillage cases, is indicative of the general attitude of the occupying armies. The *respondeat superior* defense raises one of the most serious problems in the whole subject of war-criminal prosecution, but it is outside the scope of the present discussion, which concerned primarily with problems of jurisdiction rather than of procedure.[1]

[1] It may be mentioned that Goebbels, writing on 'The Air Terror of our Enemies,' declared early in 1944 that 'No international law on warfare is in existence which provides that a soldier who has committed a mean crime can escape punishment by pleading as his defense that he followed

ALLIED PROSECUTIONS OF RHINELAND RESIDENTS

The American and British military authorities, though not directly interested in the prosecution of war criminals, were confronted with the problem when the Belgian and French armies asked for the extradition of such persons (Allen, *Occupation*, p. 66; Hunt, p. 231). In the American zone each case of this kind was subjected to a thorough examination, and the individual was extradited if it was decided that there was sufficient evidence against him. This decision of the American military authorities, though it did not entirely conform with the 'extraterritoriality' principle of American jurists, was in accordance with the attitude of the American peace delegation toward the war-criminal problem. On 29 March 1919, the Commission on the Responsibility of the Authors of the War and on Enforcement of Penalties had presented a report to the peace conference which contained the statement that 'every belligerent has, according to international law, the power and authority to try the individuals alleged to be guilty of the crimes of which an enumeration has been given in Chapter II . . . if such persons have been taken prisoner *or have otherwise fallen into its power*' (*American Journal of International Law*, 1920, vol. 14, p. 121; italics mine). Although the American members of that commission, Secretary of State Lansing and Professor Scott, disagreed on some points with the opinion of the majority of the commission, they explicitly expressed their approval of the passages of the majority report which are quoted here (ibid. p. 140).

Two quite different types of cases are to be distinguished in considering the actions of French and Belgian military authorities against war criminals resident in the Rhineland. One type concerned persons accused of outright occupation crimes—crimes committed in Belgium and northern France during the wartime occupation of those territories; in most of these cases the indi-

the commands of his superiors. This holds particularly true if those commands are contrary to all human ethics and opposed to the well-established international usage of warfare' (*Berliner Börsenzeitung*, 28 May 1944).

vidual's connection with the crime was discovered quite by accident. The second type of case concerned persons who were found in possession of machines that had been 'confiscated' in the formerly occupied Belgian and French territories.

Cases of the first type were not very numerous, as identification and the production of evidence were extremely difficult. It is usually almost impossible to identify the individual soldiers and officers of the hostile army who are guilty of having committed specific crimes. In both the Vogelgesang and the Courjou cases, mentioned above, arraignment was possible only because both men, at the time of their capture, were in possession of diaries in which they had given detailed reports on their criminal activities.

In the first weeks of the Rhineland occupation five German officers were arrested by the French military authorities and indicted for acts of pillage, theft, and violence committed against the population of the formerly occupied zones of northern France (*Journal du droit international*, 1919, vol. 46, p. 1258); the decisions in these cases are not known. In addition, about 150 warrants of arrest were issued, and several French courts sentenced members of the German occupying army *in absentia* (ibid. 1920, vol. 47, p. 857; 1921, vol. 48, pp. 781, 1076). In one of these trials the German General von Nathusius was sentenced to prison for larceny. When Nathusius went to France in 1924, in order to visit a soldiers' cemetery, he was arrested and the execution of his sentence was attempted (Feilitsch, pp. 971-3); it was only after long negotiations that he was released. On all these cases the reports are extremely brief, and they give the impression that the French authorities were not very interested in the prosecution of this type of war criminal.

The Belgian cases in this category were far more significant, but in considering them the peculiar character of Belgium's situation must be borne in mind. The invasion of that country, in open violation of a solemn neutrality pledge, introduced a special element into the problem of war crimes committed during the occupation.

The outstanding Belgian case concerned with a crime of violence was an action against a German miner, Bockstegen, who had served during the war in the German occupation army in Belgium. One day early in January 1919 a Belgian soldier on guard at the entrance of Bockstegen's working place identified the German as the individual who had killed several persons in the Belgian's native village in August and September 1916. On 23 January Bockstegen was arrested in accordance with a decree of the Belgian Minister of Justice, of 11 January 1919, which declared that any person residing in the occupied zone could be deported to Belgium if he was under suspicion of having committed during the war either a political or an ordinary crime in occupied Belgium. As De Jaer has said (p. 127): 'During the armistice period the Belgian courts were entitled to exercise in the occupied zone all powers which were necessary for the enforcement of the Belgian penal statutes. This power was an absolute one, and was based on the transfer of the de facto power in the occupied zone.'

After Bockstegen had been convicted for murder by the trial court he appealed to the Cour de Cassation. There his plea was based on three contentions: first, that Belgian courts had no jurisdiction in his case, since he 'had belonged to the armed forces at the time at which he had committed the crimes'; second, that if jurisdiction was vested in the Belgian courts at all, it was in this case vested not in the ordinary courts but in the military tribunals, by virtue of the 'war criminal' provisions of the Versailles treaty; and third, that he had been punished for the same crimes by a German military tribunal, and therefore was protected by the principle *ne bis in idem*. On 23 March 1920, the Cour de Cassation rejected the appeal and affirmed the judgment of the trial court (*Pasicrisie belge*, 1920, 1, p. 104; *Annual Digest*, 1919-22, case 324, p. 458; *Journal du droit international*, 1920, vol. 47, pp. 718 ff.).

Bockstegen's claim to immunity on the ground that he had been a member of the German occupying forces was regarded by the high court as 'contrary to the spirit of the written law as well as to the universally recognized rules of ethics' (this question was dealt with more explicitly in the Kauhlen case, discussed below). The plea that jurisdiction, if it existed, belonged to the military tribunals was rejected by the argument that de jure the right of the Belgian courts to prosecute members of the German occupying forces had never ceased to exist; the war-criminal provisions of the Versailles treaty 'were not intended to, and did not, affect the rules as to jurisdiction which in Belgium apply to the prosecution of crimes committed within the kingdom by aliens not surrendered by virtue of the treaties.' *Ne bis in idem* was excluded as a defense, on the ground that if Belgium had an original right of prosecution this prerogative could not be affected by trials of a foreign sovereign's courts; here the Cour de Cassation had a precedent in its decision in the Gebhardt case, rendered on 16 December 1919 (*Pasicrisie belge*, 1920, I, p. 10).

In the Kauhlen case (*Pasicrisie belge*, 1921, I, p. 100) the defendant was indicted for malicious denunciation of Belgian subjects to the German military authorities. His plea that he had belonged to the German occupying forces was rejected. Said the court: 'Malicious denunciation to the enemy during the period of occupation is punishable by Belgian courts even if the author of the denunciation belongs to the hostile army. No principle of international law requires that a person who belongs to the military forces of the enemy be granted immunity for giving information to the enemy.'

The attitude of the Belgian Cour de Cassation in the Norz case (*Pasicrisie belge*, 1920, I, p. 7) was even more radical. In October 1916 and March 1917 the Belgian Government in Exile had enacted statutes according to which all persons were punishable who rendered assistance on Belgian territory to armed forces of the hostile state, or who shook the allegiance of Belgian subjects to their king and country, or who maliciously fostered the policies and plans of the enemy. And on 16 December 1919, the high court decided that Austrian citizenship was no defense for violation of these statutes. In thus subjecting members of the occupying forces to war statutes that had been enacted with a view to strengthening resistance against the invader, the supreme court was apparently motivated by the theory that the invasion of Belgium was not a belligerent occupation, in the meaning of international law, but was rather an international wrong subject to special legal principles. These Belgian cases cannot without reservation be regarded as precedents in international occupation law.

Although the Belgian Cour de Cassation declared on 10 August 1920 (*Pasicrisie belge*, 1921, I, p. 84) that arrests of war criminals were permissible in the occupied Rhineland also after the ratification of the peace treaty, the Belgian Government did not make use of that privilege. In June 1921 the question was raised in the Belgian parliament why a certain Tesmar—a German war criminal who resided in the occupied zone—had not been arrested; the Minister of Justice answered that the Minister of Foreign Affairs had prevented the prosecution of Tesmar because the occupying powers had decided to refrain from further actions against war criminals in the occupied territory (*Journal du droit international*, 1921, vol. 48, p. 773). This is the last official statement on the prosecution of war criminals in the Rhineland.

Far more important than this first type of case, in long-run implications, were the actions arising out of the confiscation of French and Belgian machinery. During the war, according to Farquhar's report, the Germans 'had carried away from the occupied portions of those countries all the machinery and everything that would be valuable in the reorganisation of the factories' (quoted in Garner, 'Contributions . . .' p. 92, note 1). Since it was not feasible, in most cases, to prosecute the persons responsible for the confiscations—who, if identifiable at all, were likely to be German authorities outside the jurisdiction of the victorious powers—actions for 'the receipt of stolen goods' were instituted against those Rhenish entrepreneurs who were in possession of the machines. These actions, unlike the rather incidental prosecutions of other war criminals, aroused considerable discussion both in the occupied and in the occupying countries. They are dealt with here as a problem of war-criminal prosecution, but it should not be overlooked that at the time they occurred their economic implications were at least of equal importance, as most of the leading industrialists of the Rhineland were affected.

Though in most cases of this kind the accused, himself, was not the author of the original crime, but was merely considered to be punishable as a beneficiary of it, in the most sensational case—that of Robert and Hermann Röchling, leading industrialists of the Saar basin—the defendants were accused of the actual confiscation. The Röchling brothers were indicted for having transferred 8,000 tons of machines and materials from French factories to their own enterprise. Hermann, however, was a member of the German armistice delegation, and therefore the American authorities did not extradite him to the French authorities when he was passing through Trier in December 1918. Thus proceedings were instituted against Robert, and at the same time Hermann was tried *in absentia*.

Robert's defense, that he had acted on command of superior authorities, was rejected by the French military tribunal in Amiens which tried the case (*Journal du droit international*, 1921, vol. 48, pp. 362-3). The looting of foreign factories for one's own benefit was considered to be punishable, even if it had been done on the command of superiors; the Röchling brothers were considered to have acted not as soldiers but as industrialists. It is worth emphasizing, however, that in a total war, where there is no clear line of demarcation between military and industrialist activities, any distinction between non-military persons and soldiers, in regard to the recognition granted the *respondeat superior* defense, may lead to very arbitrary results. Robert and Hermann Röchling, the latter *in absentia*, were sentenced to ten years' imprisonment and a fine of 10 million francs (Grimm, pp. 58 ff.), but the decision of the Amiens court was reversed, on appeal, by the superior military tribunal in Nancy. The reversal, according to a French writer (Cadoux, p. 459), 'was motivated by the fact that the responsibility for the incriminating acts—however verified and vile these were—rested on the German authorities whose orders were executed by both brothers as officers.'

Almost all the leading Rhenish industrialists were in danger of criminal prosecution for possession of French or Belgian machinery, and after several others had been arrested, the German Government asked R. von Hippel, the Göttingen professor of international law, to prepare a memorandum on the legality of the German measures and of the arrest of German managers for the purchase of such machines. Von Hippel (whose memorandum was published in 1920 in *Niemeyers Zeitschrift für internationales Recht*, vol. 28, pp. 183-206) contended that the German military authorities had exercised the right of eminent domain in the occupied Belgian and French territories, with respect to all property that they considered essential for the pursuit of the war. He admitted that no exception had yet been recognized to the rule of international law according to which the private property of the residents of an occupied territory should be protected. He maintained, however, that such protection should be granted only under the same reservations that the Hague Convention (Article 23 g) stipulates in regard to private property in an area of actual fighting, since urgent necessities justify infringements of property rights in an occupied as well as in a fighting zone. This principle, he said, was particularly applicable to the German confiscation of Belgian and French machines, because Germany, under the British blockade, was in a 'state of distress' (*Notstand*), and was entitled to take all measures necessary to overcome it. Von Hippel concluded this sec-

tion of his memorandum with the words (p. 194) that such procedures as those against German industrialists, 'which may prove
of basic significance in the future, can hardly be reconciled with
the true French interests. France would implicitly deny that in
case of war, recognition should be granted to a right of distress,
aimed at the preservation of [the nation's] existence, and thus
would create a precedent which might be applicable to herself,
in the event of a future war.' At the time this memorandum
was presented to the victors of the war, the peace treaty had not
yet been signed.

From the point of view of criminal law, von Hippel denied
that the French had jurisdiction in regard to crimes committed
by Germans in Germany, even if French interests were violated.[2] This contention raises the question of evidence, which
was almost as difficult in the confiscation cases as in the more
general war-criminal cases, though for quite different reasons.
The military authorities in the Rhineland followed the principle
that possession of such machines was sufficient to subject the
holder to the suspicion that he had violated the criminal provisions on receiving stolen goods. But if the defendant declared
that he had bought the machines on German territory it was
almost impossible for the prosecuting government to refute his
statement. And von Hippel had a strong argument in his favor
when he said that the French had no jurisdiction in criminal
cases of this kind if the crime was committed in Germany.
Neither French nor German law permits the prosecution of a
foreign subject for a crime violating individual rights of nationals if the crime was committed on foreign territory—though
both permit such prosecutions if the crime was an attack on the
security of the state. In an article on the German confiscations,
published in 1919, Nast explicitly stated ('Les sanctions

[2] Cf. the Cutting case, in which the Government of the United States
denied the right of the Mexican Government to punish an American citizen
for having insulted a Mexican citizen on American soil (Moore *Digest*,
vol. 2, p. 233).

pénales . . .' pp. 120, 127) that criminal prosecution for the purchase of stolen goods was out of the question if the goods had been acquired on German territory. Actually all evidence difficulties concerning the Rhenish industrialists could have been overcome by applying the maxim *res ipsa loquitur*, but this was impossible so long as the 'territorial' principle was adhered to.

In a conference in Brussels, on 23 March 1919, the Industrial Sub-Committee of the Inter-Allied Armistice Commission decided to abstain from further criminal prosecution of Germans who had benefited from the looting of Belgian and French factories, provided that Germany enacted a statute permitting the return of the material. Such a statute was enacted on 28 March (*Reichsgesetzblatt*, 1919, p. 349), and thereafter, in accordance with orders of Marshal Foch, proceedings were instituted only against persons who had not declared or had destroyed the confiscated material (Nast, 'L'occupation . . .' p. 157; *Der Waffenstillstand*, vol. 3, pp. 99-103, vol. 2, pp. 265-331). The material returned to Belgium and France during the armistice period alone amounted to 164,000 tons, with a value of 135,000,000 gold marks (*Der Waffenstillstand*, vol. 2, p. 331). The delicacy of the whole problem is indicated in the fact that on several occasions German workers threatened to demolish the machines rather than see them removed (Hunt, p. 233).

The Brussels decision represented a German victory in the war-criminal question. The available sources do not reveal whether the occupying powers were unable or unwilling to overcome the legalistic objections that were used as justification for this gesture of conciliation. Shortly afterward, the occupation authorities extended their lenient attitude from the criminal to the administrative side of the looted-machinery problem. On the ground that many of these machines were in the hands of 'virtually innocent purchasers' they decided to apply 'business arrangements' rather than 'arbitrary' methods to the question of retransfer (Allen, *Occupation*, p. 67).

Although the Reich was compelled to return the confiscated

machines to Belgium and France, the Germans clung to the theory that because of German 'distress' during the war, the confiscations had been lawful. This principle was adopted by the German supreme court in a civil case decided on 1 November 1922 (105 RGZ 326; *Annual Digest*, 1919-22, case 296, p. 427). The court declared that the requisition, although contrary to the Hague Convention, was lawful, for 'it is a principle which is recognized in international law, and which must be applied also to the Hague Conventions, that a state's right to self-preservation is superior to all obligations undertaken in treaties, and that in case of necessity a state may depart from and go beyond the provisions of the Hague Convention.' Thus the Reichsgericht, four years after the end of hostilities, repeated the principle which Germany had used during the war as justification for her violation of Belgian neutrality and for many other violations of international law. This principle, contained in the German Manual of War, 'when carried out to its logical conclusion leads to the absolute supremacy of strategical interests as expressed in the ancient maxim, "omnia licere quae necessaria ad finem belli" ' (Garner, *German War Code* . . . p. 11).

A POSSIBILITY FOR THE FUTURE

The handling of the war-criminal problem during the armistice period clearly indicates that no proper solution was found. Some jurists have even suggested that there is no solution except that of practical politics. Thus James Garner, who shortly after the war adhered to the territorial principle in the interest of justice (*International Law* . . . vol. 2, p. 477), by 1925 had come to the conclusion, regarding the right to prosecute war criminals, that 'it really makes no difference, however, whether such a right can be founded on international law or not. It is simply a question of policy and expediency, to be exercised by the victorious belligerent' (*Recent Developments* . . . p. 457).

Such a purely political approach amounts to an adoption of opportunist rather than legal considerations as the basis of action in this matter. But the punishment of war criminals for violations of law loses its very meaning if it is not conceived as a legal problem. Even from a political point of view the exclusively political approach is dangerous, for it provides the former enemy with moral weapons in those other conflicts that are so likely to accompany the termination of a war. Moreover, at the moment the victorious nations disclaim the necessity of legal justification for their punitive actions the war criminals will be enabled to play the role of political martyrs.

After the last war the principles governing the handling of this problem were neither wholly legal nor wholly opportunist, but a kind of unstable amalgam of the two. This lack of a procedure that was both legally justified and practically efficient made it possible for Germany to escape the execution of the war-criminal provisions of the peace treaty. The course of events actually strengthened the prestige and power of those inside Germany who were supposed to have been penalized.

The experience of the armistice period should make it clear that the territorial principle of war-criminal jurisdiction is not tenable. The war-criminal problem is legally solvable only if it is treated in the framework of international law, but the territorial principle transfers it to the realm of municipal law. And no country will be complacent about the unreserved submission of its own soldiers to the jurisdiction of the enemy. Moreover, the territorial principle contains a logical difficulty that may be impossible to resolve except on the reasoning of *force majeure*. To translate this difficulty into terms of the last war: if the occupation authorities in the Rhineland were not prepared to recognize, as a matter of principle, the immunity of the German forces that had occupied Belgium and northern France, then it was only by virtue of the terms dictated in the armistice agreement—not by any innate right—that they could claim for their own troops immunity from prosecution by German courts for crimes against the Rhenish population. Such considerations make it clear that the territorial principle leads indeed to the conclusion that the punishment of war criminals is 'simply a question of policy and expediency.'

On the other hand, the maxim that any army is extraterritorial, and subject only to its own statutes, is basically sound and is in conformance with recognized rules of international law. Can this principle, the substance of the Anglo-American attitude, be accepted as the answer to the problem of war-criminal prosecution?

An essential reason for the difficulties beclouding this problem, not only after the First World War but, even more, during the present struggle, is that there are two quite different elements involved. On the one hand is the indictment against individual members of the German armed forces for violations of municipal criminal law. In addition, however, the German authorities themselves frequently approved or encouraged these crimes; 'the instances in which such offenders were tried and punished by the German courts were distressingly rare' (Garner, *International Law* . . . vol. 2, p. 476). The attitude of the German Government toward certain of the war crimes committed by members of the German armed forces represents in itself a violation of international law, an international wrong.

The only writer who stressed this crucial point in the war-criminal discussion after the last war was the Austrian international jurist Alfred von Verdross, in a work which Garner (*Recent Developments* . . . p. 458, note 1) has called 'an excellent and on the whole a very fair discussion.' Both in war and in peace, Verdross maintained, international law has some bearing on the criminal law of the individual states. Under peace conditions the citizens of a state are subject to prosecution for criminal acts committed against the citizens of a foreign state; and similarly in time of war, a state that is in belligerent occupation of enemy territory has the obligation to punish its soldiers if they violate basic rights of the resident citizens. Articles 41 and 56 of the Hague Convention, and Article 28 of the Geneva Convention, explicitly lay down this principle in regard to property rights. And it is obvious, said Verdross (pp. 20-21), that if an occupying power is obliged by international law to punish violations of residents' property rights it cannot be entitled to refrain from punishing such crimes as homicide, assault, and other attacks on the personal integrity of resident citizens if these crimes are contrary to established rules of warfare. Extraterritoriality grants the privilege of immunity from prosecution only because the members of the occupying forces are subject to prosecution by their own administrative and judicial agencies; therefore extraterritoriality implies also a duty—the duty to prosecute those violators of the law who are exempted from the jurisdiction of the courts of the occupied country.

But to claim the privileges of extraterritoriality without adhering to the duties is an abuse of law. Thus if a state in belligerent occupation systematically violates its duty to prosecute members of its army for crimes against the resident population, it forfeits the privileges of extraterritoriality. There is nothing in international law that would oblige any state to refrain from prosecuting those violators of law who would otherwise be inadequately punished or not punished at all: if violators of the rules of warfare are not punished by their own state 'a concurrent criminal jurisdiction of the violated state seems to be justified' (Verdross, p. 25).

This theory not only clarifies the Lieber provisions for the punishment of war prisoners but also explains why it was only war prisoners that were considered subject to prosecution by the other side—why Coleman, for example, could not be prosecuted by the courts of Tennessee. The justification of the captor's right to punish a war prisoner for crimes committed before his capture, for which he has not been punished by his own authorities, lies in the impossibility of his being brought to trial by his own sovereign. Lieber's Instructions take it for granted that the enemy has a responsible government and that unless circumstances make it impossible that government will mete out adequate punishment if a member of its armed forces commits a crime. The criminal's own government may be actually prevented from prosecuting him, but in all other cases each belligerent may rely on the decency of the enemy government and the honesty of its courts.

During the Civil War the crimes of members of the armed forces were viewed as isolated acts of individual soldiers. War crimes were not considered the product of a systematic campaign sponsored or encouraged by the hostile government. As James F. Rhodes has remarked (vol. 5, p. 504), in discussing a famous war-criminal case—the maltreatment of Northern prisoners by the Confederate Captain Wirz: 'Nowhere did [Lincoln] charge the Confederates with cruelty. In no message to Congress, in no public or private letter did he make a point of the alleged barbarous treatment of Northern soldiers held captive at the South.' And the American war-criminal cases of the Civil War are even today reliable precedents for cases that arise in a war in which both parties adhere to the rules of international law as a matter of principle.

But in a war in which one belligerent defies the rules of international law in its treatment of inhabitants of occupied territory, the factual situation is so different that the old cases can no longer be regarded as precedents. A belligerent that is unwilling to punish its own war criminals must be treated as if it is unable to enforce its criminal statutes. In that situation there is no longer any meaning in the basic distinction between war criminals who have been taken prisoner and those who have otherwise fallen into the hands of the opponent. Both are subject to prosecution on the ground that their own government fails to hold them liable for their actions.

If in the present war we adopt the 'international-law' principle of war-criminal prosecution we can, on a sound legal basis, refuse the privileges of extraterritoriality to those who have participated in the occupation of our allied nations, and at the same time claim those privileges for our own troops in occupation of enemy territory. Denial of the privileges of extraterritoriality to the members of an army which has defied the duties of that status represents a 'negation of a negation,' in the meaning of Hegelian legal philosophy, and leads to the restoration of law. Thus the punishment of war criminals on the basis of the 'international-law' principle is not an act of vengeance but is rather the exercise of a judicial power which the hostile government has failed to apply to its own subjects. Far from being an expression of political expediency, such procedures against the German war criminals will restore the principle of equality before the law. Enforcement of the rules of international law against the German occupation agencies will have its final justification in the adherence of the United Nations occupation agencies to the principle that the rule of law must govern military occupation as well as the less turbid procedures of peace.

PART II

THE PEACE PERIOD

1920-23

IV

The Rhineland Agreement

DURING the armistice period, the government of the occupying powers in the Rhineland had represented a combination of improvisations and political experiments, with the authority of the military being gradually replaced by that of civilian agencies. During the peace period it was based on a carefully prepared plan. But the entire regime represented a compromise settlement of one of the most far-reaching controversies that developed around the peace table.

The decision reached at the Peace Conference in April 1919, that the Rhineland should remain an integral part of Germany but should be occupied for fifteen years, as guarantee for the execution of the treaty, meant a rejection of the French demand for a separation of that territory from the Reich. France waived this demand in return for a promise received from Wilson and Lloyd George that she would be guaranteed against German aggression. After it became evident that the United States and England would not recognize the promise of their representatives, France concentrated her hope for security on her power position in the occupied territory, using the methods of economic pressure, propaganda, and military force. Thus the occupation, during the peace period as well as the armistice period, was characterized by internal conflicts among the victorious powers, with France attempting the line of self-help on the ground that her allies had broken a gentlemen's agreement. It was only after the Locarno pact of 1925 had temporarily put an end to the diplomatic tensions between England and France, and to the political, economic, and military feuds between

France and Germany, that the Rhineland occupation ceased to be one of the chief causes of unrest for the whole European continent.

France had a rather good case when she tried to find new safeguards for her security after it became clear that the American and English promises could not be realized. But she did not have a good case when she tried to do this by escaping the strict application of the international treaty governing the occupation. In this effort she was compelled to use artificial arguments: the true motives for her actions against Germany would have had no legal standing, as the Wilson-Lloyd George promise of guarantee was not a part of the occupation agreement. Even before the Paris compromise had become legally binding, and before she had any reason to doubt the promise of her allies, France had weakened her position, by sponsoring the Dorten putsch. Her role in that affair led the other powers to seek special safeguards against a repetition of such an adventure (Noyes, pp. 38 ff.). Thus the political compromise by means of which the status of the Rhineland had been settled in general was supplemented by a technical compromise concerning the methods of occupation.

The peace instrument itself contained no details concerning the occupation, but it required Germany to observe all the conditions laid down in a special occupation agreement. This document, the 'Rhineland Agreement,' had a somewhat turbulent history.

In a meeting of the Peace Conference on 6 May 1919, Marshal Foch pleaded his objections to the Rhineland compromise which had been reached, shortly before, by Clemenceau, Wilson, and Lloyd George. The conference rejected his arguments and on 8 May it requested the Supreme War Council to draft a statute for the planned Rhineland occupation. Three days later a plan was presented. This draft (published in Miller, vol. 19, p. 490) followed very closely the precedent established by Germany after the Franco-Prussian war, and in several passages it was even a literal copy of the Rouen convention of 1871.

The most significant provisions of the War Council's draft were that the existing state of martial law should be continued, with its enforcement entrusted to the military authorities; and that the German administrative agencies should be obliged to comply with any measures that the military authorities of the occupying powers, or the civil officials attached to them, found necessary 'in the interest of the security, maintenance and distribution of the troops.' Both these provisions were taken almost bodily from the convention of Rouen. In addition to other stipulations concerning military courts, railway regulations, and the appointment and dismissal of German officials, the draft contained a clause declaring that the military authorities should have the right to veto German legislative acts, including 'industrial regulations, awards, or agreements.'

This last provision deserves a special word. Certainly its formulation was too vague, and, if adopted, it would probably have been strongly opposed by labor all over the world as a dangerous attempt to interfere with the domain of the unions, for it permitted identical treatment of cartel regulations and collective labor agreements. The history of the Sherman Act during the last few decades is ample evidence that such identical treatment is not practicable. Collective agreements are the result of social conflicts between capital and labor; cartel regulations represent internal business affairs. In collective agreements the power of capital is confronted with the power of labor; in cartel regulations the power of capital is not restricted but rather strengthened. Collective agreements are concluded under the control of public opinion; cartel regulations are the product of secret negotiations. The different character of the two makes it essential that they be treated differently, not only in domestic affairs but also when military occupation introduces a condition of international control.

But aside from this ambiguity in formulation, the proposal to allow a veto of 'industrial regulations, awards, or agreements' revealed a clear understanding of the fact that in so thoroughly organized a country as Germany was in 1919, social and economic organizations play as important a legislative role as do parliaments and administrative agencies. The Supreme War Council at least realized that supervision of German economic and social life was practically impossible unless cartel regulations were treated in the same way as statutes and ordinances.

This draft met with fierce objections from Noyes and Stuart, American and British representatives on the Inter-Allied Rhineland Commission. Pierrepont Noyes characterized it (p. 42) as 'an extremely brutal document,' and in a historic letter to President Wilson declared that 'force and more force must inevitably be the history of such occupation long continued.' The letter ended with a 'skeleton plan' (Baker, vol. 3, pp. 255-6; Hunt, pp. 313-14) which will be quoted in extenso because it was of basic importance in the history of the Rhineland occupation under the Versailles treaty:

SKELETON PLAN

I. As few troops as possible, concentrated in barracks or reserve areas with no 'billeting,' excepting possibly for officers.
II. Complete self-government for the territory, with the exceptions below.
III. A civil commission with powers:—
    (a) to make regulations or change old ones whenever German law or actions
        (1) threaten the carrying out of Treaty terms, or—
        (2) threaten the comfort or security of troops.
    (b) To authorize the army to take control under martial law, either in danger spots or throughout the territory whenever conditions seem to them to make this necessary.

Noyes said in his letter that in sketching the plan he was 'forgetting the apparent ambitions of the French.' Actually, however, he had by no means forgotten them but was making every

effort to cope with them. On 21 May General Mangin, commander of the 10th French Army, had approached General Liggett in matters concerning the Rhineland republic. It was on
27 May that Noyes sent his letter to President Wilson. In the
words of General Allen (*Occupation*, p. 85), 'Doctor Dorten's
efforts in attempting to foment revolution in the occupied territories had considerable influence in causing the drafting of this
letter and yet more in determining the future policy there.' General Mordacq, French commanding general in Wiesbaden, who,
as late as 1926, vehemently criticized the basic ideas of the skeleton plan, also held General Mangin chiefly responsible for Noyes'
action (Mordacq, *La mentalité allemande . . .* p. 158). The history of that famous letter is ample evidence that the modalities
of an occupation by allied armies may be determined by considerations of inter-allied policy rather than by the necessities
arising out of common interests against the conquered enemy.

It is evident at a glance that the skeleton plan overturned the
two basic characteristics of the draft submitted by the Supreme
War Council: martial law was no longer to be the rule, but only
the exception; and administration of the occupied territory by
military agencies was to be replaced by the supervision of a civil
commission. Though this 'civilian' plan was vehemently opposed
by Marshal Foch and his aides (Noyes, p. 47), a special committee was appointed to examine the two drafts. And it was this
committee, under the chairmanship of the French minister
Loucheur, which formulated the final text of the Rhineland
Agreement, on the basis of a compromise between Lloyd George
and Loucheur (Lloyd George, vol. 1, pp. 485 ff.; Carles, p. 302;
'La France sur le Rhin,' 1929, p. 124). The text of the Rhineland
Agreement is presented in Appendix I of this study.

The Loucheur committee adopted two fundamental ideas of
the Noyes skeleton plan: the rejection of a continuation of
martial law; and the substitution of a civil commission for military agencies as supreme representatives of the occupying powers. But it made one fundamental change: whereas Noyes had

suggested that the legislative power of the civil commission should extend to all situations in which the carrying out of the peace terms was threatened, the final Rhineland Agreement allowed the High Commission to issue ordinances only 'so far as may be necessary for securing the maintenance, safety and requirements of the Allied and Associated forces' (Article 3). During the next years this change in wording was to prove of the greatest significance in the development of European history. Adoption of the much broader Noyes proposal would have given grounds for intervention in nearly all fields of German internal affairs. In the matter of reparations, for example, there were innumerable German 'actions' in social and economic politics that could have been held to 'threaten the carrying out of treaty terms.'

In the discussions concerning the final form of the occupation agreement, organizational questions completely overshadowed the functional side of the problem. The skeleton plan made no explicit recommendations concerning the administration of economic agencies, and the draft finally agreed upon was almost equally silent on this matter. During the negotiations of the Loucheur committee the British delegates had suggested that the jurisdiction of the civil commission should include economic questions. These, they said, are closely interrelated with social problems, and therefore with the maintenance of public order. But the British suggestions were not incorporated in the Rhineland Agreement ('La France sur le Rhin,' 1929, p. 125). In its final form that document took no notice of cartels, and touched upon collective agreements only indirectly, in a special provision concerning arbitration of labor conflicts in vital industries and public utilities. During the Ruhr conflict, early in 1923, the powerful coal syndicate was converted into an agency of the occupation authorities, but because of the peculiar situation of that period the results of the experiment have little relevance for the general problems of occupation government. During the period reviewed in this study the occupation authorities exercised no cartel control whatever—though this does not mean, of course, that no cartel problems arose.

The Rhineland Agreement contained thirteen articles, in which the principles of the occupation were laid down. In Article 2 it provided that the governing authority, known as the Inter-Allied Rhineland High Commission, should be a civilian body, and in Article 13 it gave that body the power to declare a state of siege and to delegate to the military authorities the enforcement of martial law. Article 3, its most important provision, defined the general jurisdiction of the High Commission and gave that body the authority to issue ordinances which 'shall have the force of law.'

Article 3 also provided that, except in regard to offenses by or against the members of the occupying armies, the German courts should 'continue to exercise civil and criminal jurisdiction.' And Article 5 declared that civil administration should be exercised by German authorities under German law and under the authority of the central German Government, 'except in so far as it may be necessary for the High Commission by Ordinance . . . to adapt that administration to the needs and circumstances of military occupation.' The remaining articles dealt principally with such matters as arrest, tax exemption, the maintenance of railways, telegraph and telephone systems, and the postal service, problems of requisition, billeting, and the like (Articles 4 and 6-12).

This was a particularly liberal document. The jurisdictions of the High Commission and the military tribunals were restricted to a minimum. In the field of administration, agencies of the occupying powers were almost unmentioned. It soon became evident, however, that not all the ordinances issued by the High Commission were in entire conformance with the text and spirit of the Rhineland Agreement. The variance between them and the reasons for that variance constitute one of the most significant lessons to be learned from the occupation.

The Rhineland Agreement was signed by representatives of

the victorious powers and Germany, along with the peace treaty, on 28 June 1919. Thereafter several notes were exchanged in clarification of problems that might arise, and these diplomatic instruments were considered authentic interpretations. A German questionnaire of 12 July was answered on 29 July by Clemenceau, President of the Peace Conference, and this note, usually referred to as the Réponse de Versailles, was the most important document in that diplomatic correspondence. The Germans expressed their attitude toward the Réponse de Versailles in a second note of 7 August, which was answered on 14 October. Finally, immediately after the peace treaty had been ratified and the High Commission had passed five basic ordinances, which the Germans regarded as at least partly contrary to the agreement, the Germans protested in a note of 12 January 1920. On 2 March Millerand, who had succeeded Clemenceau, answered the protest in the negative, and his note concluded the diplomatic correspondence on the Rhineland Agreement. (The text of all this highly important correspondence is contained in Kraus and Rödiger, vol. 2, pp. 1094-1157.)

The German attitude toward the Rhineland Agreement and its application by the High Commission has found no better expression than in this diplomatic protest of 12 January. German writers like Vogels and Heyland, who later published elaborate treatises on the Rhineland occupation from the German point of view, added few new ideas to this excellent brief. Looking upon the Rhineland Agreement as the Magna Charta of the occupation, the German Government raised the question whether ordinances contrary to its provisions should not be treated as null and void. True disciples of Hegel, the Germans juxtaposed to the thesis of High Commission supervision of Germany the antithesis of German supervision of the activities of the controller. Unfortunately no synthesis was ever found.

So far as the European parties to it were concerned, the Rhineland Agreement, again along with the Versailles treaty, became effective on 10 January 1920, after these nations had ratified the treaty. The United States' failure to ratify created a particularly difficult situation in the occupied territory, for no provision of the treaty or the agreement envisaged a situation in which one of the occupying powers remained in a state of war with Germany. It was out of the question to uphold the armistice regime after peace had been concluded with the majority of the powers; this would have represented an open violation of the peace at the very moment at which it came into force. On the other hand, an application of the Rhineland Agreement to the entire occupied territory, including the American zone, would have openly contradicted the non-ratification by the United States.

In a session of 13 December 1919, the Supreme War Council decided that the jurisdiction of the High Commission should extend also to the American zone, but this resolution was vehemently opposed by the American authorities in the occupied territory (Allen, Occupation, p. 120). After long negotiations General Allen's suggestion was adopted, according to which the American zone should, in theory, continue to be controlled by the armistice provisions; the American commander declared his readiness, however, to proclaim binding, by virtue of his military command, the ordinances of the High Commission (Allen, Occupation, pp. 122-4, 216-17). Since the United States could not permit ordinances to be introduced in her zone of occupation which had been enacted without participation of an American delegate, the necessity arose for the United States to participate in the deliberations of the High Commission even though she was not an official member of that body. This difficulty was overcome by a compromise according to which the highest American authority attended the meetings unofficially.

Even after November 1921, when the United States ratified the German-American peace treaty of 25 August 1921, the legal situation did not change, at least as far as the practical side of the problem was concerned. According to that treaty, the United States was privileged to participate in international commissions established under the Versailles treaty or its supplementary agreements, but she did not make use of this privilege with respect to the Rhineland High Commission. In theory the armistice regulation remained in force for the United States army until it left Germany early in 1923. But though the United States never officially recognized the jurisdiction of the High Commission her representative in the Rhineland played as important a role as the representatives of the countries that had ratified the Versailles treaty.

French writers, who have maintained time and again that the Americans, because of the skeleton plan, should be considered the spiritual fathers of the peacetime occupation regime, indicted the United States for inconsistency (for example, Carles, p. 302). They pointed out that although the United States had been largely responsible for the substitution of civilian for military administration, she was the only one who did not officially recognize the sovereignty of the High Commission in the territories under her supervision, that she was not officially represented in that body, and that for the greater part of her participation in the occupation her representative was a general. In view of the circumstances, the quite logical criticism that the American attitude was 'paradoxical' appears legalistic.

V

Institutions of the Occupying Powers

THE Rhineland Agreement represented an attempt to apply basic ideas of constitutional government to the rule of an occupation authority. But it included very few provisions that stipulated how these principles were to be carried out in actual practice. Thus the governmental structure that functioned during the peace period was, except for the military courts and police, the creation of the High Commission, in its capacity as highest authority in the occupied territory. In the following pages only the broad outlines and general functioning of these institutional arrangements will be discussed. The more far-reaching implications of the powers vested in the occupation authorities will be left for the final chapters of this study.

THE HIGH COMMISSION

The Rhineland Agreement provided that the High Commission should be composed of four Commissioners, one for each of the four occupying powers. Each Commissioner's appointment required the approval of the three other governments. The Commissioners were assisted by general secretaries and a technical staff, and questions regarding such personnel were decided by the individual Commissioners. In December 1920 about 1,300 persons were employed by the High Commission, 115 of whom had the rank of officials, the remainder performing clerical or mechanical tasks; of the 115 officials 14 were employed in work for the Americans, 16 for the British, 20 for the Belgians, and 65 for the French (Schneidewin, p. 11). The High Commission as a whole appointed only the two Inter-Allied general secretaries, who assisted in preparing and directing the meetings, one of these general secretaries belonging to the Anglo-American group, the other to the French-Belgian group.[1]

The seat of the High Commission was Coblenz, capital of the Prussian Rheinland province and chief city of the American zone of occupation. It was considered to be a council permanently in session; as a rule it met once a week, but during the first months of its existence it frequently held several meetings a week. The French Commissioner was ex officio chairman, and his task was to preside over the meetings and to represent the body both to the governments of the occupying powers and to Germany. The Commissioners were supposed to attend the meetings in person, but if this was impossible the absentee was represented by a member of his staff. Technical advisers were admitted if any one Commissioner expressed a desire for their assistance. The meetings were not public.

Decision was by a majority vote, and in case of a tie the vote of the chairman, the French delegate, had double weight. Since most of the controversies arose between England and the United States on the one hand and France on the other hand, Belgium's vote was frequently of decisive importance; but in most cases unanimity was reached (Rousseau, La Haute Commission . . . p. 54). During the Ruhr conflict, however, after the United States had left the Rhineland, England was often outvoted, and the measures enacted in 1923 against the opposition of England were labeled 'special ordinances.' If a delegate was outvoted he was entitled to ask for a suspension of the decision in order to facilitate diplomatic negotiations among the governments concerned, and an agreement reached in that way was transformed into a decision of the High Commission.

The High Commission appointed special committees com-

---

[1] The text of the 'Règlement intérieur de la Haute Commission' is published in the Recueil . . . 1923, pp. 4-11. The most detailed analysis of the internal organization of this body is to be found in the article signed by A. I., pp. 245-73; to a considerable extent the following description is based on that article.

posed of members of the technical staffs of the individual Commissioners. In the course of time some committees disappeared
and new ones were created, but at the end of 1922 the following ones were in existence (Rousseau, *La Haute Commission*
. . . p. 55, note 2): Administration, Traffic, Finances, Legal
Questions, Information and Public Security, Requisitions, Economic Affairs, and Coal Questions, the last two being, in part,
hangovers from the sanctions period of 1921. The committee for
Food Questions had practically ceased its work in 1921, but
it was not officially dissolved and it could be summoned at any
time at the request of its president. (A German statement concerning the work of these committees may be found in W.
Vogels, 'Die Organe . . .' p. 413.) By a resolution of 4 January
1922, the High Commission created a special committee for
School Questions, which will be discussed later in this study;
though only temporary in character and limited to mere investigations, this body aroused a great deal of opposition from the
Germans.

The chief task of the High Commission was the enactment
of ordinances. As soon as an ordinance was enacted, notification was sent to the commanders of the occupying armies and
to the German Government. The ordinances were published, in
French and English, in an official *Gazette*, and a German translation was published by the German authorities of the occupied
territory. The *Gazette*, which contains not only the ordinances
but also the so-called 'instructions,' and short extracts from the
minutes of the Commission, was published over a period of
nine years (1920-28), and is, of course, indispensable source material for this period. In addition, the French published, in several volumes, a collection of legal material concerning occupation questions (*Recueil* . . .), in the nature of a commentary on
the provisions of the Rhineland Agreement. Most important of
all the ordinances were those published on 10 January 1920,
particularly the first, which was concerned with questions of
legislation, the second, which dealt with judicial problems, and

the third, which contained administrative rules regarding publications and public meetings. These three ordinances and the Rhineland Agreement represent the basic law of the Rhineland occupation (see Appendices I and II).

Whereas the ordinances of the High Commission contained provisions applying to the general public, the instructions (according to Ordinance 93 of 1 July 1921) pertained exclusively to public authorities or officials. By making this clear distinction, the High Commission co-ordinated occupation law with the German legal system and thus considerably facilitated its understanding by the German agencies. Ordinances corresponded to the German concept of *Rechtsverordnungen*, instructions to *Verwaltungsverordnungen* (on this basic German distinction see Fleiner, p. 62). Co-ordination of those parts of 'municipal' law which are enacted by the occupation authorities with the remainder, which originates from the legislative branch of the occupied country, is particularly important in a state like Germany, where the classification of a legal instrument is an important datum in its interpretation.

Only the High Commission could enact ordinances. Other tasks that belonged to its jurisdiction it delegated to subordinate administrative agencies, reserving for itself, however, the right of supervision and of decision in important cases. The activities of the High Commission were partly direct, through its own exercise of governmental power, and partly indirect, through its control over the governmental powers of German agencies. On the whole it was in the field of administration, where the individual official is dependent on the commands of his superiors, that the occupation authorities exercised their powers indirectly, and in the field of judicial functions that their activities were direct; in legislation the High Commission exercised direct and indirect governmental power of almost equal importance.

But the powers of the High Commission cannot be separated into legislative, judicial, and executive. There is no profit in examining, for example, whether its right to approve German statutes was a legislative power, whether its right to cancel court decisions was judicial power, or whether both were attributes of executive power. Occupation represents not a constitutional government, characterized by a balance of powers, but rather a sort of emergency government in which all forms of power are concentrated in one centralized body. As Ireton, American analyst of the Rhineland occupation, has expressed it (p. 460):

The High Commission . . . is the antithesis of the legal doctrine enunciated by Montesquieu and so readily accepted by the framers of our Constitution: the triune distinction of power, the separation of governmental authority into executive, legislative and judicial departments, each distinct and independent of the others, yet all so correlated as to make one consistent, harmonious and logical system of government. The Commission itself exercises executive, legislative and judicial authority, and not infrequently issues its administrative mandates, enacts important and far-reaching ordinances, and reviews, as would an appellate court, the action of a German civil or criminal court at one and the same sitting.

The direct legislative power of the High Commission was explicitly provided for in the Rhineland Agreement, and therefore the Germans never challenged it. Without such an explicit provision they would not have recognized the validity of the ordinances, as is clear from a decision by the Reichsgericht on 2 November 1920 (55 RGSt 109). On that occasion the Reichsgericht had to decide whether a rule issued by the Allied military command in occupied Upper Silesia could be pleaded as a defense in a German court. It decided in the negative, and declared that military occupation in time of peace involves no right of legislation unless that power is provided in an international treaty.

The ordinances enacted by the High Commission, though originating in an international body, formed an integral part of German law. In the words of 'A. I.' (p. 253): 'These ordinances must be considered incorporated into the German legal system;

consequently the German legal system was changed substantially for the duration of the occupation in the occupied territories.' Here again there is a confirming Reichsgericht decision (106 RGZ 59), which this time dealt with the German occupation of Belgium. It should be mentioned that according to the German law of procedure, appeal to the Reichsgericht is admissible only if the appellant pleads a violation of a German federal statute. In this case the appeal was based on the contention that the trial court had misinterpreted an ordinance enacted by the German occupation authorities during the war in Belgium. The Reichsgericht rejected the appeal, declaring that the ordinance, enacted by a German authority, was substantially a part of Belgian law. It is noteworthy that this case was decided on 15 December 1922, when foreign occupation authorities were in Germany.

But the High Commission's indirect exercise of legislative power—its assertion of the right to decide whether German legislative acts should be applicable in the occupied territory—gave rise to one of the most controversial issues of the occupation. In the armistice period this problem had been handled differently by the different army commands. At that time, according to Ernst Zitelmann, professor of law at Bonn university (pp. 131-2), the Belgian authorities did not recognize the right of the German central legislature to enact statutes applicable in the territory under Belgian control; the Americans and the British did not object to the enforcement of newly enacted statutes in the zones occupied by their armies; and in the French zone 'the legal situation is said to resemble the Belgian.'

The Germans, however, held that legislative power is inherent in sovereignty, that the German state was still sovereign in the occupied territory, and that therefore German statutes came immediately into force in that area. This attitude of the political authorities was approved by the Reichsgericht on 29 September 1921, in a decision concerning an armistice case (56 RGSt 194; *Annual Digest*, 1919-22, case 315, p. 450). The defendant, a resident of the French zone, was indicted for violating a decree issued by the revolutionary government in December 1918, according to which persons infected with a venereal disease were forbidden to have sexual intercourse. He pleaded that the statute had not been approved by the French authorities, but the court rejected his defense, on the ground that German statutes became automatically valid in the occupied territory.

After the ratification of the peace treaty, the High Commission regulated this problem in Ordinance 1, issued on 10 January 1920 (Articles 7-9). According to these provisions all newly enacted statutes had to be submitted to the High Commission, which decided whether they might prejudice the maintenance, safety, or requirements of the troops. If not vetoed by the Commission they came into force in the occupied territory, but even then the Commission could 'subsequently order the suspension' of such statutes.

The Germans, however, continued to maintain that statutes came into force automatically in the occupied territory.[2] They interpreted the veto power as a 'condition subsequent' to the applicability of a statute, whereas the High Commission looked upon it as a 'condition precedent' to that validity. The distinction was merely theoretical so long as the German Government submitted all newly enacted statutes to the High Commission for examination. It assumed considerable practical importance, however, at the time of the Ruhr conflict, when the German Government ceased to respect Articles 7-9 of Ordinance 1. This issue was the basis of the famous coal-tax decision, which will be discussed in a later chapter.

In declaring that the occupation should be governed by an international civilian body, the framers of the Rhineland Agreement attempted an experiment that was unprecedented in mili-

[2] The leading cases are a decision of the Bavarian supreme court of 29 July 1922 (reported by Silberschmidt, p. 211) and a decision of the Bavarian supreme administrative court of 5 December 1928 (reported in *Annual Digest*, 1927-28, case 80, p. 119). See also the decision of the Reichsgericht of 24 October 1921 (56 RGSt 196).

tary occupations. It is therefore worth examining how successful this effort was to subject the army to the authority of a civilian commission.

The investiture of the High Commission with supreme authority did not mean, of course, that the army was completely excluded from the exercise of immediate governmental functions. By the Rhineland Agreement the military commanders were entrusted with certain powers of great significance, such as the right to requisition (Article 6); the right to bring before military tribunals those who committed offenses against the persons or property of the armed forces (Article 3); the right to exact obedience from the personnel employed on all means of communication (Article 10), in the telegraph and telephone services (Article 11), and in the postal service (Article 12).

On the delicate question of who was empowered to declare a state of martial law the Rhineland Agreement was unequivocal. Article 13 declared that this prerogative belonged to the High Commission, though once a state of siege had been declared, the military authorities were entrusted with its enforcement, having 'the powers provided in the German Imperial Law of May 30th, 1892.' But the framers of that document were so imbued with a fear of military dictatorship that they concluded a special agreement on this subject: in a memorandum of 13 June 1919 (Miller, vol. 20, p. 396) they declared that in the event of a state of martial law, the Commander in Chief was to act in consultation with and only after approval of the High Commission, unless purely military problems were at issue. The Germans were informed of this regulation in the Réponse de Versailles.

The same principle of subordinating the exercise of military power was evident in Instruction 9 of 1 April 1920 (*Gazette*, 1920, No. IV-V, p. 67). In case of emergency the local military authorities were empowered to take the necessary military steps on their own initiative, but were obliged to inform the High Commission at once. Instruction 9 (enacted immediately after the breakdown of the Kapp putsch and during a state of civil war in the Ruhr valley) provided that the local German police officer should apply to the local representative of the High Commission for military assistance, if he considered his own forces too weak to maintain public order. The High Commission or its representative would decide whether military forces were to be employed to assist the German police forces.

The provisions concerning the application of martial law were more significant in theory than in practice. During the whole period of the Rhineland occupation, martial law was declared only once in the territory entrusted to the guardianship of the High Commission (Düsseldorf and Duisburg and the Ruhr valley, which were not occupied by virtue of the Versailles treaty, were not subject to the Rhineland Agreement). On 6 April 1920, on the occasion of the Allied occupation of Frankfurt and Darmstadt (which took place against strong American protests), General Degoutte, with the authorization of the High Commission, declared a state of siege; it ended on 2 May, by virtue of a decision of the Commission on 1 May (*Recueil* . . . 1923, p. 33). Paradoxical as it may seem, martial law was proclaimed less frequently in the occupied than in the unoccupied part of Germany during these turbulent years.

Just as the Germans in 1871, after the Franco-Prussian war, had followed a French statute of 1849 in regulating the application of martial law, the drafters of the Rhineland Agreement followed a German statute of 1892 in their provision on this subject. But before the Rhineland Agreement became effective, the Weimar Constitution of 11 August 1919, in its fateful Article 48, had replaced the earlier statute by a provision allowing the civilian authorities themselves to exercise all the prerogatives of martial law. In less than fifteen years that provision was to be utilized for purposes wholly alien to its intention.

The High Commission's pre-eminence over the army under normal conditions was undisputed after 7 August 1920 (*Recueil* . . . 1923, p. 31). Before that date the military commanders had issued an order generally forbidding the singing of the *Deutsch-landlied* and the hoisting of certain flags. The High Commission declared that the military authorities did not have the power to issue general regulations, and had transgressed their jurisdiction. The military order was annulled. This is the only case on record which deals with a jurisdictional conflict between the military and civilian occupation authorities in the Rhineland.

But the absence of case material does not indicate, of course, that such conflicts did not occur. Indications of their nature may be gleaned from the memoirs of General Mordacq, military adviser to Clemenceau, who outspokenly disapproved of the distribution of jurisdictions between the military and civilian authorities (Mordacq, *La mentalité allemande* . . . pp. 158-9). According to him the Germans never knew whom they should obey, and it was a miracle that a true disaster was avoided, in view of the 'unbearable' dualism of governmental powers. Mordacq declared that either the jurisdictions should have been separated more clearly or a regime should have been introduced similar to that which obtained in the French colonies.

The French general's opposition was not confined to theory: in his practice he exercised powers that corresponded far more to his own ideas than to the regulations laid down in the Rhineland Agreement. In regard to a strike in Wiesbaden, for example, Mordacq declares that at the beginning he did not interfere with the activities of the High Commission, but when he saw that the strike continued he summoned its leaders: 'I addressed them in a very clear and outspoken way. I informed them that they had three hours in which to resume their work. One hour later they informed me that the strike was terminated. I had commanded, they had obeyed' (ibid. p. 54).

An even more significant instance concerned the arrest of the local leader of the German Nationalist party in Wiesbaden, a Dr. Fresenius. After Mordacq had arrested Fresenius, the High Commission ordered his temporary release. Although the French army commander suggested that Mordacq should obey the decision of the High Commission, Fresenius was not released from prison. It is not without interest that the suggestion of Mordacq's superior was coupled with a criticism of the weak policy of the High Commission (ibid. p. 52).

General Mordacq's attitude is ample evidence of the particular difficulties that arise if self-confident military commanders who enjoy great authority, as a result of the successful termination of a war, are subjected to the control of an international civilian authority with regard to the administration of an occupied territory. The generals, of course, are inclined to consider such an administration their proper domain. And it is quite possible that the great reputation of the highest military commander will prove a far stronger force than the most elaborate regulations and definitions of treaties and statutes by virtue of which civilian authorities are recognized as bearers of the supreme power. Thus in the occupied Rhineland, 'Whenever Marshal Foch's name appears on any communication, the French members of the Commission lose sight of the fact that this tribunal or institution is declared the supreme representative of the Inter-Allied and Associated Powers in the occupied territories' (Allen, *Journal,* p. 158).

Local Representatives of the High Commission

According to Article 5 of the Rhineland Agreement the civil administration of the provinces, 'districts,' 'circles,' and municipalities making up the occupied territory was to remain in the hands of the German authorities. In its diplomatic note of 12 July 1919, the German Government interpreted this provision as an implicit abolition of the local controllers and administrators of the armistice period. Paragraph 29 of the Réponse de Versailles recognized the German interpretation in so far as the supervision of the local German administrations was concerned, but added that 'in the interest of the population the High Commission has the power to maintain permanent representatives charged with establishing liaison between the local German authorities and the local military authorities, as well as with the High Commission itself.' This paragraph was the legal basis of the local representatives of the peace period.

In their answer of 7 August the Germans suggested that the German Reichskommissar should serve as such an intermediary between the military and civilian occupation authorities and the local German agencies. Characterizing the activities of the Allies' earlier local administrators as 'a particularly dark chapter in the history of the armistice period,' they emphasized the necessity for a drastic change if the occupying powers insisted on appointing local delegates of their own, and proposed that such agents be restricted to routine work and the communication of suggestions. This note remained unanswered.

The first ordinances published by the High Commission, on 10 January 1920, contained several provisions (in Ordinance 3) dealing with the tasks allotted to the local representatives. Their duties were to include not only routine work, such as the granting of travel permits and the handling of information concerning change of residence, but also matters of executive significance. They were authorized, in case of emergency, to seize books and pamphlets, to suspend for three days the publication of daily newspapers, and to forbid the bringing in of newspapers from the unoccupied territory. The required notice of all political meetings was to be addressed to them, and they were empowered to supervise political meetings, and, if necessary, to dissolve them. They had the right to cancel shooting licenses, to supervise the trade in arms and ammunition. They had the right to supervise the German prisons (Ordinance 2 and decision of the High Commission of 24 March 1920, *Recueil* . . . 1923, pp. 13 ff.).

In its protest of 12 January the German Government accused the High Commission of having transgressed its rights regarding the powers of the local representatives. This protest was of no avail, and local representatives were appointed in all administrative units that had any significance, with the exception of the provincial government of the Prussian Rheinland province; the governor of that province, who resided in Coblenz, had direct relations with the General Secretary of the High Commission (decision of 28 February 1920, *Recueil* . . . 1923, p. 13).

The German protest was repeated in a letter of the Reichskommissar to the High Commission, but this protest, too, was rejected, in a letter of 11 June 1920, written by Tirard (*Gazette*, 1920, No. VI-VII, p. 61). Its most important passage declared that the German authorities were required not only to comply with all ordinances and instructions of the High Commission but also to reply to all questions addressed to them by the local representatives, 'without disputing them and without previously referring them to their superiors.' This amounted to a considerable interference with the hierarchical structure of the German bureaucratic machine, for it was likely that the German officials, wholly subject to the directions of their superiors, would frequently have difficulty in explaining to the local representatives, without assistance, administrative acts that originated not in their own initiative but in orders from above. Such a drastic rule seems justified, however, in view of the fact that it was a favorite trick of German administrators to deny their own jurisdiction and shift responsibility to other authorities.

Tirard's letter further declared that the local representatives were the usual intermediaries between the High Commission and the German authorities, but that the military authorities could decide for themselves whether they preferred to have their own agents. The High Commission, said Tirard, would normally communicate with the local German administrative agencies through its representatives; only in exceptional cases would there be any immediate contact between the High Commission and the local German administrators. Although the representatives were not empowered to issue ordinances or instructions, they had the right to address to the German authorities all requests for information that they considered necessary and proper in the framework of occupation law.

The final word in the dispute was spoken in the sittings of the High Commission on 19, 20, and 22 July (*Gazette*, 1920, No. VIII-IX, p. 73). At that time the Commission repeated that it had not conferred on its representatives 'powers of administration or control which might enable them to interfere in German administration by approving or countersigning official documents.' But it stressed that the representatives were appointed for the purpose of insuring that its ordinances, instructions, and decisions were observed, and that for this purpose they were authorized to take the 'necessary executive measures,' within the limits of the powers conferred upon them.

Thus the local representatives had threefold powers: they were liaison officers between the civilian and military agencies of the occupying countries on the one hand, and the German agencies and population on the other hand; they exercised certain executive powers; and they were authorized to supervise the German administration in matters that the High Commission considered related to its jurisdiction. It may be said that the local representatives were the executive agents of the High Commission, or, as Rousseau has formulated it (*La Haute Commission . . .* p. 63), they were 'the eyes of the High Commission.'

In his book Tirard (p. 117) defined the tasks of the local representatives as follows: 'they were to make sure that the German authorities applied the decisions of the High Commission without reservation; that they did not conduct themselves in contradiction to the Rhineland Agreement; and that they did not act in a way contrary to our security and prestige.' These last words are of particular interest. The right to interfere in matters concerned with the 'prestige' of the occupying powers, by dissolving meetings and confiscating books and periodicals, makes it quite understandable that the local representatives formed one of the chief grievances of the peacetime period of occupation, and that the dispute on their powers never came to an end. In the English and American zones, however, their duties were considerably less extensive (Allen, *Occupation*, p. 151; Apex, p.

160). On 1 November 1921, there were 11 district representatives and 75 circle delegates, 49 of the latter being in the French zone, 13 in the Belgian, and the remaining 13 in the British and American zones (Schneidewin, p. 12).

Tirard's statement in his letter of 11 June 1920, that the German complaints were 'entirely unfounded,' does not find confirmation in General Allen's book on the occupation. There Allen gives a rather long list of instances (*Occupation*, pp. 150-51) in which the representatives transgressed their jurisdiction and interfered in economic life, in the autonomy of the municipalities, and in the hierarchical structure of the German administration. Such transgressions were particularly frequent during the first phase of the peacetime occupation, because in most cases the local representatives were merely the former military *administrateurs* under a new name (Schweisguth, p. 317), the actual personnel remaining virtually unchanged.

The institution of local representatives of the High Commission was abolished in 1925, after the Locarno agreement converted the open occupation into an 'invisible' one. At that time the tasks of these agents, so far as they had not become obsolete, were entrusted to civil-affairs branches of the army. It is noteworthy that six years after the Americans had suggested, for the sake of the German population, that civilian authorities be entrusted with the administrative side of the occupation, the Germans themselves desired the replacement of the local civilian administrators by administrative sections of the army.

A British local representative before and after Locarno, writing under the pseudonym 'Apex,' has said (pp. 201-2): 'The fact that the Germans preferred that power to be exercised by soldiers rather than by civilians showed how the local delegates must have been detested. So much so, that Gaye and I were ordered always to wear uniform on duty so as never to be mistaken for civilians.' Apex wondered at the German attitude, because 'civil administrations are generally supposed to have such a horror of interference by the military.'

This remark reflects a typical Anglo-American attitude toward interference in the administrative process. With a military-minded bureaucracy the interference of foreign civilians may create more psychological difficulties than the interference of foreign army officers. The basic ideas of the Rhineland Agreement originated from and corresponded to Anglo-American political concepts. And neither the Germans nor the French knew how to put these principles into practice in accordance with the spirit that animated them. The Germans, especially, have no true understanding of the significance that common-law countries attribute to the supremacy of civilian government. If the local representatives had been ordered from the beginning 'always to wear uniform,' much trouble could probably have been avoided.

But important as this psychological aspect is, it should not minimize the fact that the German opposition to the local representatives was founded also on valid legal considerations (for a German statement of the legal problems involved see Heyland, *Die Rechtsstellung* . . . pp. 241 ff., especially p. 247). Since the local representatives exercised functions that went beyond the spirit of the Rhineland Agreement and the Réponse de Versailles, functions that were clearly beyond those of liaison officers, their activities discredited the rule of law as basis of the Rhineland occupation.

It is another question whether an efficient control of the Rhineland would have been possible under a strict application of the Rhineland Agreement and the Réponse de Versailles. And this is doubtful, as these documents failed to provide the High Commission with a hierarchical executive machine able to cope with the German bureaucracy. In an occupied territory the supremacy of law is possible only if law is in accordance with the practical requirements of occupation. If an occupation statute is too 'liberal,' if it underestimates the strength of the bureaucratic forces in the occupied country, and overlooks the necessity for an efficient control of these agencies, there is a danger that those entrusted with its application will be led to adapt even its most vital provisions to the demands of expediency. This is what happened in the Rhineland between 1920 and 1925.

COMMERCIAL ACTIVITIES

On 3 June 1919, President Wilson and the American Ambassador Norman H. Davis were discussing the French attempts to penetrate the left bank of the Rhine by economic means. Wilson characterized the Rhineland Agreement, then in process of formulation, as a 'fifteen-year convention under which there would be no interference with the economic or industrial life of the country whatever.' Norman Davis was less hopeful. He pointed out that there was already an agreement that there would be no interference, and it was not being followed. President Wilson closed the discussion with the words, 'My only hope is that when we sign the peace those things will be settled' (Baker, vol. 2, p. 95).

For more than a year after the ratification of the peace treaty, on 10 January 1920, this hope was fulfilled. The provision in Article 5 of the Rhineland Agreement, that, in general, civil administration should 'continue under German law and under the authority of the Central German Government,' had three immediate effects in the economic field: the German customs officers and officials of foreign-trade agencies could be reinstated; in general the German statutes on foreign-trade matters were again applicable in the occupied territory; and the activities of the *sections économiques* were no longer permissible. During its first fifteen months the High Commission enacted no ordinances concerning economic matters. It was supposed to have no jurisdiction in this field, and it even had no special committee for economic questions.

But from the very first day of the peacetime occupation there was a duel between the French political, military, and business forces working toward a penetration of the Rhineland, and the German anti-French state machine and no less anti-French business organizations. Through its restored control over trade agencies the German administration 'was able to refuse licenses without indicating any reasons for its decision, and to ruin, by these machinations, a great number of French businessmen' (De Pange, p. 208). On 22 March 1920, Germany redrafted the law covering her foreign-trade agencies, and though the French Commissioner objected to the new statute on the ground that it would create bad feelings and a state of uneasiness in the occupied territory, which might result in unrest and thus endanger the security of the occupying troops' (Aulneau, p. 351), the High Commission rejected the French protest, and the foreign-trade statute was admitted in its new form. It was probably because of·this dispute that Jacques Carles (p. 357) suggested that the Allied powers should agree upon an interpretation of the Rhineland Agreement 'which does not bring the High Commission into a position in which it is defenseless against the Berlin trade policy,' a policy that he characterized as openly hostile toward France.

The practice of the German foreign-trade agencies was the more objectionable to the French because the Germans not only refused to grant licenses to French businessmen but were 'very liberal in granting such licenses to businessmen of other nations' (De Pange, p. 209). Georges Blondel analyzed the German methods very well when he declared, in a speech given on 13 May 1921 ('L'importance . . .' p. 110): 'Germany went so far as to make use of her cartel organizations for the purpose of organizing her trade for the benefit of certain countries and for the detriment of France, by openly discriminating against French businessmen.'

A hint of the results of these procedures is contained in the diary of Albert Malaurie (pp. 103 ff.). Malaurie there expressed his astonishment that he found no French products in the villages occupied by the French armies. And he learned from Rhenish businessmen that it was too late for French buyers to come to terms with them, because weeks earlier Americans and

Britons had bought all available products of the German factories (the fall of the mark had made German industrial products the cheapest in the world). On 30 May 1920, Malaurie remarked in his diary (p. 119) that in all the towns of the occupied territory the French and Belgian businessmen had organized themselves in economic defense organizations, posting on the walls of the German cities placards in which they strongly protested against the measures taken by the Reich since 10 January. These posters seem to have had little effect, however, for according to Blondel ('L'importance . . .' p. 110) the French businessmen were subjected to so many vexations that many of them left the occupied territory; Aulneau, too (p. 352), says that French merchants were compelled to leave the Rhineland.

But this situation was completely changed in the spring of 1921. On 7 March the London Conference of Allied Governments sent Germany an ultimatum ending with a long list of military and financial sanctions that might be imposed on her if she did not accept the Allies' requirements concerning reparations. Interference with the German foreign-trade administration was not mentioned (the text is reprinted in Keynes, p. 199). The idea of interference originated with France, and was opposed by England; only after strenuous internal struggles among the Allies was England's opposition overcome (Keynes, pp. 24 ff.). The United States took no part in the sanctions policy of her former allies.

The very important provisions regarding foreign trade, included in the sanctions when they were actually imposed, were not primarily concerned with the enforcement of the reparations payments. Rather they were an attempt to adapt the conditions of the Rhineland occupation to the peculiar situation that had developed from the French interventionist policy and the German boycott movement.

So far as they concerned the Rhineland, these sanctions, imposed on 8 March 1921, were as follows:

1. The cities of Düsseldorf and Duisburg were occupied by the Allied armies;

2. The customs duties collected in the occupied territory were seized, a special customs line was established on the eastern border of the territory, trade between the occupied and unoccupied zones was subjected to a special tariff, and the High Commission was given the right to alter the German customs duties and fees;

3. The German state-owned alcohol monopoly was placed under the control of the High Commission, so far as its sections were situated in the occupied territory, and certain income of these sections was placed at the disposal of the Commission;

4. The German foreign-trade agencies in the occupied territory were placed under the direction of the High Commission.

Although reparations problems were outside the jurisdiction of the High Commission, that body was made the executive organ of the London Conference of Allied Governments. In that capacity it acted not on the basis of the Rhineland Agreement but in the name of the governments of France, England, Belgium, and Italy, and exercised a legally unrestricted authority, primarily in economic questions. Its position as bearer of all powers provided for in the Rhineland Agreement remained, of course, unchanged. Thus two systems of occupation control, of wholly different legal character, were administered by the same agency. On 18 April the German Government, without avail, forwarded to the Conference of Ambassadors a note protesting against this use of the legal forms of the Rhineland Agreement for matters wholly outside the scope of that international treaty.

The High Commission created three special bodies to deal with activities arising out of the sanctions: the Customs Managing Board, the Alcohol Committee, and, under the Economic Committee, the Department for Import and Export Licenses (*Emser Amt*). In addition, the jurisdiction of the Allied military courts was extended to cases concerning violations of the ordinances on customs and foreign trade (Ordinance 84 of 27 April 1921)—a provision that gave rise to the highly important Florange case before the French Cour de Cassation, which will be discussed in a later chapter. Finally, the German personnel of railways, postal and telegraph services, and state monopolies was compelled to comply with the orders and instructions of the High Commission bearing on the execution of the sanctions (Ordinance 86 of 28 April 1921).

The High Commission's exercise of its functions concerning the customs and alcohol sanctions needs no detailed examination. In regard to customs it may be mentioned only that a precedent of the armistice period was followed in the provision (Ordinance 88 of 2 June 1921), that the customs functions at the German frontiers could be exercised by Allied officials if the German functionaries were not present or were unwilling to fulfil their legal obligations; but there was a significant change from the armistice period in that the Allied customs officials were expected to apply the German statutes.

And in regard to the alcohol sanctions the most significant development grew out of the attitude of the German officials themselves. On 6 May the High Commission instituted its control over the Rhineland sections of the alcohol monopoly, but the Berlin central management of that agency refused to collaborate and encouraged its local officials in the Rhineland not to comply with the Commission's orders (De Pange, p. 211). This attitude taken by a rather unimportant federal agency—a rehearsal of the methods used in the Ruhr conflict of 1923—was not authorized by the German Government but it reflected the feelings of the vast majority of German officials in that period. On 9 June the High Commission responded to this passive resistance by enacting its drastic Ordinance 89, subjecting the local sections of the alcohol monopoly to direct supervision. Within five weeks licenses were granted for no less than 23,000,000 liters of spirits to be sent from France to Germany—an amount corresponding to the regular imports for eight years (Tuohy, 'France's Rhineland Adventure,' p. 34).

The new powers regarding the German foreign-trade agencies, though they were not mentioned in the original list of sanctions with which Germany was threatened, were generally regarded as the most important part of the whole sanctions complex. The so-called Emser Amt, the special department created by the High Commission to supervise those agencies (Ordinance 82 of 8 April 1921), had the function of issuing import and export licenses, and of conducting the investigations of license applicants. During the period of sanctions such licenses were required not only for trade between Germany and other countries but also for trade between the occupied and unoccupied parts of Germany. More than 500 employees were needed to handle the applications for these intra-German trade licenses (De Pange, p. 212), which amounted on some days to 20,000 (Wachendorf, pp. 111 ff.); according to German reports these activities of the Emser Amt resulted not only in considerable economic disturbance but also in bribery, graft, and corruption (Strobel, p. 54).

The Emser Amt exercised direct administrative powers. As the President of the High Commission declared in a letter of July 1921, addressed to the German Reichskommissar:

In the occupied territory German foreign-trade agencies no longer exist. There exists only an agency which is composed to a considerable extent of German employees who work under the control of officials appointed by the High Commission. The German employees are not entitled to make suggestions which are later approved by the representatives of the High Commission. Rather the latter give commands to the officials of the Ems agency . . . In the occupied territory no German authority exists which is entitled to grant licenses. There are only German employees who receive their instructions from the High Commission and its delegates. [The German text is reprinted in Strobel, p. 52.]

Even in the armistice period the German agencies had not been actually operated by representatives of the occupying powers. But now the High Commission was not only an agency of government but also an instrument of active economic policy. During the sanctions period the Emser Amt was the executive organ of the High Commission in its second capacity.

As long as the High Commission had been only an institution of the Rhineland Agreement, entrusted primarily with police functions, no problems had arisen concerning 'collaboration' between occupation authorities and the German officials and population. All that was expected was obedience to the orders and instructions of the High Commission; the occupying powers had created no institutions that the residents of the territory might make use of or not, as they saw fit. But as soon as the High Commission took over the functions of the German foreign-trade agencies, the German businessmen were confronted with the problem whether they should 'collaborate' by applying to the Emser Amt for licenses, and once this dilemma became general, the practice of boycotting the collaborationists inevitably developed.

Thus legal safeguards had to be devised. On 30 April, about three weeks after the creation of the Emser Amt, the High Commission decreed (Ordinance 87) that any person 'who shall unlawfully injure or attempt to injure the holders of such licences shall be liable to the penalties provided for offences against ordinances of the High Commission.' And on 16 June, through Ordinance 90 (see Appendix II, below), this protection of collaborationists in foreign-trade affairs was extended to collaborationists in general; Ordinance 90, which will be discussed in a later chapter, became for the remainder of the occupation the chief weapon of the High Commission against boycott, sabotage, and ostracism. Thus the assignment of completely new functions to the High Commission necessitated not only a new type of administrative agency but also a basic change in the substantive law of the occupation.

During the sanctions period the foreign-trade situation in the occupied territory was similar to what it had been in the armistice period. The sanctions had hardly been imposed before the *sections économiques* reappeared in their old form. These had never been dissolved, and according to Blondel (*La Rhénanie . . . p.* 109), it was due to this act of 'political wisdom' that the application of the economic sanctions became possible. The 'hole in the west' was reopened, and once again the Rhineland became the favored market for French cosmetics, perfumes, cigarettes, wines, liquors, and similar luxury goods (London *Economist,* 11 June 1921, vol. 92, p. 1277). 'Up to now imports to Germany were practically reserved to the businessmen of those countries that had been neutral in the war, and to Germany's friends, but now they are possible also to French businessmen. This is the chief result of the economic sanctions, the one that France cannot renounce' (De Pange, p. 213). And on the other hand, the particularly cheap products of German industry were now available, practically without restrictions, to those foreign businessmen who had grasped this unique chance, for the German statutes were rendered virtually ineffective.

Late in the summer of 1921 the German Government, promising to fulfil the economic stipulations laid down by the London Conference, succeeded in persuading the Allied governments to abandon the policy of sanctions. Thus on 29 September the High Commission, following a resolution of the Supreme Council on 13 August, repealed the ordinances enacted in connection with that policy (Ordinance 98). But there was one important exception: the Emser Amt was continued so far as it had jurisdiction over trade between the occupied territory and non-German countries. Indeed, its continuation in this capacity was a condition for the removal of sanctions, and on 26 August the German Government expressed its consent to this measure. The Emser Amt was not abolished until October 1924.

But it was necessary, of course, to change the Emser Amt considerably after the sanctions were removed. The Germans suggested that the German agencies be restored as independent institutions, with license applicants whose requests were refused having the right of appeal to an agency of the High Commission. The French considered this unthinkable and insisted upon a direct participation in the administrative activities of the German foreign-trade agencies (De Pange, p. 214). A compromise was finally reached along the following lines: the Emser Amt was to be subject to general supervision by the High Commission; the central foreign-trade office in Berlin was to inform the High Commission about the regulations and principles followed by its individual branches (that is, the cartels); in regard to applications concerning business transactions between a German merchant and a national of one of the occupying powers, the representative of that power had to countersign the decision of the German official.

Thus the long struggle between the Germans and the French in the field of foreign trade ended with what was in effect a joint administration. Once this compromise had been concluded, problems of foreign-trade policy ceased to be an issue between the High Commission and Germany.

INTERALLIED COMPARISONS

In an attempt to make clear the wide differences in the spirit behind the administration in the various zones of occupation, nothing would be gained by referring to the 'national character' of the countries involved. The decisive point is that the Americans, English, Belgians, and French had quite different attitudes toward the occupation itself.

To France the Rhineland occupation was the chief safeguard against a new war, a safeguard that was made imperative by the failure of Britain and the United States to confirm their pledge to guarantee France's security. This feeling that the occupation was a national necessity was clearly expressed by General Mordacq in an article published in 1929, in which he warned against a premature evacuation of the Rhineland. Mordacq, who maintained that the United States had completely abandoned France in the Rhineland, and that England had gone almost as far as the United States, declared ('L'évacuation . . .' p. 768):

As a consequence of our perpetual concessions to Germany, and particularly because of the separatist movement, our prestige in Germany is wholly destroyed. In view of these facts we need the Rhineland occupation today more urgently than ever before. At present this occupation is far more important than it was at the time of the treaty. Both from a strategical and from a financial point of view the Rhineland occupation is the only guarantee at our disposal; are we depriving ourselves of it?

This statement of 1929 contrasts significantly with an editorial that appeared in the New York *Nation* in 1921 (vol. 113, p. 518), which declared that 'horse sense alone would dictate sinking no more money in such a useless venture' as the Rhineland occupation.

The occupation represented to the United States primarily an administrative task that found its justification in the necessity to liquidate the past war. Thus it is easy to understand General Allen's remark (*Occupation*, p. 216) that 'perhaps the outstanding characteristic of American representation in the Inter-Allied Rhineland High Commission was its disinterestedness—recognized alike by Allies and Germans. The United States had no territorial or political purposes to serve through its representative on the Commission,' and its 'economic and financial interests were comparatively small.' England tended toward the same attitude, while the Belgians looked upon the occupation partly as a measure of security and partly as a retribution for the German violation of Belgian neutrality. The British, according to an officer in the English zone (Apex, p. 82), regarded the Rhineland army as a 'peacetime command which was on active service only theoretically,' while the French, feeling that 'the Boche was out for revenge sooner or later,' regarded themselves as 'definitely on active service . . . as if they might be called upon to fight at any moment.' These differences in the attitudes of the various occupants are strikingly exemplified in the figures on the number of soldiers that each of them stationed in the Rhineland. On 15 September 1922 (Brugger, p. 832), the army contingents in the four zones of occupation were of the following strength: American zone, 2,000 men; British, 10,000; Belgian, 30,000; French, 106,000.

From the American point of view, Noyes' characterization of the occupation (p. 48) is quite understandable, that 'in the Rhineland a hostile military occupation is seen at its best; and at its best, I can say from personal observation, it is brutal; it is provocative; it is continuing war.' And from the French point of view, Maurice Barrès' injunction to the Chambre in February 1920 (Barrès, p. 38) is equally understandable: 'Let us strengthen the excellent work our soldiers accomplished during the first armistice period.' A jurist may be inclined to follow Noyes' point of view, and to blame the occupation authorities for having violated the spirit and letter of an international treaty, and for having discredited the idea of military occupation in legal forms. A historian may emphasize the factors that condone the French attitude, though he might deplore the methods that implemented it.

In view of the occupants' different attitudes toward the occupation, there is little wonder that conflicts among the powers began early and increased considerably in the course of time. As early as 1919 General Liggett found (p. 136) that 'the feeling existing between our people and the French was not as cordial as it should have been.' General Mordacq was more outspoken when he characterized the relations between the Americans and the French as 'unbearable'; according to Mordacq (*La mentalité allemande . . .* p. 76) the Americans became 'more German than the Germans themselves.'

Relations were no more cordial between the French and the English. The British supervising agents, said 'Apex' (p. 88), 'felt no loyalty to the French whatever,' and when the French army was ridiculed in German cabarets interfered only because non-interference 'would have embarrassed the G.H.Q. and the British section of the High Commission'; the officers of the occupying army (p. 78) 'found Germany interesting and tried to understand her point of view.' As E. H. Carr has put it (p. 50), 'The British soldier . . . found the company of his ex-enemies more congenial than that of his ex-allies.'

The French, on the other hand, were impatient with both the British and the Americans. To the French, their allies' behavior was a mixture of sentimentality and blindness—a judgment that was certainly not without foundation. Even if the French had not been made desperate by insecurity it is scarcely conceivable that a French author could have written and found an audience for a book like that of an English writer and poetess on her life in the Rhineland, in which a chapter was devoted, without irony, to a description of 'The Sweet Enemy' (Tynan, pp. 58-69).

The Germans, of course, were on far more friendly terms with the British and Americans than with the Belgians or French. According to a Swedish observer, Ludvig af Petersens (p. 13), who published in 1922 the results of a study on conditions in the Rhineland, all the Rhenish residents that he interviewed preferred the English to the Americans, because of what was regarded as the Americans' lack of consideration in regard to billeting. Petersens mentioned, however, that the people of the occupied territory were grateful to the United States authorities for their refusal to interfere with internal German affairs. It is worth emphasizing that the Germans were the beneficiaries of the Inter-Allied conflicts. As Carl Schmitt, outstanding political scientist of the Weimar period and later apologist for the Nazis, expressed it in 1925 (p. 17), the reason that German sovereignty could be maintained after the war was not the provisions of the Versailles treaty but 'the great number of enemies to whom Germany had capitulated.'

The publication of General Allen's journal gave the Germans an occasion for an open expression of their point of view about the occupation regime. In 1924, the year after its appearance in

English, the book was translated into German, and German reviewers used it as evidence of French misdeeds. In the ultranationalist *Süddeutsche Monatshefte* (July 1925, vol. 22, p. 57) the reviewer declared: 'Allen understood that the French policy was motivated by considerations of revenge. At the conference table he fought vehemently against this sort of policy. Time and again he referred to the wording of the Rhineland Agreement, and insisted upon a policy based on honesty, decency and justice.' In *Die Gesellschaft* (1924, vol. 1, part 2, pp. 179-81) Wilhelm Sollmann, socialist deputy from Cologne and a leader of labor in the Rhineland, said that Allen was 'guided by his unbribable capacity to analyze the world conflicts from a sober businesslike point of view. He emerged as an important critic of the politics that had been pursued by all French cabinets before Herriot came to power.'[3]

German diplomacy followed the same line. There is probably no precedent in history for an occupied country trying to persuade an occupying power to give up its plan to retire before schedule. On 24 March 1922, the German Foreign Minister, Walther Rathenau, sent to General Allen the draft of a cable to the American Secretary of State. The text, which was forwarded by General Allen, read as follows (*Foreign Relations* . . . 1922, vol. 2, p. 214):

Proposed withdrawal is causing great anxiety to population of Rhineland and the frontier. The American authorities of occupation have distinguished themselves by impartial use of the privileges allotted them . . . This consideration causes German Government to request American Government not to withdraw completely from the occupation of Rhineland in favor of occupation by another power. It is desirable that the impartial and moderating influence of the American power of occupation should be asserted soon by official representation on the High Commission.

[3] See also Hajo Holborn in *Archiv für Politik und Geschichte*, 1924, vol. 3, pp. 679-82; A. V. in *Europäische Gespräche*, 1924, vol. 2, pp. 384-5; Traugott Geering in *Schweizerische Monatshefte für Politik und Kultur*, 1924, vol. 4, pp. 113-16.

Less than a year later, when General Allen took his leave from the German Reichskommissar of the occupied territory, both commissioners agreed that the United States army, which had come to Germany as an enemy, was leaving as a friend. Never before had the United States enjoyed so much popularity with the Germans as in those years of occupation.

VI

Relations with the Occupied Country

IT certainly could not be said that the years 1920-22 were for
Germany a period of peaceful development. On the contrary, it was then that the German people first began to realize
the full social and economic devastation of the war. Industry
was hampered by the scarcity of raw materials and by its unfavorable situation in foreign trade; the economy had to stand
the burden of great 'invisible' unemployment; there was a far-
reaching political unrest, an early indication of which was the
rightist Kapp putsch of 1920. And through these years, in-
tensifying all the other developments, rolled the increasing pressure of the inflation, occasionally checked but only momentarily,
until its final dramatic conquest after the hysterical horror of
1923.

This, in the broadest terms, was the background of the crucial
first three years of the High Commission's rule in the Rhineland,
the period before the latent sources of trouble erupted in the
Ruhr conflict. During that time the general principles and practices were developed that governed, throughout the years of occupation, the relations of the occupying powers with the German people and the German Government. The present chapter
is concerned only with general administrative interrelations.
Problems of judicial relations and basic legal questions of occupation government are reserved for the following chapters.

THE REICHSKOMMISSAR

In matters concerning the administration of the occupied territory the highest German official was the 'Reichskommissar für

die besetzten Gebiete.' His office originated in the struggle of the Reich against the separatists (Pinon, pp. 796 ff.), and was based on the highly satisfactory experience with such an official during the German occupation of France in 1871-3. After the collapse of the Dorten putsch, the central Berlin Government decided to create this office; and the Reichstag and the diets of the four states principally involved in the occupation (Prussia, Bavaria, Hesse, Oldenburg) named eighteen members, who, as parliamentary representatives of the Rhineland, should co-oper-ate with the Reichskommissar and his subordinates with a view to safeguarding the interests of the Rhenish population. But when von Starck, former president of the Cologne district, was appointed Reichskommissar, it became clear that this official was expected to serve not primarily as mouthpiece of the Rhenish population in its relations with Berlin, but more as a representa-tive of the Reich in dealings with the High Commission.

The appointment of such a special representative of the Ger-man Government, accredited to the High Commission as quasi-ambassador, was not provided for in the Rhineland Agreement. But in its diplomatic note of 12 July 1919, the German Gov-ernment informed the Allied powers of the appointment of a Reichskommissar who should exercise quasi-diplomatic functions. And the existence of the office was agreed to in the Réponse de Versailles, on condition that the occupying powers approved the choice of incumbent; this approval could be rescinded at any time.

Recognition of the Reichskommissar did not affect the High Commission's right to communicate directly with the local Ger-man authorities. It was specifically declared that he was not rec-ognized as channel for the transmission of communications from the High Commission to the local agencies. But as the repre-sentative of the German federal and state governments, which were resident outside the occupying powers' sphere of immedi-ate influence, he could be made the sole channel for the trans-mission of communications from the local agencies to the High

Commission, and thus the existence of his office considerably affected the position of the local authorities in approaching that body. Before the appointment of a Reichskommissar,

Each German administrative agency, from the district governor down to the mayor of the smallest community, the railway agencies, postoffices, customs officials, chambers of commerce and the like, communicated independently with the occupying authorities. The result was that none of them had any weight with the occupying powers, and that the latter played them off against each other . . . The central agencies lost control over the local and provincial authorities to a considerable extent. [*Frankfurter Zeitung*, 2 June 1921, no. 400.]

Through the appointment of a Reichskommissar German administrative relations with the High Commission were centralized in one federal agency.

The functions of the Reichskommissar were laid down in an internal regulation enacted by the Reich and Prussian Ministers of the Interior on 26 October and 12 November 1919 (published in *Jahrbuch des öffentlichen Rechts*, 1923-4, vol. 12, p. 347). It declared that as agent of the Reich he was to represent to the High Commission the interests of the occupied territory and its residents. In its most important provision it stipulated that

All written and oral negotiations with the High Commission are reserved to the Reichskommissar. All other agencies, including the municipalities, are obliged to ask for his mediation if, in case of necessity, they wish to approach the High Commission. Within their general jurisdiction the district, local, and municipal agencies are entitled to deal directly with those agencies of the occupying powers which are resident in their respective districts.

The other provisions of this regulation dealt mainly with technicalities concerning the relations of the Reichskommissar with the regular German authorities.

The Réponse de Versailles accepted the German suggestion that the ordinances of the High Commission be presented to the

Reichskommissar for a critical examination before their enact-ment. The additional German suggestion that the declaration of a state of martial law be dependent on the approval of that of-ficial was of course rejected; the Allied governments merely con-ceded that, so far as possible, the Reichskommissar should be heard before a state of martial law was declared.

Except for his routine activities in the field of administration and legislation, the first Reichskommissar concentrated his ener-gies not on the political and personal problems involved, but on writing notes of protest against what he considered violations of the Rhineland Agreement (some of his notes are reprinted under 'Die politischen Ordonnanzen der Interallierten Rheinland Kom-mission in Coblenz,' in an official collection of documents on the Rhineland occupation, published in 1925 by the Reich Ministry of the Occupied Territories, a collection, incidentally, which contains the most important German source material for this period of Rhenish history; see *Dokumente* . . . vol. 1). A crit-ical examination of these notes leads to the impression that von Starck represented the type of official Max Weber had in mind when he wrote, in 1917, that the German high bureaucracy was better educated, more intelligent and industrious, and less cor-rupt than the officialdom of any other country in the world, but its political abilities were almost below zero.

The French, not very enthusiastic about the institution of Reichskommissar, were also personally unsympathetic with the first incumbent of that office (Cornier, p. 118). They regarded it as an insult that von Starck refused to attend a dinner party commemorating the inauguration of the High Commission, and they considered him responsible for the social boycott main-tained by the German officials in the occupied territory against the agents of the occupying powers; this behavior was con-trasted with the conciliatory attitude of the French after the Franco-Prussian war, when cordial social relations had been es-tablished between the French officials and the German officers of the occupying army ('La France sur le Rhin,' 1929, p. 379).

These criticisms not only overlooked the fact that the Franco-Prussian war was more comparable to the chivalrous duels of the eighteenth century than to the totalitarian First World War; they also showed a lack of psychological understanding of the nationalistic wave that was flooding the Rhineland in those years. As Wilhelm Sollmann declared in the Reichstag on 6 November 1920 (Reichstag, vol. 345, p. 1048), within a year and a half the occupation of the Rhineland had contributed more to the growth of chauvinism than all pan-Germanist agitators combined. Public opinion in the Rhineland would scarcely have permitted von Starck's attendance at a dinner commemorating the establishment of a foreign regime on German soil.

Relations were particularly strained between von Starck and Tirard, and by 1921 they had become so tense that the High Commission proposed to the Allied governments that the whole institution of Reichskommissar be abolished, and even threatened to expel von Starck from the occupied territory. In the middle of that year, after the sanctions crisis had passed its peak, von Starck resigned. His successor was expelled from the Rhineland in April 1923, during the Ruhr struggle.

It was largely because of these personal and political difficulties that the Reichskommissar's activities did not fulfil the expectations of the German Government. What had proved in 1871-3 an 'extremely happy idea' (Robin, p. 348) was only of limited value during the Rhineland occupation. A stronger personality than von Starck, whom the Germans themselves blamed for his bureaucratic pedantry, might have given the office a greater value.

As to why the German Government appointed as first Reichskommissar a typical representative of the old regime, the answer is to be found in the peculiar political situation that prevailed in the Rhineland in that period between the signature and the ratification of the peace treaty. The Catholic party, which carried most districts in the elections, was split in regard to the question of autonomy for the Rhineland; the Social Democrats had opposed the French policy so stubbornly that an appointment from their ranks would hardly have been approved by the High Commission; the other political parties were almost without influence in the occupied territory. Thus the Government concluded that a 'neutral' official was best fit for the job. Unfortunately von Starck viewed the Rhineland problems as a chain of legal cases rather than as a political phenomenon. As General Allen put it (*Occupation*, p. 185), 'Placed between the Scylla of public opinion of his own country and the Charybdis of the dominating elements of the High Commission, the *Reichscommissar* played a rôle that must have been as little satisfactory to himself as it was to the opposing interests.'

General Administration

During the peace period, as during the armistice period, the German bureaucracy, as an institution, was maintained without change. This was explicitly provided in the clause of the Rhineland Agreement which declared (Article 5) that, in general, civil administration 'shall remain in the hands of the German authorities, and . . . shall continue under German law and under the authority of the Central German Government.' And it was reaffirmed when the High Commission, in its proclamation of 10 January 1920, asserted that it desired 'to rely on the collaboration of the German officials and magistrates to ensure, in full harmony with it, the institution of a state of order, work, and peace for the population of the Occupied Territories.' On 1 July 1921, the High Commission declared that the 'occupying authorities are in no respect the hierarchical superiors of the German officials' (Rousseau, *La Haute Commission* . . . p. 134, note 1).

In the application of this principle, however, certain difficulties were encountered. The most serious of these were in the realm of personnel problems: although the German administrative machine as an entity was maintained, individual German officials were not outside the authority of the occupying powers. But before this question is discussed, a word should be said about two other directions in which the general recognition of German bureaucratic autonomy was modified by the requirements of the occupation.

One of these modifications grew out of the fact that 'the authority of the Central German Government' and the authority of the High Commission were not necessarily compatible. From a strictly legal point of view this presented no dilemma: as was explicitly asserted on 2 October 1920, in Ordinance 48, the ordinances of the High Commission represented the highest law in the occupied territory, superior not only to acts originating in the legislature but also to those originating in the executive and judicial branches of the government. The difficulty arose not so much from the general principle as from its application to concrete cases. In effect, the local official in the Rhineland had to determine whether the directive rules and orders of his superiors in the unoccupied part of Germany conformed with the general rules of occupation law—a kind of legal review of the superior by the subordinate.

This problem is exemplified in the Dorten 'abduction' affair. In pursuit of a warrant of arrest for high treason, issued by the Reichsgericht, Dorten was arrested in the occupied territory on 24 July 1920 and taken to Frankfurt, then unoccupied. The High Commission declared that the police authorities had disregarded the provision of Ordinance 2 that 'without the consent of the High Commission . . . no punitive measures shall be taken against any person in the Occupied Territories for any . . . political act done during the period of the Armistice.' But the German officials pleaded that they were obliged to execute warrants of arrest issued by the highest German court; that it was impossible for the individual police officer to know whether the warrant had been issued in compliance with or in disregard of the occupation law; that there was no opportunity to check whether the arrest was for treasonable acts committed before or after 10 January 1920.

This affair ended with a compromise. On 6 August the Reichs-kommissar expressed to Tirard the regret of the German Government (*Gazette*, 1920, No. VIII-IX, p. 79), and thereafter the High Commission refrained from taking disciplinary measures against individual officials involved in the affair. The general problem involved in the Dorten case was solved by Ordinance 120, enacted on 21 September 1922, which provided that arrests, searches, seizures, and confiscations ordered by police or judicial authorities in the unoccupied territory could not be executed in the Rhineland without 'the intervention of the competent German authority in the occupied territories'—an effort to put the burden on officials under the supervision of the occupation authorities.

A second difficulty in applying the principle of an autonomous German bureaucracy arose in connection with the police forces. Here too the problem was the dual jurisdiction of the occupation authorities and the central German administration, but in this field the problem had special importance, because of the quasi-military character of this branch of the bureaucracy.

In both imperial and republican Germany police questions were handled by the individual states. Two kinds of police existed in each state; in Prussia, which may be regarded as sufficiently representative for present purposes, these were known as the *Landespolizei* and the *Ortspolizei*. The Landespolizei was entirely a state institution, and was concerned with all matters that were of more than local significance, especially with attacks on state and society. All its units, of which the most important was the *Sicherheitspolizei*, were under the direct command of the respective district presidents. The Ortspolizei was concerned, in general, with matters of local significance, and its functions were exercised by officials of the municipalities, but it too was a state institution. In the large cities the head of the Ortspolizei was a high state official, the *Polizeipräsident;* in the smaller municipalities the functions of that office were performed by the mayor, acting not as a municipal officer but in the name of and under the supervision of the state government.[1]

On 10 June 1920, the High Commission rendered the following decision:

Except in cases explicitly provided for by the High Commission, the police forces must be wholly municipal in character and not be dependent either directly or indirectly on the Reich or an individual state. By virtue of this decision not only the 'Sicherheitspolizei' is inadmissible in the occupied zone but also the regional police, as far as the latter is controlled by the central government . . . [*Recueil* . . . 1923, p. 185.]

By this decision the High Commission abolished, in the occupied territory, the distinction between Landespolizei and Ortspolizei, recognized only the latter, and converted it into 'local police' in the full meaning of the term. The appointment of specific Polizeipräsidents was still permitted, but these officials were made subordinate to the municipal authorities; the mayor was the head of the police, even in cities with a Polizeipräsident (see, for example, *Recueil* . . . 1929, pp. 138-42; the best illustration is the case of the Wiesbaden Polizeipräsident Froitzheim, decided on 13 July 1927, ibid. p. 140). Only in Cologne, most important city of the Rhineland, was the situation different. On 31 July 1920, the High Commission allowed a 'special police corps' to be formed in that city, and on 2 October it decided that not the mayor of Cologne but the Cologne Polizeipräsident should be in command of this special police. Even in this exception, however, the general principle of local authority was maintained: the special police corps could be used outside Cologne only if the Cologne delegate of the High Commission had approved an application of the Cologne district president.

[1] The best analysis of the German police system can be found in Hue de Grais, pp. 356 ff. Under the Nazis jurisdiction in police questions has been taken away from the states and concentrated in the Reich, but the old distinction between local and centralized police remains; the Reichspolizei and Ortspolizei exist side by side (law of 24 June 1937, *Reichsgesetzblatt*, 1937, Part I, p. 653).

According to Hans Hirschfeld, a leading official of the Prussian Ministry of the Interior during 1921-32, the new organizational measures were dutifully observed by the Prussian authorities, but their practical significance was almost negligible. The local police chiefs introduced almost literally the regulations and instructions enacted for the unoccupied parts of the country; questions of personnel were settled in collaboration with the central agencies; police officers and men were trained in the police schools of the unoccupied zone, and they were frequently transferred from one part of the country to the other. The formally 'municipal' police officials, not unmindful of their careers after the termination of the occupation, acted as if they were appointees of the state government.

By far the most important problem in the High Commission's relations with the German bureaucracy was the personnel question of appointment, promotion, punishment, and dismissal of individual officials. The Rhineland Agreement, in line with Noyes' desire that self-government be maintained in the occupied territory, made no provision for these matters, except for a statement that 'the German authorities shall be obliged, under penalty of removal,' to conform with the ordinances of the High Commission. This was a reflection of the political principle of separation of powers: the legislator formulates general rules, and the judicial and executive branches merely apply these general rules to the concrete cases. Thus occupation questions were to be regulated by general ordinances drafted by the High Commission and executed by the German bureaucracy. It was considered a sufficient precaution to empower the High Commission to remove any individual official who did not conform with its ordinances.

But German governmental tradition, shaped under the omnipotence of absolutism, was basically at variance with the idea that the executive branch of government can be confined to the application of statutory provisions. Under absolutism, what we call today the 'executive branch' covered all spheres of government activity. In the course of time the judicial, legislative, and local administrative functions were split off from the hitherto all-inclusive executive functions, but the latter remained the nucleus of the state. It is true that the doctrine of separation of powers deeply influenced German political institutions—influenced them almost as deeply as it did the American Constitution—but it did so in a quite different way. In the United States a new constitution was based on that doctrine; in Germany an existing state machinery was adapted to its pattern. In the United States the executive branch of the government exercises only those powers that are explicitly entrusted to it; in Germany the executive branch exercises all powers that are not explicitly transferred to another branch. Thus in practice administration in Germany is more than the execution of statutes: it is the state power as a whole, minus legislation and adjudication.

Article 5 of the Rhineland Agreement was based on a misconception of the German administrative system. By restricting the disciplinary power of the High Commission to cases of nonconformance with the ordinances, it relinquished control over all those activities of the German administrative agencies that were based not on statutes but on an almost unrestricted general jurisdiction. The most significant jurisdictional provisions of German administrative law go back to Frederick the Great, and represent an extremely important hangover from eighteenth-century absolutism.

In its note of 12 July 1919, the German Government maintained that the High Commission had no powers whatever in regard to German administrative personnel, except for its right of dismissal for non-conformance with the ordinances. The Réponse de Versailles declared, however, that this right of dismissal implied the right to veto the appointment of individual officials. Thus, only a month after the signing of the Rhineland Agreement, the Allies were insisting on a broad interpretation of that document in order to adapt it to the practical necessities it had ignored. And despite German protests, the High Commission, in Ordinance 29, enacted on 13 July 1920, declared its right to 'veto the appointment of any German official designated to serve in the occupied territories if in the opinion of the High Commission such action is necessary for the maintenance, safety and requirements of the Allied and Associated forces.'

Ordinance 29 distinguished between absolute and provisional vetoes. An absolute veto, which prohibited the individual's appointment to the particular job he was named for—not necessarily to another office in the occupied territory (decision of the High Commission, 2 December 1922, *Recueil* . . . 1923, p. 45)—was not controlled by any rules of procedure. No hearing was granted either to the official involved or to the German Government, and no 'written opinion' was necessary. But after a provisional veto, which was based on concrete facts, negotiations were possible between the German Government and the High Commission. It was only after its objections had been forwarded to the German Government, and answered, that the High Commission decided whether it would definitely veto or approve the appointment.

The provisions of Ordinance 29 were applicable only to certain groups of officials, which were there enumerated. The list contained two main groups: officials entrusted with executive posts; and those 'authorized to carry arms' (police officers, policemen, customs officers, and the like).

At the very beginning of its regime, in an instruction of 10 January 1920, the High Commission stipulated certain data that it desired concerning the personnel already employed; in each district the German administrative agencies were required to furnish the local representative of the Commission with exact information about their officials, in regard to sickness, furloughs, promotion, and the like. And Ordinance 54, of 29 October 1920, prescribed special forms to be used by the German authorities in informing the High Commission about the appointment of new officials. These not only asked the customary questions about birth, residence, religion, and previous positions, but also inquired about the place of origin of the individual's family and that of his wife; the answers to these questions enabled the High Commission to check whether the German Government was giving preference to non-Rhinelanders in appointments in the occupied territory.

On 17 February of the following year the Commission went further and required the German Government to indicate in each case its motives for making the appointment (*Recueil . . . 1923*, p. 50). It is to be doubted, however, whether this resulted in any very helpful information, as the personnel files of the German officials were not at the disposal of the High Commission and there was therefore no possibility of checking the statements. It was not until the Ruhr conflict had reached its most crucial stage that the High Commission (Ordinance 205) claimed access to the files of German agencies in the occupied territory—an essential measure for an efficient supervision of German administration.

The question of the Germans' right to appoint non-Rhinelanders as civil servants in the occupied territory was related, of course, to the issue of separatism. The French accused the Germans of concentrating on non-Rhenish appointments and thus trying to weaken the autonomous tendencies in the occupied territory. And the Germans believed that the occupying powers wished to exclude, or at least to discriminate against, non-Rhenish civil servants, in an effort to alienate the Rhinelanders from Prussia and even from the Reich. During the armistice period, General Fayolle had actually enacted an order (21 March 1919: Cornier, p. 42) prohibiting the arrival of non-Rhenish civil servants in his zone of occupation, and tendencies in this direction were not unknown in the peace period (Dariac, p. 17). On 26 January 1922 (*Gazette*, 1922, No. 1, p. 61) the High Commission went so far as to declare that 'no Rhineland official or employee of the *Reichsvermögensverwaltung* [federal property administration] may be dismissed with a view to replacement by an official coming from non-occupied Germany.'

This issue reached its sharpest expression in the conflict between the Prussian Government and the High Commission in regard to personnel in the school administration. The Weimar Constitution required the schools to provide classes in religion, conducted in accordance with the faith of the pupils: only Catholic teachers were allowed to teach religion to Catholic children. For practical reasons elementary school teachers in Catholic districts were almost exclusively Catholics. After the conclusion of the peace treaty, certain predominantly Catholic eastern sections of Prussia had become Polish, and subsequently Boelitz, the Prussian Minister of Education and a right-wing nationalist, transferred the teachers from those areas to the predominantly Catholic areas in the west, which were occupied by the Allies. The majority of these elementary school teachers, who had spent their lives in the center of Prussian-Polish antipathies, were among the most fanatic nationalists of all Germany. Not only were their pupils in the Rhineland educated in an ultra-nationalistic spirit, but also their chauvinism exercised a considerable influence on public opinion in the villages and smaller towns, particularly as the declining influence of the clergy meant, outside the big cities, an increasing influence of the teachers.

But the Weimar Constitution provided, too, that the schools should pursue their purposes in a spirit not only of German nationality but also of international reconciliation. And early in January 1922 the High Commission, contending that the schools in the occupied territory did not observe this constitutional provision as far as the spirit of reconciliation was concerned, created a special school committee to investigate the problem (an excerpt from this resolution is reprinted in *Journal du droit international*, 1922, vol. 49, p. 264). In the words of Tirard (p. 96), 'the High Commission could not remain inactive . . . if attempts were made to restore a political regime which might prove dangerous from the point of view of the preservation of peace.' The Germans declared, however, that the education of children had nothing to do with the security of the occupying armies, which was the only legitimate concern of the High Commission; and in a meeting of the Prussian diet, on 23 January, Boelitz defended the importation of the teachers on the ground that there was no place else to send them (Preussischer Landtag, I. Wahlperiode, 1921-4, vol. 5, p. 6428). Despite the possible dangers in this situation (dangers that were subsequently realized with the advent of the Nazis) the High Commission confined itself to the formation of a committee.

But the High Commission's assumption of veto powers, unwelcome as it was to the Germans, did not overturn the principle of autonomy for the German administration in the occupied territory. Its exercise was intended to combine the principle of autonomy with that of supervision. As long as the occupying powers did not contend that the power to veto meant the power to appoint, far-reaching clashes were avoided. Only when the High Commission assumed the power to appoint officials—in Ordinance 205, enacted on 31 August 1923, during the Ruhr conflict—did its interference with German personnel policy become a problem of crucial political significance. A strict application of that ordinance (which was repealed on 22 October of the following year) would have endangered the political status of the Rhineland.

A list of all Reich, state, and municipal officials whose appointment was vetoed between 1 July 1922 and the beginning of the Ruhr conflict on 31 January 1923 reveals that during this time the High Commission objected to only nine teachers, five customs officials, two police officers, one railway official, and one official of the general administration (*Recueil* . . . 1923, pp. 45-6). The veto power, a necessary preventive against tendencies hostile to the aims of the occupation, was not a major point in the complaints of the Germans against the civil-servant policy of the occupying powers.

The chief German grievance in this field concerned the dismissal and expulsion of officials. The penalty of removal from office, provided in Article 5 of the Rhineland Agreement for non-conformance with the ordinances, was stipulated also in Ordinance 1, of 10 January 1920, which declared that for such disobedience 'Any German Authority . . . may, in addition to being liable to the penalties provided for an offence against an Ordinance of the High Commission, be suspended or deprived of his office.' But Ordinance 1 also provided that these penalties were applicable to German officials who violated orders given by the military authorities; and for non-conformance with the ordinances it mentioned the additional penalty of expulsion from the occupied territory. And in Ordinance 29, enacted six months later, the High Commission went still further and declared its right to dismiss any German official if it regarded such action as 'necessary for securing the maintenance, safety or require-ments' of the occupying powers.

These criteria could, of course, lead to the dismissal of a Ger-man official even if he had violated no specific rule of occupation law. The more surprising, therefore, is the inclusion in Ordi-nance 29 of certain rules of procedure providing that when such disciplinary measures were contemplated the official should be served with 'definite and specific charges in writing' and be given 'an opportunity to present his defense.' This grant of procedural due process would have been understandable if dismissal had still been restricted to instances of specific disobedience, but it was little more than a farce when dismissal was made possible for reasons of expediency.

In view of the development from removal for specific viola-tions of ordinances to removal for considerations of expediency, it did not mean very much when it was declared in Ordinance 93, on 1 July 1921, that disciplinary proceedings could be initi-ated also for non-compliance with any orders or decisions issued either directly by the High Commission or by its express au-thority. By this provision the High Commission's local repre-sentatives were included in the establishment of direct super-vision of the German administrative system.

That removal from office had become a discretionary expedient, and no longer a disciplinary procedure based on concrete facts and controlled by legal safeguards, is evident from the Momm affair. Tension between the occupation authorities and Momm, president of the Wiesbaden district, had existed since the beginning of the High Commission's regime. He was held responsible for the Dorten 'abduction,' and his personal relations with Mordacq, French commanding general in Wiesbaden, were very cool. On 4 July 1922, during a big parade of the Wiesbaden republican parties and unions, occasioned by the assassination of Rathenau, two German workers were killed by the police. Similar clashes occurred in many cities of the unoccupied part of Germany in connection with these parades, evidence of the civil-war atmosphere that prevailed at that time throughout the country. But both Mordacq and Tirard declared, in public, that the events of 4 July made it essential that Momm be removed.

The Prussian Government, the political parties in Wiesbaden, and the non-French members of the High Commission saw no sufficient reason for his removal. Not only was this an internal German affair, having no direct connection with the occupation, but also, as a result of their own decision regarding the police administration, the occupying powers could not hold Momm responsible for a clash between German civilians and the German police; they themselves had declared that the district presidents, as officials of the state governments, had no responsibility concerning police questions in the occupied territory. The French, however, insisted, partly because the issue had meanwhile become entangled in considerations of prestige. Unable to convince the majority of the High Commission that the events of 4 July were adequate justification, Tirard brought forth the argument of Momm's inability to co-operate with the French occupation authorities. And on 14 August (*Dokumente . . .* vol. 1, p. 85) the High Commission informed the Reichskommissar that Momm had to be dismissed, because 'the maintenance, security and requirements of the occupying armies are dependent to a considerable extent on the personality of the German officials in the occupied zone,' and 'the good relations which should exist between the occupation authorities and the German agencies might be impaired' if Momm stayed in office. In his answer to the High Commission, on 22 August, the Reichskommissar pointed out that Momm had been served only with charges concerning the events of 4 July; no opportunity had been given him to present his defense against the charges on which his dismissal had actually been based. But this protest was ignored.

As district president, Momm was a political official, a representative of the Prussian Government. In German law political officials can be dismissed or suspended for reasons of political expediency. If the occupation authorities had based their case on this fact, and had restricted their arguments of 14 August to political officials, they would have remained on solid ground and would not have established a dangerous precedent for thousands of unpolitical civil servants. But the High Commission was not inclined toward such a method of reasoning.

It is hardly possible to overstate the significance that republican Germany attributed to the legal provisions intended to protect officials, employees, and workers from dismissal without cause. These provisions—which may be summarized in the formula that no person could be deprived of his job without due process of law—originated in the statutes governing the bureaucracy. German civil servants, appointed for life and entitled to pensions, could be dismissed from office only through court proceedings which were characterized by the same legal guarantees as criminal proceedings. And even if the official was found guilty, the court, rather than ordering his dismissal, could impose an administrative penalty, such as a fine. Through the possibility of such penalties, discipline could be maintained without infringing on the official's right in his job.

These principles, which dominated the legal thinking of the

broad masses of the German population, must be borne in mind in order to understand why the Germans reacted so vehemently to the civil-service policy of the occupation authorities. The representatives of occupying powers, educated under different economic, social, and legal conditions, are likely to be wholly unaware of the sensitiveness toward certain of their measures on the part of the population of the occupied country. Under the peculiar conditions of legally governed military occupation, comparative law ceases to be the hobby of a few scholars and becomes a matter of vital importance for the handling of delicate questions of government and administration. The civil-service policy of the High Commission is ample evidence that during the Rhineland occupation the occupying powers lacked understanding of ideas that the Germans considered progressive, social, and truly democratic.

No administrative penalties were at the disposal of the High Commission in the field of general civil administration. In this field only three punitive procedures were possible, all of them drastically stronger than ordinary administrative penalties. A German civil servant, like any other resident of the occupied territory, could be subjected to court proceedings for violation of an ordinance, if the ordinance so provided; in that event, due process of law was adequately guaranteed. And a civil servant could be dismissed by the High Commission, under the conditions that have been described above; in that event due process was formally provided for, but in practice it was almost meaningless. And finally, a civil servant could be expelled from the occupied territory—again not only for violating an ordinance but also for endangering the 'maintenance, safety or requirements' of the troops; in that event there was no legal protection whatever.

The penalty of deportation was applicable not only to civil servants but also to all 'dangerous individuals.' It was mentioned in Ordinance 1 as a possible punishment of any 'German authority' who disobeyed an ordinance, but Ordinance 3 declared that any person might be expelled 'if it appears to the High Commission that the presence of the person in the Occupied Territories is dangerous to the maintenance, safety or requirements of the troops of occupation, or to the interests of public order.'

In its note of 12 January 1920, the German Government protested that the deportation provisions were violations of the Rhineland Agreement, for they replaced regular court procedures by irregular executive procedures. And less than a week later, on 17 January, the question was discussed in the German National Assembly (Nationalversammlung, vol. 332, pp. 4466-8). Said Erich Koch, Minister of the Interior: 'The civil liberties of the Rhenish population are curtailed by no provision more seriously than by the rules concerning deportation . . . No examination of the facts, no evidence, is required. Deportation is not inflicted *after* a court procedure and a verdict, but rather *instead of* a court procedure and a verdict.' The ordinances of 10 January, he declared, would in fact inaugurate a 'perpetual state of siege' for the occupied territory. Peter Spahn, a leader of the Catholic party and one of the highest judges of Germany, asserted that these ordinances 'represent a regress from the situation that existed during the armistice period, because they subject the whole of public and private life in the occupied territory to the arbitrary discretion of the High Commission.'

At that time, just one week after the regime of the High Commission had replaced the armistice administration, it was rather early to make such statements. But notwithstanding their exaggerations the speeches of Koch and Spahn are noteworthy, if for no other reason than that they drew the attention of the German public to basic problems of the peacetime occupation.

No exact figures are available on the number of German residents who were deported from the Rhineland during the various periods of the occupation. The potential significance of the expulsion provisions is evident, however, from a detailed list published by the German Government in 1925, according to which 41,808 officials were deported during the Ruhr conflict (*Doku-*

mente . . . vol. 1, p. 92). In the armistice period, according to Koch's speech of 17 January, the French had deported 76 officials and the Belgians 12, whereas the American and British military authorities had made no use of their powers of expulsion. Even if the figure for the pre-Ruhr peace period was no higher than this, the implications of the deportation powers were by no means negligible. Figures can hardly express the full significance of the problems involved.

The uncontrolled power of the High Commission to deport civil servants as well as 'dangerous' persons, without procedural guarantees, makes it clear that in a zone occupied by foreign armies martial law conditions can exist even if such a state has not been explicitly declared. From a psychological point of view, the coexistence of two systems of government—a rule of arbitrariness and a rule of law—is probably harder to endure than an outright rule of martial law. Under a state of siege, life is wholly controlled by considerations of expediency; no standards exist by which the acts of the government might be judged. But if legal procedures are presumably respected, extra-legal measures appear arbitrary and the activities of the courts hypocritical. The deportation provisions and their application by the High Commission indicate that in reality the rule of law had not been substituted for the martial law plan of the Supreme War Council. The solution of the Loucheur committee had been converted into a mixed system of law and lawlessness.

PUBLIC UTILITY ADMINISTRATION

The problems that were solved somewhat arbitrarily in the field of general administration were handled with careful legality in the field of public utilities. In order to meet the practical requirements of occupation the High Commission, by statute and practice, so amplified and modified the Rhineland Agreement that its control over general German administration became not greatly different from its control over the vital public utility agencies. But in this process it neglected the safeguards and realistic procedures characterizing public utility administration, which had been regulated from the beginning, and with careful attention to the problems involved.

Occupation authorities must be able to rely without question on the functioning of these more technical agencies, and the Rhineland Agreement, supplemented by diplomatic correspondence and Ordinance 6 of the High Commission (10 January 1920), provided a realistic solution for the administration of railways, postal service, telephone and telegraph service, navigation and highway facilities, gas, water, and electricity works. In Germany all these public utilities had been operated for decades by the Government—by the Reich itself (postal, telephone, and telegraph services), the states (railways and navigation facilities), or the municipalities (gas, water, electricity, and highways). Thus in regulating them the occupying powers were not confronted with the problem of reconciling private interests with military necessities.

The following discussion of control in this field is concerned primarily with the railway (including tramway) administration. But control of postal, telephone and telegraph, navigation, and highway facilities followed very closely the pattern set forth for the railways. And except for certain precautions against strikes, the High Commission enacted no specific rules concerning the gas, water, and electricity enterprises.

During the armistice period, Marshal Foch had exercised full authority over all means of communication, and the Supreme War Council proposed that this complete military control be retained after the ratification of the peace treaty. The Loucheur committee did not accept this proposal. By the Rhineland Agreement the civil-service officials of these agencies, like the officials of the more general administrative bodies, were obliged 'under penalty of removal' to conform with the ordinances of the High Commission. In addition, however, they were required to obey 'any orders given by or on behalf of' the Commander-in-Chief of the occupation armies 'for military purposes' (Articles 10-12);

this provision applied not only to officials but also to all employees and workers in the communications services. It is of particular significance that the jurisdiction of the army was explicitly restricted to orders issued 'for military purposes.'

As the Germans realized at once, this formula represented a decisive improvement for them over the situation that had existed during the armistice period. In its notes of 12 July and 7 August 1919, the German Government emphasized that according to this provision the administration of the technical public agencies would be in the hands of German officials and the German personnel of these enterprises would no longer be generally subordinate to the military authorities. The Allied diplomatic note of 14 October recognized the German interpretation and stipulated several principles regarding railway administration. In almost all important points the railway occupation law of the peace period was based on this document.

The 14 October note declared that the civil administration of the railways should rest with the German authorities. German civil-service statutes and labor law were to be applicable to the personnel of the railways, and future statutes in this field were not to be subject to extraordinary limitations by the occupying powers; it is of special interest that the right of the railway personnel to be represented by its unions and workers' councils was explicitly recognized. An Inter-Allied Railway Commission was provided for, in accordance with a German suggestion that a specific body be created to serve as agent of the military high command; by creating this intermediary agency the Allied note followed the intention of the Rhineland Agreement to prevent direct relations between the military authorities and the German civilian authorities. Railway subcommissions were to be formed, which would take over the functions of the 'line commandants' of the German military railway system—a good example of technical co-ordination of occupation agencies with the administrative system of the occupied territory. It was even suggested that the Germans should appoint a delegate who should serve for the

Railway Commission, just as the Reichskommissar did for the High Commission, as liaison officer with the German administrative agencies.

The principles laid down in the 14 October note were not disputed by the Germans. They were codified in Ordinance 6 on 10 January, and one month later, on 11 February 1920, the High Commission declared that the German delegate should have all powers necessary for the execution of the orders transmitted to him by the Railway Commission (*Recueil* . . . 1923, p. 369). This institution of a special delegate to represent the German agencies before the Railway Commission worked so satisfactorily that the same principle was soon extended to the telephone and telegraph administration (Ordinance 15, 18 April), to navigation problems (Ordinance 17, 1 April), and to the maintenance of roads in the occupied territory (Ordinance 33, 5 August). Thus the military authorities exercised their powers of command through two intermediaries: a civilian agency of the occupation authorities; and special delegates of the occupied country. All possible safeguards were taken to avoid clashes between the occupying armies and the agencies of Germany.

In addition to the device of intermediary agencies, and to the fact that the occupation authorities' right to issue concrete orders was restricted to matters of military significance, there was another particularly noteworthy characteristic of the public utility regulations—noteworthy especially in view of the situation in the field of general administration. This was the provision in Ordinances 6, 15, 17, and 33 that the special commissions had the right to 'impose, or call upon the German authorities to impose, any penalties provided for by the German regulations.' Thus in this field the occupation authorities had at their disposal not only the three penalties of court procedures, dismissal, and expulsion, but also the highly important penalty of administrative procedures, which was not merely an additional means of punishment but also a protection of the officials from arbitrary measures and an intelligent adaptation to the legal tradition of the occupied country.

In the administration of public utilities, problems arose, of course, and had to be coped with. But these, on the whole, were problems of labor relations, arising out of the social unrest and economic disorganization of the period; they were not clashes on the fundamental principles of administrative procedure. Early in 1922, when a strike seemed inescapable, Degoutte suggested that the whole railway system be subjected to military control, but this proposal was frustrated by the energetic opposition of General Allen (*Journal*, p. 316). On the whole, it is no exaggeration to say that the regulations on railway questions resulted in perfect collaboration. The German protest note of 12 January, which subjected to such bitter criticism all the other ordinances enacted on 10 January, did not even mention the provisions of Ordinance 6. Until the time of the Ruhr conflict, there were no difficulties whatever in the administration either of the railways or of the other communications agencies. Indeed, so scrupulously did the railway officials obey orders that they even cooperated in the railway activities connected with preparations for the occupation of the Ruhr (Le Trocquer, p. 271); not until their own government proclaimed the policy of passive resistance did they change their attitude.

LABOR

After 1918, labor relations in Germany were increasingly regulated by legislation. Provisions of public law governed such matters as the length of the working day, the resort to conciliation and arbitration, the operation of works councils, collective agreements, public employment offices, unemployment insurance, the protection of minors and women. This trend toward a replacement of the labor contract as an institution of private law by 'the job' as an institution of public law may be described as a development 'from contract to status'; it has become even stronger under the Nazi regime.

But labor questions regarding German workers were a matter of concern to the High Commission only in two respects: first, if labor relations had a bearing on the maintenance of public order; and second, if German nationals were employed by members of the occupying forces.[2] The first situation called for a definition of the High Commission's attitude toward strikes and lockouts, especially in public utilities; the second called for a decision on how far the occupation authorities themselves, as employers, would conform with the requirements of German labor legislation.

Regulations governing strikes by German workers, and lockouts by German employers, were laid down by the High Commission in Ordinance 5, of 10 January 1920. The provisions of that ordinance referred primarily to coal mines and public utilities (railways, telegraphic, telephonic and postal services, navigation, and gas, electricity, and water works). By decision of the High Commission, however, they could be extended to any other undertaking that was 'necessary for the maintenance, safety, or requirements' of the occupying armies.

Ordinance 5 declared that no strike or lockout could take place until the dispute had been submitted to the conciliation authorities prescribed by German law. But it also provided that the decision of such authorities could be appealed before a board of conciliation appointed by the High Commission. In providing for such boards the Commission adopted the basic ideas of the American conciliation boards of the armistice period. Ordinance 5 declared that these bodies should be composed of a president, two members, and four German assessors (two repre-

[2] The limitation of the High Commission's jurisdiction in labor questions was emphasized early in 1920 by the American representative on the Commission, in connection with a dispute on whether the works council statute was to be admitted in the occupied territory. Maintaining that there was nothing in the Rhineland Agreement that allowed the High Commission to interfere with industrial affairs unless the armies were actually threatened, Noyes succeeded in overcoming a French plan to veto the enactment of that statute. (These facts are based on information received from Mr. Noyes.)

senting the employers, two the employees); in Ordinance 53 (15 October 1920) the four assessors were replaced by four representatives, or delegates, who were 'entitled to be present at the discussions of the board and to be heard by it,' but this change had little practical significance.

Unlike their American prototypes, the peacetime conciliation boards served only as appellate bodies. The only compulsory element in the provisions governing resort to them was the requirement that disputes be first taken before whatever conciliation authorities were provided by German law. In 1920 the German attitude toward labor arbitration was still in process of formation. A provision of the demobilization decree of 12 February 1920 (*Reichsgesetzblatt*, 1920, p. 218) was interpreted as giving the Minister of Labor the authority to declare binding the verdict of an arbitration board; this interpretation was upheld by the Reichsgericht on 7 March 1922 (104 RGZ 171). Meanwhile, on 10 November 1920, the German Government made the resort to arbitration compulsory in all public utilities (*Reichsgesetzblatt*, 1920, p. 1865), and declared that if the verdict was not accepted, a stipulated period of time had to elapse before a strike or lockout could be resorted to. These regulations were not, however, of great concern to the High Commission, as that body was interested not in the determination of wages and hours but in the maintenance of public order.

Negotiations before the occupation boards of conciliation were intended to provide a 'cooling off period.' Their decision was not compulsory, nor were they empowered to prohibit labor conflicts. But if their services were not successful, the strike or lockout could not occur until the expiry of a week after written notice of the intended action had been received by the relevant local representative of the High Commission. Ordinance 107, enacted on 1 March 1922, at the time of a railway strike, gave the High Commission much more far-reaching powers in regard to labor conflicts, but the provisions of that ordinance were never put into practice.

According to Thiallet (pp. 55-77), eight cases were settled by
the conciliation boards before the time of the Ruhr conflict
(three railway disputes, one streetcar, one heavy industry, two
mining, one public building), the most important of the cases
involving about 20,000 workers (A. I., p. 260). Max Gottschalk,
Belgian representative on such boards, has said that proceedings
before them were entirely amicable and satisfactory. It is noteworthy, however, that rather than resort to these boards 'employers and employees earnestly attempted to reach an agreement or to appeal to the ordinary German arbitration instances'
(Schmitz, p. 312). In fact, the disinterest of labor contrasts
sharply with the emphasis laid on the conciliation boards in
many publications of the occupying powers. As soon as the German administrative machine was able to prevent the outbreak
of labor conflicts in vital industries the function of these boards
disappeared.

Quite different issues were involved in the labor relations in
which the occupation authorities themselves participated as employers. The idea of 'complete self-administration' for Germany
called for a correspondingly complete autonomy for the occupying forces, but this hope of separation, one from the other, was
of course impossible of fulfilment. Once the occupation authorities began to participate actively in the administration of the occupied territory it was inevitable that they began to use the
services of German nationals. The latter were employed mainly
as clerical workers and servants, but also, to some extent, as construction workers.

Implicit in this situation was the question whether German
employees of the agents of foreign sovereigns retained the privileges granted them in German public law. The High Commission dealt with this matter in Instruction 18 of 21 September
1922, which exempted the occupation authorities from 'any obligation prescribed by German law in respect of employers.' This
ruling excluded not only the application of the public law provisions of German labor legislation but also the application of

private law regulations concerned with such matters as damages for breach of contract—in spite of the fact that according to general principles of conflicts of law, a contract concluded in Germany, to be fulfilled by both parties in Germany, is controlled by German law.

The records show no evidence that this issue was ever taken before the courts, but the same question, in quite different attendant circumstances, was dealt with in a very interesting decision of the German Supreme Labor Court at a much later time, when the last soldiers had left the Rhineland. On 28 January 1931, that court decided a case (7 RAG 301) in which the issue was whether a Russian commercial agency in Germany was obliged to conform with the German statute governing works councils. The Russian agency contended that since it was a part of the sovereign Russian state it was not subject to the public-law provisions of German labor law. The court decided otherwise, basing its decision on the fact that special international treaties existed between Germany and Russia, which regulated this question. *Obiter dictum*, however, the court expressed the opinion that in the absence of such special international agreements, agencies of foreign sovereigns would not be subject to German public law provisions concerning labor relations.

In spite of the fact that the question seems not to have become a serious one in the Rhineland, some of the implications of Instruction 18 are worth a brief consideration. If labor contracts between the occupation authorities and German nationals were not subject to German law, by what law were they regulated? Instruction 18 did not answer this question, but the attitude of its framers is suggested in its provision regarding wages: the wages of these employees were to be fixed either by amicable agreement or, for requisitioned services, by the Assessment Commission. Thus both collective agreements and the regular German arbitration boards were ruled out, and even the special conciliation boards of the occupying powers were not given authority. Entrustment of labor questions to the Assessment Commission, on which appointees of the occupying powers were in the majority, meant in effect that those powers took upon themselves the right to dictate the labor conditions of their employees. These workers had no legal protection whatever.

Only in one point did Instruction 18 contain a constructive solution of the problems involved. The German employees' rights to social insurance were protected by an ingenious provision according to which their wages were paid not directly to themselves but to the municipality in which the services were rendered. The municipality, serving as a kind of intermediate employer, had the responsibility of paying the social-securities dues to the respective social institutions, and of seeing that the employee punctually received the remainder of his wage. This interesting legal device of an 'intermediate employer' might well have been extended to other aspects of the labor relations between the occupation agencies and their German employees. No direct contractual relations between these two groups would have existed if the municipality had employed the workers and then provided the occupation agencies with their services. Also, this solution would have permitted a clear distinction between free workers and those whose services were requisitioned.

The employment of German nationals by agencies of the occupying powers gave rise also to two other problems not connected with labor relations. The first was how the interests of the occupation authorities were to be protected from possible abuses by the German Government in its exercise of public power over its own nationals. This will be dealt with in the next chapter, in connection with the partial exemption of such German employees from the criminal jurisdiction of their own courts. Provision for such partial exemption, as a measure of self-protection for the employer, is an indispensable part of occupation law, even if the occupying forces refrain from the slightest disposition toward abuse of their powers.

Another problem connected with this situation was the protection of the employees themselves, from their own government and their co-nationals, in the event of any attempt to ostracize or boycott the co-operative elements of the population. This will be discussed presently, in connection with the broader question of 'collaborationists' in general. It may be noted here that the protection of those whose collaboration is based on a regular labor contract raises less serious issues than the protection of those who render services not controlled by provisions of private or public law.

Social and Economic Organizations

The question whether the Rhenish population should have an opportunity to express its wishes and attitudes regarding social and economic matters, through representatives in autonomous organizations that would have direct relations with the High Commission, was wholly overshadowed by considerations of high politics. The chief proponent of the idea was Maurice Barrès, whose sponsorship was sufficient to discredit the plan in Germany. German suspicions were strengthened after the *Manchester Guardian* (2 November 1922, and 5 March 1923) had revealed the Dariac Report, a secret report by members of the French parliament, contending that the Ruhr as well as the Rhineland should be subjected to occupation, and proposing the establishment of an independent Rhenish parliament. Any idea of creating special political, social, or economic institutions for the occupied territory was regarded by the Germans as a disguise for separatist machinations.

In the first months of 1921, Tirard arranged a few meetings between the High Commission and representatives of the German clergy, press, and universities; a few months later similar conferences took place with representatives of the various professions, and of business and agriculture, and finally with spokesmen of labor (Allen, *Occupation*, pp. 233-46). But discussion of political problems was not acceptable in these meetings, and indeed, as Allen remarked, though he had at first been sympathetic with the idea, it was difficult to see why these conferences were arranged at all (*Journal*, p. 184). The German participants were strongly suspicious.

Opposition to the creation of special institutions that should act as representatives of the Rhenish population did not exclude the formation of special committees for this purpose within the existing organizations. But this, too, failed to go very far. Attempts to establish a basis for economic representation foundered on the controversy whether the political authorities, as desired by labor, or the economic organizations, as desired by the industrialists, should serve as spokesmen in dealings with the High Commission (see Strobel, pp. 77-85). These struggles reflected the divergent attitudes of labor and big business toward the problem of business and government—an antagonism that dominated the political scene in Germany during these years.

THE COLLABORATIONISTS

Events of recent years have given the term 'collaborationist' an opprobrious connotation. But it should be remembered that in circumstances different from those of Nazi occupation residents who co-operate with the regime of occupying powers are not necessarily Quislings. The significance of the term depends on the nature of the regime and the purposes that motivate co-operation with it.

One of the basic ideas of the framers of the Rhineland Agreement was to isolate completely the occupying armies from the population of the occupied country. After the ratification of the peace treaty, the function of the occupying armies was to be reduced to mere presence. But from what has already been said it is abundantly clear that military occupation without contacts between the occupying forces and the resident population is impossible. During the Rhineland occupation, in its peace period as well as in its armistice period, there were political contacts between the occupying forces and separatist elements within the occupied territory; and economic contacts between businessmen sponsored by the occupation authorities and businessmen of the Rhineland; and also personal contacts between members of the occupying armies and the resident population.

For the most part, personal contacts raised no issues of collaborationism, and thus in the present context they may be dealt with very briefly.[3] It was primarily in the matter of sexual relations between soldiers and German girls that personal contacts constituted any problem at all. This question was handled quite differently by the different occupying forces. The French military authorities had no objection to intimate relations between their soldiers and the female inhabitants of the Rhineland; the Americans tried to prevent them by means of disciplinary measures and penalties (Hunt, pp. 179-84). As for prostitution, it was regulated and controlled by the French and Belgians, outlawed by the Americans and British. Women who solicited or had illicit sexual intercourse with the soldiers were treated by the American authorities as 'vagrants,' liable to sentences of two to six months in jail; imposition of the sentence was subject, however, to the approval of the military commander. The British regulations provided that the military police had the right of arrest if German prostitutes violated the German police ordinances. French and Belgian regulations were concerned with details regarding open houses and other matters of control. No common policy could be adopted by the High Commission with respect to these questions; each army determined its procedure independently (the regulations of the American and British armies were published in the *Gazette*, 1921, Nos. III-IV, pp. 106-7; see also Hunt, pp. 83 and 127-30).

But even in the sex question the issue of collaborationism was not entirely absent. It arose for the first time immediately after the conclusion of the armistice. German peasant boys had cut the hair of a German girl who had had intercourse with French

---

[3] Particularly interesting material on personal aspects of the Rhineland occupation is presented in an article by George Boas (pp. 542 ff.). Dr. Boas served as an officer in the American army of occupation, and he has combined with his own views those of a present colleague of his, who witnessed the same events as a boy in Germany.

soldiers, had beaten her, and compelled her to walk through the streets of her native village with a placard indicating her crime. The French threatened to penalize the Burgermeisters of the villages involved if the boys were not handed over to the French military authorities. The latter did not recognize the German point of view, that quarrels between German boys and girls were an internal German affair, and that military courts had no power to punish Germans for misdemeanors committed against other Germans. On the contrary, the French interpreted the incident as a disturbance of public order (Schweisguth, p. 109).

Also on the more important question of political and economic contacts the four armies of occupation took different positions, as was evident from the earlier remarks on separatism and the 'hole in the west.' The American attitude may be classified as 'isolationist,' the French as 'interventionist.' The British attitude was an approximation to the American, although it was not enforced so rigorously; the Belgian an approximation to the French. As a result of the isolationist attitude of the American occupation authorities, the question how collaborationists should be protected was almost non-existent in the American zone. It was a matter of considerable significance in the territory under French supervision.

The Rhineland Agreement made no mention of the collaborationist problem—an omission that was due not to negligence, however, but to the fact that the framers of that document were attached to the liberal philosophy of non-interventionism. And the first ordinances dealt with it as a matter of the past. In Ordinance 2, which provided that 'no judicial proceedings shall be instituted or continued and no punitive measures shall be taken' against anyone for political, economic, or administrative collaboration during the armistice period, the High Commission intended to close a chapter of the past rather than to proclaim principles for the future. In practice, however, these immunity provisions made it possible to exercise a far-reaching control over the activities of the German courts, by enabling the High Commission to prevent the German authorities from inflicting penalties upon those whom it was willing to protect.

In Ordinance 90, enacted on 16 June 1921 (see Appendix II, below), the High Commission went farther in protecting those who had rendered services to the occupation authorities. Through that ordinance it empowered itself to decide, at will, any criminal, civil, administrative, or disciplinary cases in which collaborationist problems were involved, for it provided that by its own decision jurisdiction in such cases could be vested in itself rather than in the regular German courts or administrative agencies. Ireton has said (p. 465) that 'this is perhaps the one ordinance of the Commission open to question as to its constitutionality,' for it represented an 'unauthorized divestment of German jurisdiction' and had no plausible connection with the maintenance, safety, and requirements of the occupying forces.

This position was taken also by the Reichskommissar, in his protest of 24 June (*Dokumente* . . . vol. 2, pp. 8-9). But on 17 July Tirard answered that Ordinance 90 represented only an adaptation of the German administration to the needs and circumstances of military occupation, in the meaning of Article 5 of the Rhineland Agreement. This argument is not legally admissible. A substitution of administrative measures of the occupant for court activities of the occupied country cannot be classified as 'adaptation'; it is rather a structural change. Ordinance 90 gave the High Commission a general power of annulment, and potential jurisdiction in all fields of law and administration.

The effect of these ordinances on proceedings before German courts will be discussed in the following chapter, in connection with the broader problem of judicial relations between the Germans and the occupying powers. But the ordinances influenced the operation of administrative as well as criminal law, and it is their implications for administrative measures of discipline that should be pointed out in the present context.

The methods of influencing the German civil-service personnel policy that were discussed above concerned only the power of the occupation authorities to remove or prevent the appointment of German officials whom they considered unfit for administrative functions under the peculiar conditions of occupation. Ordinance 90 dealt with the opposite situation, for it asserted the right of the occupation authorities to prevent the disciplining or removal of officials whom they considered particularly fit for such functions. It could be said that this ordinance supplemented the power to veto appointments by the power to veto dismissals and administrative penalties.

This latter power has great potential importance in any occupation regime, because administrative penalties, unlike criminal and civil-law penalties, depend almost entirely on discretion: an official who violates the code of behavior laid down for his group can be subjected to administrative penalties. Occupation authorities depend on the co-operation of the agencies of the occupied country, but if the highest authority of that country is able to stipulate, by means of disciplinary procedures, what is the 'proper' attitude of its civil servants in their relations with the occupation authorities, it is able to dictate the forms and methods of communication between the two groups. It may even go so far as to sabotage all attempts of the occupation authorities to overcome the mistrust that is likely to characterize relations between the two groups at the beginning of a military occupation. Thus there is a close relation between protection of collaborationists and control of the personnel policy of the occupied country.

The seriousness of this problem depends, of course, on the attitude of the occupied country. If government and administration are conducted by responsible persons, who want to co-operate with the occupying powers because of a mutual desire for harmony and for a lawful adherence to the conditions of the occupation agreement, there can be no occasion to protect collaborating officials from punishment. But the problem becomes vitally important if there is bad faith on either side, or if the population of the occupied country is swept by a nationalistic hysteria which leads it to defy the acts of its own officials.

At the time of the Rhineland occupation, German civil-service personnel policy was in the hands of responsible governments, in Berlin and the state capitals, and as a whole the population accepted the principles and conditions of the occupation. In that situation Ordinance 90 had only a limited significance, at least in the period before the troubles in the Ruhr. To be sure, there were instances not only in the field of criminal law but also in the field of administrative law (see, for example, *Recueil* . . . 1923, p. 343) in which the Germans instituted proceedings against persons whom the occupation authorities deemed deserving of protection. But in most such cases the occupation authorities themselves had at best an uncertain justification, because the collaboration that they protected was a collaboration in political and economic activities that were quite outside the accepted principles of the occupation.

The situation would have been quite different if a Nazi type of regime had existed at the time of the Rhineland occupation. Under those conditions the principles contained in Ordinance 90 would have been an essential means of self-protection against attempts to replace responsible officials by irresponsible demagogues. If the democratic process is not functioning in the occupied country, the occupying powers cannot afford to neglect the exercise of a dual control over civil-service personnel policy— prohibiting not only the appointment of sabotaging officials but also the disciplining or dismissal of co-operative officials.

In such a situation, however, it is particularly essential that the occupying powers conduct themselves in such a way that they have the confidence of the resident population. Otherwise they cannot rely on the sincerity of any co-operation they may be given, and they will find themselves confronted with 'protection' cases that are not only difficult to justify but in some instances even unwelcome.

One example, though it occurred later than the period under

review here, may be cited as illustration of the tangled ramifications inherent in the encouragement of collaborationist activities that outrage the nationals of the occupied country. At the time of the Ruhr struggle, Dorten, of separatist fame, was sued by his former maid for support of her illegitimate child (*Dokumente* . . . vol. 2, p. 51). It was a matter in which the occupation authorities had no right to interfere, but the moral reputation of the defendant was to a certain extent connected with the prestige of the French occupation army; moreover, in view of the circumstances it was quite possible that the charge was merely an effort to exploit the public feeling against Dorten. Thus the High Commission interrupted the proceedings by requiring the Wiesbaden municipal court to send the files to Coblenz in order that it might check the case. When it decided, after many months, that the proceedings might continue, the defendant had left Germany. Continuation of the case was then meaningless for the plaintiff. And the High Commission found that the second horn of its dilemma was no better than the first, for the public, taking it for granted that Dorten was guilty, was incensed that foreign authorities had enabled him to escape the consequences.

Even with the most exemplary behavior, a future occupation regime in Germany, confronted with so many difficult tasks, will find that one of the most difficult is that of distinguishing between those collaborators who are motivated by opportunism and the desire to hide their past and keep their jobs, and the truly sympathetic elements of the population who realize that the future of their country depends upon the gradual reconstruction of a decent administration and the rebirth of responsible autonomous groups. The necessary protection of the responsible collaborators should not be jeopardized by a use of this power for dubious ends.

VII

Administration of Justice

THE Rhineland Agreement dealt very briefly with questions concerning the administration of justice in the occupied territory, its entire text on such matters being contained in four short paragraphs (Article 3c, d, e, and Article 4). It was therefore necessary for the High Commission to provide the detailed regulations that would govern the problems of judiciary and police, and this it did in its long and highly controversial Ordinance 2, of 10 January 1920. Ordinance 2 was of course supplemented and amplified in various later ordinances and regulations, but it represented the basic principles of the occupation authorities on this question.

Various fundamental provisions of this ordinance were hotly contested by the German Government and by German jurists, and some of the objections were not without a certain formal validity. But the root of the trouble, here as in the matter of the local representatives, lay in the fact that the well-meaning Rhineland Agreement was not an effective instrument for a military occupation after a total war. By its inexactness and its omissions it enabled the High Commission to assume practically unlimited power, and enabled the Germans to protest, with technical justification, against proper and essential actions of the Commission.

Jurisdiction of Military Tribunals and German Courts

In organization and actual functioning, there was little difference between the occupation courts of the armistice period and those of the peace period. The military tribunals remained as the judicial instruments of occupation government.

On the question of court powers, the Rhineland Agreement contained only three short provisions (Article 3c, d, e): 'The German courts shall continue to exercise civil and criminal jurisdiction,' except that the armed forces, and the persons accompanying or employed by them, 'shall be exclusively subject to the military law and jurisdiction of such forces,' and that anyone 'who commits any offence against the persons or property of the armed forces . . . may be made amenable to the military jurisdiction of the said forces.' The first of these exceptions is self-evident, as a general principle; the second is remarkable not because of its content but because of its omissions. If literally interpreted, it would afford the armies no protection from attacks directed against their existence, their inner structure, or their honor, or from actions, such as disturbances of public order, which might indirectly threaten their security.

Indeed, this conclusion was actually drawn by the German jurist Karl Heyland, theorist on Rhineland occupation law. Heyland declared (*Die Rechtsstellung . . .* p. 165) that according to the Rhineland Agreement, crimes of Germans directed against the existence or security of the occupying armies—such as conspiracy in a mutiny of the soldiers, or the cutting of telephone or telegraph lines—could be handled only by German courts, applying 'German law and the lawfully enacted statutes of the High Commission, but not the military codes of the occupying powers.' He defended his somewhat paradoxical conclusion by pointing out (ibid. p. 166) that such crimes would not remain unpunished, but would be dealt with by German courts, whose objectivity should not be questioned.

It is hardly necessary to emphasize that the High Commission did not interpret the Rhineland Agreement so narrowly. Ordinance 2, enacted on the very first day of its regime, subjected to military jurisdiction not only those who committed 'any offence against the persons or property of the armed forces' but also anyone who contravened an ordinance of the High Commission (Article 2). It also stipulated penalties applicable to any person who 'wilfully damages' any public installation, 'in a manner likely to prejudice the security of the troops of occupation' (Article 24), or who 'commits or abets the commission of any act calculated to promote bad feeling, dissatisfaction, indiscipline or mutiny amongst the troops of occupation' (Article 26).

Two days later, in its note of protest, the German Government contended that through this ordinance the High Commission vested the military courts with criminal jurisdiction almost at will, and that such provisions were contrary to the Rhineland Agreement. Here the Germans' case was formally sound, and their contention was not very convincingly refuted in the answer to their protest, sent by Millerand on 2 March (see Kraus and Rödiger, vol. 2, p. 1155). Millerand merely held that the High Commission's right to provide for the security of the troops, through the enactment of ordinances, implied the power to transfer jurisdiction from German courts to the military tribunals, the only criminal courts at the disposal of the occupying powers. Heyland, however, went a step further than the diplomatic protest, and maintained (*Die Rechtsstellung* . . . p. 168) that this provision of Ordinance 2 was void—which would mean that 10,000 or more sentences inflicted between 1920 and 1926 were illegal because the courts had no jurisdiction.[1]

Whatever may be said about Heyland's blindness to the practical necessities of efficient occupation, the fact remains that the legal basis on which the military tribunals actually functioned

---

[1] No exact figure is available on court proceedings in all zones of the occupied Rhineland. Tuohy mentions, however (*Occupied* . . . p. 143), that the British Summary Court handled about 3,700 cases between 1920 and 1926 in Cologne, and, between 1926 and 1930, about 1,000 cases in Wiesbaden. The French and Belgians brought at least as many cases to trial as the British did, and thus the estimate of 10,000 appears conservative. Only a very small proportion of the cases brought before the military tribunals were concerned with attacks on the persons or property of the armed forces. Since the Rhineland Agreement was never in force in the American zone, the court proceedings there were not subject to the German challenge.

was not strong enough—except in regard to the 'persons or property' cases provided for in the Rhineland Agreement—to vest these courts with an authority that the nationals of the occupied territory could recognize as anything further than an expression of mere force. Certainly the jurisdictional provisions of Ordinance 2 represented a realistic approach to the problems involved. But if occupying powers are compelled to use, as justification for such vital activities, arguments so flimsy as those of Millerand in his note of 2 March, the principle of military occupation controlled by the rule of law is gravely discredited.

Despite the fact that Ordinance 2 was so much more stringent than the Rhineland Agreement, there was at least one respect in which it gave the Germans an advantage: in Article 4 it empowered the military authorities, if they so desired, to allow jurisdiction to remain with German courts in individual criminal proceedings against German nationals. A choice of this kind had been provided for in the German occupation of France in 1871-3, but it had not been mentioned in the Rhineland Agreement, and it represented a considerable improvement of the German legal position. Its inclusion is particularly noteworthy, as the precedent of 1871 was not very encouraging: at that time (Robin, pp. 360-61) a French jury had, on two occasions, acquitted a French national of the murder of a German soldier, although in both cases the defendant's guilt was almost beyond doubt.

The practical importance of this provision varied in the different zones and periods. According to Heyland (*Die Rechtsstellung* . . . p. 180) the American and English military authorities left many cases to the German courts, particularly those concerned with insignificant violations of the ordinances and (in the American zone) those concerned with criminal proceedings against juveniles. At first France and Belgium did not shift jurisdiction at all, but France changed her attitude on this question in the course of time. There were quite a number of instances in which jurisdiction was relinquished in cases of more than trifling importance. Once this occurred even in a murder case: in 1921 a German national killed an American soldier, and the German district court of Neuwied was allowed to conduct his trial; that court sentenced him to death, but the sentence was commuted by the High Commission to life imprisonment (Rousseau, *La Haute Commission* . . . p. 192, note 3; Allen, *Journal*, p. 108). In 1928, according to Tirard (p. 140, note 1), 1,424 violations of ordinances were detected in the occupied territory, of which only one-third were handled by the military tribunals (the *tribunaux militaires de simple police*); nearly half were left to the German courts, and the remainder did not come to trial.

A decision of the military authorities that a case should be handled by a German court was not final. Another provision of Ordinance 2 (Article 4) reserved to the High Commission 'the right at any stage of a case to make any order transferring any such case to any other court.' In its diplomatic note of 12 January 1920, the German Government branded this rule an open attack on the independence of the judiciary and a revival of *Kabinettsjustiz*. But this protest seems hardly justified, for derivative jurisdiction does not entail the same status as the original jurisdiction of constitutional courts. When jurisdiction was shifted to a German court, the latter acted as an agency of the occupying powers, and in the contested provision the High Commission merely reserved the right to restore the original situation if its confidence in the objectivity of the German court should prove unjustified. The provision afforded a legal possibility of preventing the German courts from sabotaging occupation law. No case is on record, however, in which the High Commission actually made use of this privilege of transferring jurisdiction in a pending case. Indeed, Tirard himself declared (p. 141) that 'the German courts loyally fulfilled their duty,' punishing those whom they considered guilty, 'in accordance with law and justice.'

It has been mentioned that exemption from German original

jurisdiction applied not only to the armed forces but also to those 'persons accompanying them' to whom a revocable pass had been granted, and to 'any persons employed by, or in the service of such troops' (Article 3d). This provision referred primarily to the families of soldiers and officers of the occupying armies, and to servants and employees. Its political significance lies in its applicability to German nationals.

Such a provision represented a necessary protective measure, not only for the German individuals involved but also for the occupying armies. Persons closely affiliated with the armed forces were inevitably aware of many facts concerning the internal working of the occupation regime, and it would not have been desirable to allow them to remain unconditionally subject to German jurisdiction, particularly to the pressure that could be exercised through the methods of criminal procedure. But the exemption provision was capable of serious abuse, for it could have been used to protect not only co-operative elements engaged in bona-fide occupation activities but also those engaged in activities not connected with the professed aims of the occupation. Thus the interpretation of this clause was one of the important questions that arose in connection with the ratification of the Rhineland Agreement.

In its diplomatic note of 12 July 1919 (Kraus and Rödiger, vol. 2, pp. 1102-9) the German Government held that this provision should in no circumstances be regarded as applying to German citizens. The note pointed out that if it applied to German nationals it would lead to an insupportable situation in which two classes of Germans existed in the occupied territory, one that was subject to, and one that was exempt from, the jurisdiction of the German courts. In commenting on this passage of the note the Belgian jurist B. De Jaer has discussed the question (p. 103) whether international law recognizes extraterritoriality of nationals from the courts of their own country. In the Réponse de Versailles (Kraus and Rödiger, vol. 2, pp. 1115-16) the Allies recognized the German contention, in regard to the general exemptions mentioned in the Rhineland Agreement, but they declared that the German courts were not entitled to institute proceedings 'in respect of political or commercial acts relating to the armistice period' if such acts had not given rise to legal proceedings by the occupation authorities.

When the High Commission enacted its first ordinances the Germans found that Article 1 of Ordinance 2 was virtually an exact repetition of Article 3d of the Rhineland Agreement, with no mention of the exception recognized in the Réponse de Versailles. In their note of 12 January 1920, they objected to this omission, but Millerand, in his reply of 2 March, reiterated the assurance given in the Réponse de Versailles. And indeed, so far as the exemption of employees was concerned, the German fear of an abuse of privilege proved unjustified. In the first days of October 1920 the High Commission even improved the German position: in Ordinance 43 (1 October) it provided that German nationals should be exempted from German court proceedings only in cases specified in an ordinance of the High Commission; and in Ordinance 44 (2 October) it provided that for German employees of the occupying armies or authorities such exemption should be allowed only 'where the acts alleged against them were done by them in the course of, or arising out of, their duty.' It is worth mentioning that on 26 April 1921 (Bruns, p. 299) the Reichsgericht interpreted Article 3d of the Rhineland Agreement exactly as the High Commission did in Ordinance 44.

Nine months later, in Ordinance 94 (1 July 1921) the High Commission declared that German employees of the occupation authorities could not, without the consent of their employer, be summoned as witnesses in criminal proceedings in German courts. The ordinance declared, however, that permission would be granted unless 'the matters in respect to which the evidence is required concern or relate to the official duties of such persons,' in which case the High Commission would decide at its discretion. Ordinance 94 met no objections from the Germans, as the German codes of procedure contained similar provisions for all 'officials.' In fact, the employee aspect of the exemption question, which played so great a role in the notes exchanged early in 1920, was hardly touched on in later discussions.

But the situation was quite different in regard to another, related provision of Ordinance 2, which was not mentioned at all in the German note of 12 January. Article 31 of that ordinance contained a general amnesty for all persons involved in business transactions carried out during the armistice period with the expressed or implied permission of the occupation authorities, and declared that without the consent of the High Commission no judicial proceedings should be instituted or continued against residents of the occupied territory for any political or administrative activity during the armistice period. This article constituted an *ex post facto* legalization of the 'hole in the west' and separatist activities. And as has already been mentioned, Ordinance 90, enacted on 16 June 1921, gave the High Commission the power to transfer to itself the jurisdiction of German courts and administrative agencies in cases involving collaborationist problems.

Besides their significance in the field of civil-service administration, which has already been discussed, these provisions had far-reaching implications for the relationship between the High Commission and the German criminal courts during the following years. It is true that until the time of the Ruhr conflict they were not applied very often. And they were used mainly in connection with minor matters. In the Korn case, for example, decided on 23 November 1922 (*Recueil* . . . 1923, p. 343), Korn, a baker, was arraigned before a German court for violating the German eight-hour day statute, having permitted his employees to work overtime in order to produce and deliver bread on time to the French military agencies; and the High Commission canceled the judgment of the German court. But the powers of the High Commission in regard to the protection of collaborationists led to at least one *cause célèbre*—the Commission's interference with the judgment of the Cologne court in the libel case of President Ebert against the separatist leader Joseph Smeets.

In 1921 Smeets had published an article in his Cologne paper in which he attacked the chief executive of the Reich for having violated the German food-rationing statutes. After examining numerous witnesses the court decided that not the slightest evidence existed for his statements, and Smeets was found guilty of libel as well as of certain other charges brought against him. General Allen reports in his *Journal* (p. 283) that on 10 September 1921 he was invited to a session of the High Commission in order to 'discuss a political matter for which the lawyers would not be required'; and thereafter, despite the strong opposition of the American and English representatives, the High Commission decided that Smeets should be released (ibid. p. 286). According to a High Commission note of 7 October 1922 (reprinted in *Dokumente* . . . vol. 2, p. 27) the sentences given Smeets were sanctions imposed upon a resident of the occupied territory to end his relations with the occupying powers. General Allen called this intervention decision of the High Commission the 'least worthy act' of that body (*Occupation*, p. 201; important documents of the Smeets case are published in the same book, pp. 325-32).

The Smeets affair was discussed with indignation in the German Reichstag and the Prussian Diet (Reichstag, sitting of 23 October 1922, vol. 357, pp. 8872-6; Preussischer Landtag, sitting of 23 October 1922, I. Wahlperiode, 1921-4, vol. 9, pp. 12875-93). In the Prussian diet (pp. 12883-93) Prime Minister Otto Braun declared the High Commission's decision 'an unheard of infringement of the legal power of the Prussian courts. Never before has the High Commission violated Germany's sovereignty in such an arbitrary way.' The German Government sent a sharp note of protest to France, England, and Belgium, in which it pointed out that Smeets' article was a copy of another article published in Cologne, whose author had been punished for his libel without interference by the High Commission (the text of this note is available in *Dokumente* . . . vol. 2, pp. 28-9).

The Smeets affair was one of the most important occurrences undermining confidence in the Inter-Allied regime as a rule of law. At an official reception held by the High Commission for delegates of labor, the workers, 'after noting that several political matters had been discussed,' took the occasion to present their formal protest against the interference of the Commission (Allen, *Occupation*, pp. 245-6). They fully realized that the authority of the new republican government was seriously threatened if the personal honor of the President of the German Republic was not respected and protected within the German borderlines. On 12 December 1921, representatives of five major political parties of the Rhineland met at Königswinter, on the Rhine, and published a statement branding the action of the High Commission in this case as an 'interference with the most sacred sphere of civil liberty' (*Dokumente* . . . vol. 3, pp. 10-11). Since in the Germany of 1921 a joint declaration of five major political parties was almost unthinkable, it is evident how deeply public opinion in the Rhineland was affected by the affair. Separatist politics and its backing by the High Commission, rather than producing disunity among the German population, actually brought about a united front in the Rhineland. It was of little help that in average cases the occupation authorities observed the law satisfactorily. Public opinion does not notice the everyday activities of the courts. One big case like that of Smeets overshadows the wisest application of the law in a thousand small cases.

As for cases in which members of the armed forces were arraigned for crimes against residents of the occupied territory, these were of course within the jurisdiction of the military tribunals. In the majority of such cases the decision met no objection from the Germans, a strong indication that the judgment was reached in accordance with the requirements of justice. But in some cases, particularly those concerned with crimes of violence, such as homicide, assault, and rape, it was inevitable under the peculiar conditions of occupation that the question should arise whether the military tribunals were biased in favor of their co-nationals or influenced by considerations of the prestige of the occupying forces.

In 1923 the Reich Minister of the Interior published a list of 300 crimes committed by members of the armed forces against residents of the occupied Rhineland (Reichstag, vol. 376, Aktenstück No. 5448). The list, which was based on careful investigations by the German authorities and was asserted to include only the gravest cases, contained 65 instances of homicide, 65 of maltreatment and assault, and 170 of rape and similar crimes. In some of the cases the accused soldier was acquitted, but the report mentions several instances in which severe penalties were inflicted on soldiers who were found guilty. A French Moroccan soldier was given the death sentence for murder; an American soldier was sentenced to three years of imprisonment for manslaughter; French soldiers were given sentences, for rape, ranging up to eight years; and, for the same crime, three Moroccan soldiers were given ten years at hard labor.

The latter cases belong in one of the most publicized chapters of the Rhineland occupation, the so-called *Schwarze Schmach*. It would be of no avail to discuss the very elaborate German and French literature on this subject. It should be mentioned, however, that a commission appointed by a Swedish Christian society made a careful examination of the allegations against colored soldiers in the Rhineland during the first two years of occupation, and concluded that in that period no more than a hundred offenses of all kinds were attributable to the 24,000 colored troops in Germany; the report asserted that according to the French authorities four-fifths of this number remained unsubstantiated, but 'the German authorities with equal emphasis declare that they have no reason to withdraw a single case.' The report was published in July 1921 in the *New Statesman* (vol. 17, pp. 353-4), and the author of the article declared that 'viewed solely from the standpoint of actual outrage and violence, the inhabitants of the occupied regions might even be better off with a larger proportion of coloured troops, who, it must be remembered, have no painful memories of the hardships of '71.'

From a historical point of view the German propaganda campaign against the French army for using 'black' soldiers is far more important than the crimes themselves, for it represented a rather successful attempt to influence public opinion in the United States in favor of the German cause in the occupied Rhineland. As Norbert Sevestre has said in an illuminating analysis of this issue (p. 418), the immediate purpose of the German propaganda in this field was to alienate the United States from France by exploiting American race prejudice.

An indication of the Germans' success is contained in a speech delivered in Congress on 31 August 1922 by Senator Hitchcock of Nebraska (Hitchcock, p. 12020):

We may sit idly by while France in her folly proceeds to cripple, if not to crush, the German Republic by demands for reparations which all the world knows Germany can not possibly meet at this time. We may even witness in silence the fall of the German Republic, and see the German people driven in desperation back to the grasp of the plotting monarchists or into the arms of Bolshevism. But we as a Nation are in part responsible for the Rhineland being under military occupation and it is our right, as well as our duty, to protest against quartering half-civilized black troops among white people, where they appear as conquerors and act as criminals.

A courageous article in the *Nation* by Lewis S. Gannett, in which he declared after careful investigation that 'There is no such thing as a "Black Horror on the Rhine"' (Gannett, p. 733), produced numerous letters of violent indignation (New York *Nation*, 1921, vol. 112, p. 815; 1921, vol. 113, pp. 44, 264). It was of no avail that Maximilian Harden (pp. 293-9), a German writer of international reputation, published statements in *Zukunft* that independently corroborated what was said by Gan-

nett, Sevestre and the *New Statesman*. The official German
propaganda, and the will to believe, proved stronger than the
truth, and, as E. H. Carr has put it (p. 51), the 'black shame'
issue provided Germany, for the first time since the war, with
'a cause in which British and American opinion sided emphatically with Germany against France' (see also Tuohy, 'France's
Rhineland Adventure,' p. 33).

But even in cases in which no race prejudices were involved,
nationalistic feelings were frequently aroused. After the decision
in the Rouzier case, for example, in which a French lieutenant
was acquitted of the murder of a German citizen, public opinion in the Rhineland was highly incensed. G. E. R. Gedye, who
believed that this decision constituted an open violation of law,
declared in 1927 ('La Justice Militaire,' p. 556): 'Across the
Rhine, German extremists thank God and the French chauvinists for this new weapon afforded them to drive home their fa-
vourite text—that *rapprochement* is folly, and that only force
will drive out the regime of force instituted by France in their
country.'

Under the influence of Gedye's brilliant and provocative article, which appeared in the London *Nation*, Horace G. Alexander (p. 656) proposed in a letter to the editor of that periodical
that a mixed commission with a neutral chairman be created as
an appellate body for all cases involving crimes committed by
members of the armed forces against German nationals. 'I believe,' said Alexander, 'this would bring a source of real assurance of legal equality to the German population, and it would
therefore be a great encouragement to the Locarno policy.' This
proposal, made in the final period of the occupation, was scarcely
feasible, as the occupying armies were agents of individual sovereign states and not of an international authority, but it is
worthy of consideration for a future occupation in which this
condition may be different.

In most instances it was clear whether a particular case belonged to the jurisdiction of the military tribunals or to that

of the German courts, but there were a few borderline cases in which this decision depended on the classification of the crime in the various legal systems. An example is a situation in which a German witness, under examination by a military tribunal, took an oath which later proved false. In these circumstances would the military tribunal or a German court be entitled to arraign him for perjury? German criminal law classifies perjury as an offense against religion, and it is obvious that it was not within the jurisdiction of the occupying powers to prosecute violations of religion. But it can also be held that perjury is a form of contempt of court, and that the religious formulation of the oath is incidental to the statement of facts. On 10 November 1920, in Ordinance 56, the High Commission took the latter view. The ordinance, which dealt both with contempt of court and with perjury, declared that the taking of a false oath in a military tribunal was punishable in accordance with the national laws of that tribunal.

During the last phase of the occupation the Reichsgericht had occasion to decide a case in which a German was arraigned for having committed perjury in a Belgian military tribunal. For reasons not stated in the report, Belgian perjury provisions did not cover the case, and on 20 February 1930 (64 RGSt 15) the Reichsgericht rejected the defendant's plea that his oath had been taken in a non-German court, reversed the decision of the trial court, and delivered sentence. The case was not of great importance, but it is further evidence of the unforeseeable situations that arise in the course of military occupation.

COURT PROCEDURES AND PRACTICES

In cases concerning an attack on 'persons or property' of the occupying armies, the court, whether German or military, applied the substantive and procedural law of its own country; for the German courts the decision regarding procedure was contained in Ordinance 2 (Article 7), and that regarding substantive law was contained in the general provision of the Réponse de Versailles that German courts should apply German law. But in cases concerning violations of ordinances, both the German courts and the military tribunals, though applying their own laws of procedure, were obliged to decide on the basis of a substantive law which was not the law of their own country but that of an international body—specifically occupation law.[2] In the peace period, unlike the armistice period, the substantive law of the occupying powers constituted a closed system of criminal law (De Jaer, p. 88), covering not only special but also general problems, such as conspiracy and the like. The 'general' part of criminal occupation law was regulated by a provision of Ordinance 2 (Article 23), which was replaced on 17 December 1920 by Ordinance 66, and this regulation, summary as it was, represented more than a mere legalistic technicality. A mixture of occupation law, enacted by an international body, with municipal law of one of the occupants or of Germany, would have led to serious confusion.

Ferdinand Tuohy has presented (*Occupied . . .* pp. 141-8) an interesting picture of the everyday activities of military tribunals in the occupied Rhineland. His description pertains to Summary Court procedure in the British zone, but it may be assumed that the situation was about the same in the American tribunals. 'The Summary Court,' he remarked (p. 142), 'was like nothing in our own lauded judicial system.' Although it had no jury, in spite of the fact that it handled criminal cases, it was nevertheless a true court 'and in no sense a court martial.' Tuohy says that a 'legal purist would have turned from the hybrid in horror,' but this consternation would have been restricted to Anglo-American visitors of the courts, for the 'omnipotence' of the presiding judge in the Summary Court was wholly in accordance with German experience (at the beginning of the

[2] On 10 July 1924, the Conseil de Revision de l'Armée du Rhin decided that French soldiers could not be punished for violations of High Commission ordinances, because the latter were not French law (*Journal du droit international*, 1926, vol. 53, p. 649).

occupation the jury system had been used in German courts in exceptional cases, but it was abolished entirely early in 1924). German lawyers, on the other hand, sometimes 'looked at one another in puzzled, even in pained, surprise' when a German defendant was acquitted because 'a case broke down'; this astonishment, and the question, 'Were the *verdammte Engländer* playing with them?' (p. 148), were due to the great differences between common law and continental procedure. In the occupation tribunals the defendant's position was considerably weaker than in ordinary procedure, but the guarantees enjoyed by a defendant in common law are so strong that they surprised the German lawyer even after they had been accommodated to the peculiar situation of an occupation court.

The military tribunals of the occupying armies were foreign courts on German soil, and double jeopardy was not recognized as a defense, either in them or in the German courts. In the military courts this problem was of no great importance, but in the German courts it had rather significant implications.

In a case decided by the Reichsgericht on 23 February 1920 (54 RGSt 139) the defendant had threatened another person with a pistol in order to obtain money. He had committed the crime in the British zone and had been punished by a British military tribunal for violation of an ordinance concerning the unauthorized possession and use of a weapon. Thereupon he was arraigned before a German court for having committed blackmail with a dangerous weapon, and in his second trial he pleaded *ne bis in idem*. The Reichsgericht rejected the defense, characterizing the crime as a violation of German as well as of occupation law.

This decision, which dealt with an armistice case, was rendered shortly after the ratification of the peace treaty, but the principle it expressed was maintained during the subsequent years. On 19 December 1924 (59 RGSt 9) the Reichsgericht, in rejecting a defendant's plea that he had been sentenced by a French military court *in absentia* for the same crime for which he was indicted in the German court, made the statement: 'The decisions of foreign courts have, in principle, no legal effect inside Germany. Such decisions do not eliminate the right of the Reich or the states to punish in an individual case.' Here the Reichsgericht was prepared to apply only that section of the German criminal code which provided that the execution of the judgment of a German court must be suspended to the extent that a sentence passed by a foreign court, for the same offense, had been executed.

In still another case (DJZ 1927, vol. 32, p. 1243), decided during the last phase of the occupation, a certain Reine, a German citizen, had invited a French soldier Landreau for a ride in his automobile. Reine permitted Landreau to drive for a while, though the latter was unfamiliar with the operation of a car. The result was that Landreau killed a child. The French military tribunal arraigned not only Landreau but also Reine. In doing so it based its jurisdiction, improperly, on a provision of the French Code de Justice Militaire, though it had full authorization to try Reine as a result of a provision in Ordinance 2 (Article 2) which declared that if German and Allied nationals were jointly concerned in the commission of an offense the case should go to the military tribunal. The French court gave Landreau a sentence of three months (but released him on probation), and fined Reine. After this conviction Reine was arraigned before the regular German court and punished for a second time. Burkhard, who reported this case, maintained that the second indictment was justified because the fine imposed on Reine was not an 'adequate punishment.'

The German courts' assertion of a right to subject German nationals to a second trial for the same offense was, in effect, an assertion of a right to review decisions of the military tribunals. It is true that this practice made it possible to assure the enforcement of German law, but in doing so it could lead to excessive punishment of the defendant. In actual fact, however, it was not so much for considerations of justice as for considerations of national prestige that the German courts excluded the plea of double jeopardy.

In regard to cases tried by the military courts, Ordinance 2 (Article 11) declared that the power of pardon and of commutation or reduction of sentence should be exercised 'in conformity with the laws and regulations of the nation concerned.' If sentence had been passed by a German court, acting by virtue of derivative jurisdiction, this power was vested in the High Commission (Article 10). It is not without interest to learn from Tirard (p. 141) that in considering the pardon of a person sentenced by a German court, the High Commission regularly followed the recommendation of that court. He characterizes this attitude as a recognition of the German courts' conscientious fulfilment of their duties.

The Rhineland Agreement (Article 5) declared it to be understood that 'the German authorities shall be obliged, under penalty of removal, to conform to the Ordinances,' but it was never determined whether 'authorities' here included also the judges. According to the French jurist Alléhaut (p. 50) neither the Rhineland Agreement nor any ordinance excluded interference with court proceedings; in fact, the High Commission, he declared, 'has affirmed its right to remove judges and has made use of this right.' Alléhaut, who published his book in 1925, apparently had in mind a decision of the High Commission rendered on 12 June 1923 (Recueil . . . 1929, p. 69), which explicitly stated that judges were among the officials who would be prosecuted for the application of statutes that were not admitted in the occupied territory.

Actually, however, both in principle and in fact the occupying powers recognized during this peace period, as during the armistice period, that except in case of direct military necessity the full independence of the judiciary is essential for a continuation of court activities in an occupied territory. Before the turbulent period of 'passive resistance' during the Ruhr conflict, when several judges were arrested and punished by the French military authorities (*Dokumente* . . . vol. 1, pp. 128-9), the occupying powers fully respected the personal independence of the German judges.

It may be noted that after the present war the situation regarding judicial freedom will be wholly different. In its meeting of 27 April 1942, the German Reichstag adopted a resolution, introduced by Göring, according to which the 'leader' of the German nation is empowered summarily to remove from office any state official, including judges. A future occupation of Germany will be confronted with the problem not of preserving but of restoring judicial independence.

Civil Cases

During the armistice period the German courts had not been entitled to deal with cases against persons exempted from their criminal jurisdiction. This meant that in civil cases too the members of the occupying forces were exempt from the jurisdiction of the German courts. German plaintiffs were advised to sue in the courts of the soldier's country of origin, and it goes without saying that this regulation, understandable during the armistice period, amounted practically to a denial of justice under the peculiar conditions of that time.

The Germans contended that after the ratification of the peace treaty German courts should be entitled to decide all civil cases against members of the armed forces in which German courts would have jurisdiction according to German law. Even if it is held that the members of the occupying forces were not 'domiciled' in the Rhineland, the application of this principle would have given the German courts jurisdiction in almost all civil cases. In continental law 'domicile,' although not without significance, is by no means so important as it is in common law. Under German law, contract claims can be raised in the courts of the district where the contractual obligation is to be fulfilled (§29 ZPO); tort claims, in the district where the tort has been committed (§32 ZPO); claims based on a will, in the court where the testator resided at the time of his death (§27 ZPO). Of special importance is the provision in the German code of civil procedure (§23 ZPO) which stipulates that for all claims presenting a money value, persons without residence in Germany can be sued in the courts of those districts in which property of theirs can be attached; the significance of this provision arises from the fact that it covers claims for the support of illegitimate children, which are the most important civil actions likely to arise in a military occupation.

The question of civil jurisdiction was not explicitly mentioned in the Rhineland Agreement provision, in Article 3d, that the armed forces (and also the persons accompanying or employed by them) should be 'exclusively subject to the military law and jurisdiction of such forces.' In its note of 12 July 1919, the German Government held that 'military law' is concerned only with questions of public and criminal law, and that therefore the jurisdiction of the German courts in civil actions was not restricted. The Réponse de Versailles, of 29 July, conceded that contract claims concerning military persons or their families as private individuals should be heard by the German courts, 'subject to a right of evocation reserved to the High Commission in cases of abuse'; but it declared that 'cases which are at the same time civil and criminal must be judged by the military courts.' On 7 August the Germans objected that if the High Commission were given a right of evocation it would seriously interfere with German jurisdiction and constitute a reflection on the impartiality of German judges.

It is noteworthy that Marcel Nast, chief legal adviser of the French High Commissioner, fully agreed with the German point of view and severely criticized the position taken in the Réponse de Versailles ('De la situation . . .' p. 391). Vanard, too, declared (p. 206) that the phrase 'military law' was lacking in precision and must be considered 'incomplete,' but he ably shifted the discussion from mere text interpretation to a basic analysis of the problems involved. Vanard contended (p. 208) that the members of an occupying army remain in the occupied territory not voluntarily, as private persons, but as agents of a foreign state, and that therefore they should be given a privileged status in regard to civil as well as criminal proceedings.

The High Commission tried to solve this problem in Ordinance 2 (Articles 15-21). There it declared (Article 15) that the German courts should 'continue to exercise their civil jurisdiction,' except over the armed forces and the persons accompanying or employed by them; and that even in regard to these exceptions the German courts, as a general rule, should be competent in civil cases in which such persons were involved in their private capacity. For extraordinary cases the ordinance established special 'High Commission Courts' to serve both as courts of first instance and as appellate courts. In the first of these capacities such a court had jurisdiction in regard to those cases which the High Commission decided should not be handled by a German court, 'by reason of their character or the status of the persons named as parties.' In its appellate capacity a High Commission Court was entitled to review civil decisions of German courts if a person who was exempt from German criminal jurisdiction 'considers he has suffered injury from a miscarriage of justice on the part of the German Court' (Article 19).

Each High Commission Court ('one or more' were provided for) was intended to have three members, two of them, including the president of the court, being Allied nationals, the third a German citizen. But this plan of a mixed Allied-German judicial committee could not be realized. The German Government, insisting on a literal interpretation of Article 3d of the Rhineland Agreement, refused to appoint a German delegate, and thus the High Commission Courts were composed only of Allied nationals (Rousseau, *La Haute Commission* . . . p. 213). In their appellate capacity these courts, according to Tirard (p. 143), did not reverse a single German court decision. During the Ruhr conflict the local German chambers of commerce appointed assessors to the special mixed judicial commissions which were pro-

vided for in Ordinance 244; these commissions were empowered
to adjudicate damages caused by the Rhenish railways, at that
time under French and Belgian management. According to a
Belgian judge on such a body, the collaboration of the German
assessors and the other members of the commissions was highly
satisfactory.

In regard to the most important type of case that arose in the
field of civil law—the claims for support of illegitimate children
—the High Commission decided, on 24 March 1921 (*Recueil
. . . 1923*, p. 332) to inform the commanding generals that German plaintiffs had no other remedy at their disposal than to sue
the members of the occupying forces in the latters' national tribunals; this meant, of course, that such actions were practically
out of the question, because the plaintiffs could not afford to
employ a lawyer and prepare a case in a foreign country. The
High Commission suggested, however, that in each instance the
superior of the accused soldier should examine the case, and try
to influence the soldier to fulfil his duties if the examination revealed his liability. On 29 July the Commission converted into
a rule of substantive law (*Gazette*, 1921, No. VII-IX, p. 239) its
decision that affiliation or alimony actions against persons belonging or attached to the Allied armies could not be heard by
German courts, military tribunals, or High Commission Courts,
but could only be brought before the national courts of the defendant's country of origin.

This decision was motivated by the practical consideration
that the soldiers should be protected from suits brought for
'vexatious motives,' and by the general principle that the armies
'constituted in the Occupied Territories a body, governed in
principle by its own laws, which could not be obliged to conform to German laws, especially where the latter were of an
essentially national character, as was the case in respect to affiliation law' (ibid.). The financial results of the decision were
not very important, for even if German jurisdiction had been
recognized in such cases, the German plaintiffs would have had

the greatest difficulty in executing a favorable decision. Far more important were the indirect effects. A defendant who is threatened with an affiliation action may prefer to marry the girl who is the mother of his child, and it is safe to say that the occupying armies, which were not in favor of such marriages, were well aware of the practical consequences of excluding German jurisdiction in these cases.

In practice the members of the occupying forces were subject to German civil jurisdiction only in those cases in which their own national courts would have applied German law. This principle was never expressly formulated, but it stood behind the actual practice of the occupation authorities. It was primarily in contract cases, and in certain tort cases, that the members of the armies were subject to German civil law.

PUBLIC LAW CASES

In conformance with general principles of international law, German court's had no jurisdiction in cases against one of the occupying powers. The situation was not quite so clear, however, in regard to cases in which one of the occupying powers raised a claim against a German defendant.

An interesting case in this field concerned a collision of a German streetcar with a truck of the French army (see Rousseau, *La Haute Commission* . . . p. 221, note 1). The French commanding general decided that the tramway corporation was responsible for the accident; he assessed the damages due and required payment to the French army. The German Government, characterizing the case as purely 'civil,' denied the right of a military authority to handle it, since a German party was the defendant; the army commander, however, declared the case 'administrative' in character. On 14 June 1922, the High Commission denied its power to review the decision of the army commander, and referred the corporation to the German courts. This recommendation was, of course, without meaning, as the French army could not be made to plead its case in a German court. The case raises difficult questions of occupation law. In denying the right of a military authority to decide a typical negligence case without 'due process' the German protest was well founded. On the other hand, it is quite understandable that the French army would not sue in a German court. If the German corporation had pleaded contributory negligence, or had raised a counterclaim, the German tribunal would have had to decide on the action of an agent of the occupying powers.

As was discussed above, members of the occupying armies could, as a rule, be sued in the German courts in civil cases in which they had acted not as agents of the occupying powers but as private individuals. Thus on 31 March 1922 (Rousseau, *La Haute Commission* . . . pp. 219-21, note 1c) a French commanding general decided that the army was not responsible for damages in an accident caused by an automobile of the French army at a moment when the car was not in military use but had been placed at the disposal of private persons for extra-military purposes. Liability rested with the soldier who was in charge of the car, and with the persons to whom he had entrusted it.

In its meetings of 10 November 1921 and 18 May and 14 June 1922, the High Commission considered a plan to institute a 'Conseil de Justice de la Haute Commission,' a body that would be similar to the French Conseil d'État (Rousseau, *La Haute Commission* . . . pp. 229 ff.). This body was to be given wide powers to examine all matters excluded from the jurisdiction of the German courts, either by virtue of specific ordinances or by virtue of general rules of international law. It was planned as a mixed agency composed of two representatives of the Allied nations and one German; one of the Allied representatives was to belong to a nation that had no specific interest in the case, the other to the nation directly or indirectly involved in the conflict, and curiously enough the latter was suggested as chairman. The Council of Justice was to have ultimate authority in those civil law cases reserved for the High Commission Courts, and it was to have jurisdiction also in those cases that directly involved either the Allied governments or the German Government. In these public law cases, however, it was to be empowered not to render a decision but only to advise; its awards would have to be ratified by the interested governments in order to become binding, but the authors of the plan hoped that in most cases its award would be voluntarily adopted by the parties involved.

The importance of this plan, which was never adopted, lies not in its details but in the fact that it was drafted. The very contemplation of such a plan indicates that the High Commission was dissatisfied with the exclusion of legal remedies in all questions of public law. As Rousseau commented ('Le régime . . .' p. 817), 'It is highly desirable that the efforts made by the High Commission will immediately result in and contribute to a regime in which the protection of the rights of each individual in the occupied territory will be supplemented by the necessary guarantees.' This remark has considerable significance, coming as it does from a French staff member and legal adviser, at the peak of the Ruhr conflict.

An important aspect of the public law relations between Germany and the occupying powers concerned reimbursements for damages caused by the occupying forces, and for requisitions made by them. According to the Versailles treaty (Article 249) such payments, as part of the costs of occupation, were owed to the occupying powers by the German Government. On 2 March 1919, the German National Assembly enacted a statute according to which persons who had suffered damages in connection with the occupation could file their claims with a special German administrative authority (*Reichsgesetzblatt*, 1919, p. 261; executive decree of 22 April 1919, ibid. p. 405). Only the English, however, recognized this statute as valid in the Rhineland (see the German diplomatic note of 7 August 1919, in Kraus and Rödiger, vol. 2, pp. 1127-8); the other occupying powers were not willing to abandon their control over proceedings of this kind. When the German Government on 17 July 1922 enacted a new statute regarding compensation for personal damage caused by the occupation of German territory, the High Commission decided not to admit the statute in the Rhineland (*Gazette*, 1922, No. VII-IX, p. 257).

Article 6 of the Rhineland Agreement provided that local commissions, composed of appointees of both the German and the occupation authorities, should determine the charges for requisitions and damages. Subsequent ordinances and regulations of the High Commission dealt with this question in more detail. Ordinance 49, of 7 October 1920, concerned with questions of billeting and quartering, provided that the compensation paid by the German authorities was subject to control by the occupying armies. Ordinance 59, of 22 November 1920, was concerned with questions of requisition and damages, and declared that the local commissions, although entitled to assess damages, had no power to 'adjudicate upon the question of responsibility.' Details were dealt with in an internal regulation enacted on 30 September 1921.[3]

It is diverting to learn that one German Burgermeister had the ingenious idea of classifying support for an illegitimate child as a damage caused by 'requisition' of the occupying troops. The municipality, which was obliged to support the child, was entitled under German law to sue the person nominally responsible for support. The Burgermeister pleaded that the municipality was for practical reasons unable to sue in an American court the American soldier who was considered to be the child's father, and contended that the Reich should reimburse the municipality on the basis of the German statute concerning dam-

---

[3] See *Recueil* . . . 1923, pp. 154-8. These regulations, which were frequently altered, were published in final form in the *Gazette*, 1924, No. VII, pp. 386-94. They were supplemented by regulations of the individual armies. The texts of the British, French, and Belgian army regulations were published in W. Vogels, *Die Bestimmungen* . . . which contains the most comprehensive collection of material in this field. Since it was published in 1925, when the American army was no longer in the Rhineland, it does not contain the American material. An extract from the American 'Instructions . . . regarding the Assessment of Damage to Quarters' can be found in the *Gazette*, 1922, No. VII-IX, pp. 217-24.

ages caused by the occupation (RWG 1923, vol. 1, p. 264). The action, it may be added, was denied.

Powers of Military and German Police

Members of the occupying forces were, as a general rule, exempt not only from German criminal jurisdiction but also from arrest by German police. Exceptions were made, however, for certain serious offenses: Ordinance 78 (24 March 1921) provided that persons belonging to the armies could be arrested by German police officials if they were 'found committing any of the following acts: murder, assault with arms or violent assault, rape, robbery with violence, arson or unlawfully entering any building by breaking or scaling any wall, fence, or other enclosure,' or if they were caught in an attempt at murder, rape, or arson. The ordinance declared that the arrested person should be handed over immediately to the nearest military authority. On 19 March 1920 (*Recueil* . . . 1923, p. 31) the High Commission decided that the commanding generals of the individual armies could, by military orders, exact from their subordinates obedience to the German police regulations.

Much more important, however, was the question of military police authority over residents of the occupied territory. The Rhineland Agreement made no mention of such authority. On the contrary, its only police clause (Article 4) provided that the German authorities, if so requested by military officers of the occupying powers, were obliged to arrest and hand over to those powers any person charged with an offense, who according to Article 3 was subject to the jurisdiction of the military courts.

No document exists which might explain the astonishing fact that Article 4, with its reliance merely on the co-operation of the German police forces, was apparently considered sufficient. Whatever the explanation, the omission of any provision for police authority over Germans who were subject to the jurisdiction of the military courts revealed a serious lack of understanding of German political and administrative traditions, as well as of the practical requirements of occupation government. Although 'supremacy of law' has been recognized under all governments of western civilization, there are basic differences between the Anglo-American concept of 'rule of law,' the French idea of *droit administratif*, and the German concept of *Rechtsstaat*. The German Rechtsstaat is characterized by the recognition of a strong executive branch of the government, controlled by an elaborate system of legal provisions. In order to create a rule-of-law occupation within the legal system of a Rechtsstaat it is not sufficient to proclaim the principle of 'supremacy of law.' There must be a structural co-ordination of occupation law with the law of the occupied country. If the authors of the Rhineland Agreement had written that document not in the spirit of Anglo-Saxon mistrust of the executive branch of government but with an effort to achieve a structural co-ordination of occupation law with the German Rechtsstaat system, they might have accomplished their purpose—an efficient occupation government, controlled by law, smoothly co-operating with German agencies.

A reliance solely on the police of the occupied country, in occupation cases concerning its own nationals, cannot seem sound even to that country. The latter's police agencies will either come into conflict with the occupation authorities, on the ground that their attitude is too lenient, or lose the confidence of their countrymen, on the ground that they enforce the occupation law too strictly. The latter danger was particularly great in the Germany of the Weimar Republic: German chauvinists did not miss an opportunity to declare that the republican government and its executive subordinates were agents of the Allied governments. The idea of autonomy, which was given expression in the Rhineland Agreement, had limits that were not recognized. The enforcement of statutory law imposed by occupation armies does not allow of autonomy for the occupied country. Police agencies entrusted with the enforcement of occupation law are necessarily agents of the occupying powers.

The theoretical question whether the military police had the right to proceed against German nationals was raised early in 1920 by Tirard. On 28 May he received as answer from his government a legal opinion of Inter-Allied jurists which declared: 'We are of the opinion that strictly from a legal point of view the occupation authorities have no other jurisdiction in criminal matters than that laid down in Article 3 of the Rhineland Agreement. Consequently they themselves are not entitled to arrest persons who are guilty of a crime' (*Recueil* . . . 1923, p. 307).

The police provisions of Ordinance 2 (Articles 3-6) cannot be reconciled with this opinion. They adapted police regulations to the enlarged jurisdiction of the military tribunals by subjecting the German police, both in the occupied and in the unoccupied parts of the country, to the command of the military officers, not only in cases concerned with attacks on 'persons and property' but also in all cases concerned with violations of the High Commission's ordinances (Article 3). And, far more important, the execution of the ordinances was entrusted to Allied as well as German police: the monopoly of the German police over German nationals was replaced by a dual jurisdiction of the two police forces. In criminal violations of ordinances the Allied military police had exactly the same power as the German police to 'collect evidence, present charges and arrest accused persons' (Article 5); the only difference was that the German police applied German law of criminal procedure, while the military police applied the law of its country. In general the military police had the powers of arrest and search 'whenever persons are caught in the act, or in cases of urgency, or when proceedings are being taken before the Allied Military Courts.'

Thus the legal position of the High Commission was even weaker in regard to the rights it granted the military police than it was in regard to the power it vested in the military tribunals.

To be sure, the provision in the Rhineland Agreement (Article 5) that civil administration should 'continue under German law and under the authority of the Central German Government,' was followed by the qualification, 'except in so far as it may be necessary for the High Commission by Ordinance . . . to adapt that administration to the needs and circumstances of military occupation'; but this exception did not actually empower the High Commission to subject German citizens to arrest by Allied police officers. And since the powers vested in the police did not derive from the Rhineland Agreement they were subject to no 'constitutional' limitation and to no possibility of legal review. The implications of this aspect of the situation will be discussed in the following chapter.

In 1925 a German writer declared (*Süddeutsche Monatshefte*, December 1925, vol. 23, p. 200): 'Such provisions concerning the jurisdiction of police authorities look prima facie rather insignificant. In reality this change in the jurisdictional regulations has shifted a tremendous amount of power to the military police. Here is the "legal" basis of the whole system of political supervision.' American and British critics of the Rhineland regime never stressed this point. Unfamiliar with the continental methods of a 'police state,' they could not understand the significance either of the Rhineland Agreement's inadequacy on this subject or of the High Commission's grant of a power unlimited by statutory restrictions. But though they did not appreciate the full implications of the situation, they were able to see its results. As an English writer put it, in an article entitled 'The French War on Germany' (H. W. M., pp. 644 ff.): 'A civil face is indeed given to the administration. But the amenable Tirard is little more than a mask for the martinet Degoutte.'

In his answer of 2 March to the German protest of 12 January, Millerand asserted that the right to declare a state of martial law implied the right 'to take preventive and naturally less rigorous measures, if necessary in order to preserve the safety of the armies and eventually public order.' Alléhaut followed a different line (p. 85), contending that the extended jurisdiction of the military police was justified because it was not expressly forbidden in the peace treaty or the Rhineland Agreement; only an explicit treaty provision, he maintained, could prohibit the High Commission from exercising its general power to do whatever was necessary for maintaining the security of the armed forces. No legalistic sleight-of-hand can minimize the fact, however, that the exercise of practically unlimited powers by the military police was entirely contrary to what the framers of the Rhineland Agreement had in mind when they formulated that document.

Their effort to prevent such a concentration of power, even in the interests of 'public order' and the security of the troops, may have derived from an understanding of its possible misuse—a consideration that was of course at the root of the German protests. And that this fear was not entirely unfounded is evident from a decision of the High Commission on 1 July 1921 (*Recueil* . . . 1923, p. 286), according to which the military authorities were entitled, provided the procedure was regularized as soon as possible, to arrest suspicious persons without a court writ not only in cases belonging to the jurisdiction of the military tribunals but also in cases in which the person involved was accused of no specific crime but was to be expelled from the occupied area for reasons of expediency.

The propagandistic significance of the High Commission's arrogation of powers in these matters should not be overlooked. The Germans appealed to world public opinion, using the situation in the Rhineland as evidence for the contention that they had been deceived. The Rhineland Agreement, they said, was a trap: once signed by Germany it had been broken by the agents of the occupying powers. Their arguments were so strong that they succeeded in convincing a considerable part of Anglo-Saxon public opinion. If the wisdom of the Rhineland Agreement itself had been questioned, the German attacks on transgressions of it might have lost a good deal of their force. But in the United

States and England, the Germans had an audience that was sympathetic with the basic ideas of that document.

The High Commission would have been helpless in dealing with the strong bureaucratic machine of Germany if it had not had an executive apparatus at its disposal. In general administration it solved this problem by the creation of local representatives; in matters of law enforcement it was forced to rely on the military police. Entrusted with the task of maintaining the peace of Europe, it could justify its actions in these matters by reference to a 'higher law' of political necessity. But the fact remains that from a strictly legal point of view the police provisions, like the powers vested in the local representatives, were not reconcilable with the Rhineland Agreement. And in the long run this transgression of an international treaty proved unfortunate for the occupying powers themselves.

The need to rely on the military police for the task of law enforcement produced a paradoxical result. The framers of the Rhineland Agreement had intended to establish an occupation government that would be civilian in character, but their failure to provide the High Commission with civilian executive officers necessitated a reliance on the military police, and thereby produced a regime that had all the appearance of military government. Public opinion in an occupied country is not so much concerned with the top agencies as with the executive officers who represent the occupant in everyday life. It is scarcely surprising that the Rhineland occupation appeared wholly military to the 'man on the street.'

Since offenses against occupation law belonged originally to the jurisdiction of the military tribunals it is wholly understandable that the German police officials, when they had 'taken cognizance of the commission of an offence, or arrested an accused person,' were required by Ordinance 2 (Article 4) to forward the papers immediately to the Allied military authorities. Nevertheless, this clause provides a good illustration of the way in which a lack of technical co-ordination between occupation and municipal law can impede the administration of justice, or even encourage its sabotage.

Vogels, legal adviser to the Rhineland Reichskommissar, construed this provision (*Das Rheinlandabkommen* . . . p. 61) to mean that the German authorities were entitled to keep the case in their hands until all preliminary steps had been taken, such as the questioning of the suspected person and the summoning and the examination of witnesses; only after such a complete clarification of facts, he held, could they determine whether an offense was actually committed, and thus 'take cognizance' of it. Since such proceedings were outside the control of the occupation authorities, this interpretation was obviously almost an invitation to the German police agencies to abstain from arrest until they had, in effect, decided the case.

The significance of this interpretation should not be underestimated. As Robin has pointed out (p. 336), only the agents of the occupied country are 'in a position to perform these indispensable investigations efficiently, as in the very nature of things foreigners would be unable . . . to penetrate into the recesses of the country in order to discover and seize the guilty persons.' According to Vogels' interpretation, this natural responsibility of the local police agencies was supplemented by the legal privilege of deciding whether the facts justified a conclusion that the examined person had actually committed the offense of which he was accused.

Under the procedure followed in the examination of suspects and witnesses by German prosecuting authorities—police officials, state attorneys, and judges—no shorthand record is taken of the questions and answers; it is up to the examining official to summarize the statements made. Tuohy has characterized the German judge as 'something of a Torquemada,' but, if he was opposed to the statute that he was called upon to enforce, Torquemada, far from burning his victims, was in a position to act as co-conspirator with his fellow nationals. Masters in the art of legal manipulation, the German police and court officials were able to concoct records that could not have been disproved even by the most elaborate examination of the files.

Vogels' interpretation of the 'cognizance' clause of Ordinance 2 is, of course, a matter of the past, but it is significant because it raises the question how such attempts can be prevented in the future. An efficient occupation is a matter not only of power but also of techniques. If this provision of Ordinance 2 had followed the wording of the German code of criminal procedure in dealing with the duty of the police agencies to inform the state attorneys (§163 StPO), Vogels could hardly have interpreted it as he did. Such a conformance of occupation law with the technical rules of the occupied country would be to the interest of everyone concerned. The occupying powers could then be confident of the way in which the agencies of the occupied country would execute the ordinances, and could hold them responsible if they deviated from their usual practice without good reason. And the agencies of the occupied country could regard the application of occupation law as part of their routine work if the technique were not different from their usual activities. In the enforcement of occupation law, the co-operation of subordinate police officials is particularly important, and these officials, primarily bureaucratic in character, will co-operate the more efficiently the more their techniques of work are respected.

VIII

Jurisdiction of the Occupying Powers

THE fundamental issue of the degree of power vested in the occupation authorities, since it hinged on what may be called the 'enabling statutes' of the occupation, took different directions in the armistice and the peace periods. In regard to the armistice period the question was whether the occupation was a purely 'belligerent' one, subject to the rather broad principles of international law. And in the peace period the controversy lay primarily in the interpretation of the 'maintenance, safety and requirements' clause of the Rhineland Agreement.

ARMISTICE PERIOD

During the period before the peace treaty was ratified the occupation of the Rhineland was certainly not what is called in international law a 'pacific occupation.' On the other hand, the Allied and Associated armies did not seize the Rhineland by military force, but entered it after the factual end of the war, and in accordance with an armistice agreement between the hostile powers. These circumstances made possible a legitimate difference of opinion on whether this was technically a 'belligerent occupation.'

Pacific occupation is based on a special agreement or treaty covering the rights and duties of the occupant; but under a purely belligerent occupation the powers of the occupying country are limited only by the precepts of international law, as embodied in the Hague Convention. In a belligerent occupation, according to that code (Article 43), 'The authority of the legitimate power having in fact passed into the hands of the oc-

183

cupant, the latter shall take all the measures in his power to restore, and ensure, as far as possible, public order and safety, while respecting, unless absolutely prevented, the laws in force in the country.' Marshal Foch's basic order 562 CR, of 15 November 1918 (Boyer, p. 239), explicitly referred to the Hague Convention as basis of the supervision exercised over German 'administrations' during the armistice period.

At first the Reichsgericht, reflecting the general attitude of vanquished Germany, regarded the armistice occupation as a belligerent one. Thus on 23 February 1920, in a decision concerning an armistice case (54 RGSt 139), the high court justified its reasoning by reference to the provisions of Article 43 of the Hague Convention, concerning, in the words of the court, the obligations of an occupying power 'in case of a belligerent occupation.'

Another acknowledgment of the conditions of purely belligerent occupation during the armistice period was contained in the Uhlmann decision of 25 October 1920 (Bruns, pp. 575-8). This, though one of the first occupation cases decided by the Reichsgericht, was based on events that occurred after the termination of the armistice period; the court's decision referred, however, to the armistice as well as the peace period of occupation. For several reasons the Uhlmann decision was of outstanding importance, and it will be discussed in the following chapter in another context; here it is sufficient to point out that in sustaining the acquittal of the defendant the Reichsgericht implied that the armistice period was one of belligerent occupation. The court declared that the occupation authorities had 'the right to exercise state power' and therefore also legislative power; it drew no distinction in this respect between the armistice and the peace periods, except to declare that in the armistice period the power was derived from Article 43 of the Hague Convention, and was vested in the military authorities, while in the peace period it was derived from Article 3 of the Rhineland Agreement and was vested in the High Commission. By thus referring only to the Hague Convention as the legal basis of the armistice period, the Reichsgericht clearly showed that it regarded that regime as a belligerent occupation.[1]

Meanwhile, however, Karl Strupp, eminent German writer on international law, had developed a theory (Strupp, 'Das Waffenstillstandsabkommen . . .' pp. 252 ff.) according to which the armistice regime was a mixed type of pacific and belligerent occupation, for which he coined the word *Mischbesetzung* (p. 266, note 3). For another example of an occupation occurring after the termination of hostilities, on the basis of an armistice convention, he referred to the one that followed the Prussian-Austrian armistice of 26 July 1866; six years later, German international lawyers were able to present an impressive list of historical precedents of *Mischbesetzung* (Heyland, 'Besetzungsrecht,' p. 686).

Strupp held that *Mischbesetzung* is controlled primarily by the conditions of the armistice agreement. In regard to the Hague Convention he maintained that for each question a special investigation is necessary in order to find whether the nature of the particular provision of that code is in accordance with the peculiarities of an occupation that is based on an agreement rather than on war operations. Under no conditions, he held, could the occupying powers claim more rights under *Mischbesetzung* than under the international law of land warfare. Strupp looked upon the Rhineland armistice occupation as one of 'an eminently pacific character,' and from his analysis of its special legal nature he concluded that state power in the Rhineland had not shifted to the occupation authorities but remained with the authorities of the occupied country (for a criticism of this theory, see Feilchenfeld, pp. 111-14).

In 1921, the year after Strupp's analysis was published, Marcel Nast of Strassburg University, the French High Commissioner's chief expert on occupation law, published an article advancing a similar theory ('L'occupation . . .' pp. 140-41). The armistice regime in the Rhineland, he contended, was a 'belligerent occu-

[1] For an American interpretation of the same kind, see Colby, p. 911.

pation on a contractual basis.' According to his interpretation, the powers of the occupation authorities derived primarily from the armistice agreement, and the Hague Convention, while also applicable, had only the importance of a stop-gap rule.

The publication of Strupp's article gave the Reichsgericht a new point of view, and by 29 September 1921 it was declaring that 'the occupation . . . took place in pursuance of the Armistice Agreement. It was a contractual, not a war occupation' (56 RGSt 194; *Annual Digest,* 1919-22, case 315, p. 450). The high court was even more explicit in dealing with a case decided on 7 March 1922 (56 RGSt 288), concerned with whether a Rhineland resident could be sentenced for violating a German pricing order of November 1919, and whether such orders were automatically applicable in the occupied territory. This time the Reichsgericht reversed the acquittal ordered by the lower court, and declared:

Since this did not represent a belligerent occupation in the meaning . . . of the Hague Convention and the corresponding agreement of October 18, 1907, between Germany on the one hand and France and other powers on the other hand, which is still in force, the question whether German state power was subjected to restrictions can be answered only by reference to the wording of the international treaty in question, that is, the armistice agreement.

The court continued that it 'no longer upholds the theory that the occupation of the Rhineland under the armistice agreement was a belligerent occupation, as it originally held in its decisions of February 23, 1920, and October 25, 1920.' The latter was, of course, the Uhlmann case. But that case had never been published, and no jurist, except members of the high court itself, had any opportunity to find out what the overruled decision had said about occupation law. The court presented no reasons to explain why it now overruled the basic principles it had enunciated less than a year and a half earlier.

The new theory that the Rhineland occupation during the

armıstice period was contractual in character enabled the Reichsgericht to escape the application of precedents established by
itself during the war period in regard to belligerent occupation.
At that time, when it was French territory that was occupied,
French jurists had attempted to minimize the rights of the occupation authorities, and German jurists had tried to justify
their extension. In the leading cases decided during the war,
the Reichsgericht had declared that in an effective occupation
the state power of the occupying country replaces the state
power of the occupied country, which is *de facto* prevented
from exercising its functions (DJZ 1916, vol. 21, p. 134; JW
1917, vol. 46, p. 721). Thus, so long as the Reichsgericht regarded the Rhineland occupation as a belligerent one, it had to
acknowledge—if it followed its own precedents—that German
state power in that territory was replaced. But the *Mischbesetzung* theory made it possible to apply one interpretation to the
cases arising in the Rhineland, and another, quite different interpretation to any remaining cases regarding previous occupations
by the German armies. Therefore in 1921, at the very time the
Reichsgericht was declaring that the state power of the Rhineland occupants was restricted by the armistice agreement, it decided a case arising from the German wartime occupation of
Poland (103 RGZ 231), and repeated, almost word for word, its
old contention that the occupation authorities exercise full state
power; it even implied that in a belligerent occupation the occupant is entitled to change the currency of the occupied territory.

This point of view was significantly abandoned in another currency case decided by the Reichsgericht on 14 November 1923,
a case in which the circumstances were reversed (107 RGZ 282).
On 4 July 1919, a Swiss firm had sent two bales of silk from
Alsace to Germany, and the silk had been lost by the German
railway. The issue in the case was whether the German plaintiff was entitled to damages in German marks or in French
francs—a question of considerable interest to the plaintiff, since
the mark was practically worthless at that time. The plaintiff

contended that the shipping contract had been concluded after the introduction of French currency in Alsace, but the Reichsgericht declared that France was not entitled to change the currency in that territory before the peace treaty was ratified; until then the armistice conditions prevailed, and the occupation 'did not eliminate German state power in the occupied zones' (a similar decision was rendered on 29 September 1924, in a comparable case; JW 1925, vol. 54, p. 138). The court's decision was hardly reconcilable with the Versailles treaty, which declared (Article 51) that Alsace-Lorraine was considered to have been incorporated into France on 11 November 1918 (the court held that this clause could not change the relations already established under civil law between the two partners to the contract); and the decision was the more remarkable since the treaty had been signed by both Germany and France at the time the shipping contract was concluded.

Thus in regard to the armistice period the German attitude was, on the whole, that the occupants were not entitled to the rather broad exercise of state power that would have been their right if they had been in belligerent occupation of German territory. On the contrary, according to the general German interpretation, they could exercise only those powers that were expressly granted to them in the armistice agreement. At the time these principles were laid down by German jurists the armistice period had already ended, and in any case they would scarcely have affected the actual course of the occupation. But such pronouncements, once incorporated into legal writings and court decisions, may be cited in the future by German courts and jurists as 'the law of the land,' unless special precautions are taken to make them inapplicable.

There is one aspect of belligerent occupation that is worth mentioning for its possible relevance to the problems of the present war. The phrase in the Hague Convention concerning the occupant's duty to respect the existing laws of the occupied country, 'unless absolutely prevented,' represents an obligation of international law. Nevertheless, international law, which originates in and is deeply imbued with the principles of natural law, does not oblige any military government to respect existing laws that violate basic ideas of justice. An occupying power that conforms with the principles of international law is for that very reason obliged to disallow any municipal law that is contrary to the *ordre public* of the international community.

When Marshal Foch declared that the laws and regulations in force in Germany at the time of the armistice would be respected unless they were contrary to the rights and security of the occupying powers, he implied that existing German law was in accordance with the *ordre public* of the international community. Whether or not he was right in 1918, it is scarcely possible to make the same assumption regarding German law twenty-five years later.

The Hague Convention envisaged, primarily, reasons of military expediency when it recognized that the occupant might be 'absolutely prevented' from respecting the laws of the occupied country. Today, however, war is not only military but economic and social, and there may be reasons just as urgent as military expediency for disallowing the existing laws of the vanquished nation. It is true, as Lauterpacht has recently warned (p. 95), that there is a possibility that 'we may get into the habit of treating the "totality" of modern war as a general license to lawlessness'; but it is essential that in applying the traditional concepts of international law we do so with regard for present and not past conditions. It would be a tragic mistake if conformance with the letter of international law should entail a violation of its spirit and intentions.

Peace Period

In regard to the source of the occupants' powers after the ratification of the peace treaty, the most concise expression of the German point of view is contained in a speech delivered by Peter Spahn in the National Assembly on 17 January 1920 (Na-

tionalversammlung, vol. 332, p. 4464). Spahn, a leader of the
Catholic party and chief justice of the Frankfurt appellate court,
declared:

> The occupation of the Rhenish provinces is not an *occupatio
> bellica*. I have to use the expression because some of the provisions
> of the ordinances are obviously derived from the ideas of the
> Convention regarding Land Warfare [the Hague Convention],
> and are therefore regarded as justified . . . Neither that Conven-
> tion nor other general regulations of international law, but only
> and exclusively the provisions of the treaties—the peace treaty
> and the Rhineland Agreement—control the law, the scope and the
> jurisdiction of this occupation. The treaties are based on the as-
> sumption that all specific questions concerning the Rhineland oc-
> cupation have found their regulation in these documents. The
> idea must be rejected that the Allied powers possess any power
> whatever to issue commands of any kind beyond the scope of
> these treaties.

This attitude regarding the source of their powers was followed, in the main, by the occupation authorities themselves. The
important jurisdictional issue in the peace period of the occupation was not so much the source of power as the intricate question of 'constitutional' interpretation.

The Rhineland Agreement defined the jurisdiction of the High
Commission only in the most general terms, and failed to provide
specific executive powers for the fulfilment of its tasks. The crucial clause in that document was the provision in Article 3 that
'The High Commission shall have the power to issue ordinances
so far as may be necessary for securing the maintenance, safety
and requirements of the Allied and Associated forces.' The decision in regard to what constituted 'maintenance, safety and requirements' and to what was 'necessary' for securing them was
left to the discretion of the Commission. It is obvious that this
authorization was so broad that it could be applied to practically
any situation. The controversy over its interpretation could be
regarded, from one point of view, as the whole history of the

Rhineland occupation during the peace period, and there is no need to recapitulate what has already been said regarding specific aspects of this problem. But certain of its implications are worth emphasizing for their relevance to the question of occupation law in general.

It was evident from the very beginning that the High Commission considered the task of protecting the security of the occupation forces equivalent to the task of preserving public order. In a proclamation issued on 10 January 1920, the first day of its government, it declared (*Gazette*, 1920, No. 1, p. 17):

The Inter-Allied High Commission desires to rely on the collaboration of the German officials and magistrates to ensure, in full harmony with it, the institution of a state of order, work and peace for the population of the Occupied Territories. Responsible for public order, of which the burden lies finally on the troops of Occupation, it means to guarantee to the people of the Rhineland justice, the enjoyment of their public and private liberties, and the development of their legitimate aspirations and of their prosperity.

An even more concise expression of its attitude was contained in the preambles of the first ordinances, where the Commission spoke of its duty 'to secure the maintenance, safety and requirements of the Armies of Occupation, and the consequent preservation of public order.'

The German Government emphatically disagreed with this assumption of responsibility for public order. On 6 November 1920, Erich Koch declared in the Reichstag (Reichstag, vol. 345, p. 1044):

There exists a basic difference between our point of view and the theory of the High Commission concerning its jurisdiction. This difference has so far proved unbridgeable. The High Commission tries to justify its ordinances by reference to the necessity of protecting public order and security. We deny emphatically that the High Commission is entitled to exercise such powers, and emphasize that the Rhineland Agreement gives the High Commission only the power to enact ordinances which are necessary for the maintenance, safety and requirements of the occupying forces.

Much the same objections had been raised during the first week of the peacetime occupation, in the German diplomatic note of 12 January and in the National Assembly on 17 January.

The most extreme expression of the German point of view was contained in an article by Nelz, who declared (p. 245) that occupying forces are entitled to exercise a general responsibility for public order only if they are in belligerent occupation, with their rights derived from the Hague Convention. Therefore, he maintained, the High Commission had no power whatever to exercise that responsibility; on the contrary, the occupying armies had the right of protection, by the police forces of the occupied country, from disturbances of the public order.

What the Germans actually opposed was not so much the claim to responsibility for public order as the discretion inherent in that responsibility, and its possible abuse. The maintenance of public order was certainly entrusted to the High Commission so far as it affected the safety of the occupying troops. But in any particular case it was a matter of discretion whether the safety of the armed forces was at issue. If the Germans had formulated their point more exactly, they would have demanded that the High Commission concern itself with public order only for the purposes explicitly stated in the Rhineland Agreement, and that those purposes be narrowly interpreted, in accordance with the maxim that presumption rests with the freedom of the individual.

On this question of broad or narrow interpretation of what was necessary for the security of the troops, it may be worth while to mention a famous Belgian case decided on 26 January 1920 by the Cour d'Appel of Brussels (*Journal du droit international*, 1920, vol. 47, pp. 732 ff.). The case grew out of events that occurred during the armistice period, before the Rhineland Agreement was in force, but it clearly reveals the type of rea-

soning against which the German protests were directed. The
issue was whether it was within the jurisdiction of the occupation courts to proceed against a German national who had forged
German banknotes in the occupied territory. The Belgian court
decided in the affirmative, maintaining that Belgian soldiers in
the occupying forces received and spent German money and
were consequently exposed to the danger of taking forged banknotes for good ones. The court considered it insignificant
whether evidence existed that the forged notes had actually been
received by Belgian soldiers: the mere possibility was regarded
as sufficient. Offenses committed in the occupied territory, said
the court, 'must be punished as if they had been committed in
Belgium if they caused, or risked causing, to Belgian soldiers in
their private capacity any injury that the criminal statutes of
Belgium intended to prevent, even as a mere possibility.'

This decision of a high Belgian court was criticized even by
a Belgian writer, B. De Jaer, who published in 1928 the most
penetrating study that has been produced on the legal problems
of the Rhineland occupation. The court's principle of possible
injury, said De Jaer, was based on a misunderstanding of the
true nature of occupation law; 'Belgian law is applicable only in
exceptional cases' (p. 17), and exceptional provisions should not
be interpreted broadly.

Almost inseparable from this question of broad or narrow interpretation of 'maintenance, safety and requirements' is the
question whether the rights of the High Commission were defini-
tively set forth in the Rhineland Agreement, or whether the occupation authorities had also certain 'incidental or implied
powers.'

An early indication of the Commission's attitude toward this
question was contained in a decision it rendered on 28 May 1920,
a few months after it took office (*Gazette*, 1920, No. VI-VII, p.
45). The problem was whether the families of married non-commissioned officers and privates could be billeted in German homes.
The Rhineland Agreement (Article 8) dealt with the billeting

of officers and their families, and provided that privates and non-commissioned officers should be accommodated in barracks; but it made no provision for the accommodation of married privates and non-commissioned officers. The High Commission therefore referred to the general clause of Article 3, and based its decision on consideration of 'whether the necessities of the maintenance, security or requirements of the military forces . . . were consistent with authorization for married non-commissioned officers and privates to bring their families into the Occupied Territories.' The Commission added that 'The basis of discussion would be different only if authorization of this nature were either formally prohibited in the Agreement or were in contradiction with the military regulations of the various armies.'

Thus the High Commission made it clear that it regarded its responsibility for public order as a general power, entitling it to take any measures not expressly forbidden in the Rhineland Agreement. Thereby it followed the continental conception of the executive branch of government. In continental political theory, the executive enjoys a presumption of legality, and its general police power is limited only by specific prohibitions. Whereas in American law the police power is viewed as 'the judicial defense against the charge of an invasion of "the constitutional rights to liberty and to property"' (Hamilton, pp. 191-2), in continental law the rights to liberty and property are viewed as judicial defense against the exercise of the police power.

In Germany the police power of the executive was defined, in the eighteenth century, as the task of maintaining public order and protecting the public from imminent dangers. This famous definition, contained in the Prussian Code of Frederick the Great, became generally accepted throughout Germany as one of the basic provisions of public law. But while it represented a limitation upon the power of the sovereign to do as he pleased with the life, liberty, and property of his subjects, it nevertheless left ample scope for abuses.

One of the chief purposes of the enactment of a bill of rights was to restrict this general police power of the executive. In the words of Gerhard Anschütz, one of the most eminent authorities on German constitutional law (Meyer-Anschütz, vol. 3, p. 956):

The civil liberties of the individual represent limitations on the executive branch of the government, particularly on the so-called 'inner administration.' The significance of civil liberties must be found in the fact that wherever such liberties have been guaranteed by statute, the executive agencies of the state, particularly the police agencies, cannot exercise the power to issue prohibitive writs.

In a footnote Anschütz emphasizes that in German law the bill of rights restricts not so much the power of the legislative as the power of the executive branch of the government. The High Commission, however, when it assumed a general police power, in the continental sense of the term, was circumscribed by no such statutory guarantees of individual rights. And no international bill of rights existed which might have curbed the discretion permitted by the Rhineland Agreement.

The Commission's own interpretation of its powers was followed also by various French jurists who dealt with this matter. Thus Nast asserted ('De la compétence . . .' pp. 283-4) that the High Commission had the power to 'intervene in all cases in which public order and social peace are about to be disturbed, and it is entitled to make an end, with all means at its disposal, to anything that could directly or indirectly jeopardize the security of the troops.' Jean Rousseau formulated not only his own point of view but also the official attitude of the French High Commissioner, for whom he acted as legal adviser, in the words (La Haute Commission . . . pp. 72-3): 'It is not possible to arrive at a limitative enumeration of the matters connected with the maintenance and safety of the armed forces. This question is a function of the circumstances, of the moment.' And after the end of the occupation, Tirard himself declared (pp.

157-8): 'The occupation authorities could not be indifferent to any question that touched upon the interests entrusted to their defense. All events that might disturb public order, even if they were not directed against the occupying troops, might jeopardize their safety or maintenance.'

An analysis of the foregoing statements reveals that the three French writers propounded theories which, although *prima facie* only variations of the same proposition, actually represent different approaches to the basic problem of occupation law. Nast's formulation, in which he restricted the jurisdiction of the occupant as bearer of the police power to the preservation of public order and security, was in accordance with the traditions of continental police law. According to Nast, the occupant had only the right to take negative measures, to act in self-defense. It may be admitted that the broad interpretation he gave to the phrase 'security of the troops' could in many cases justify an exercise of police power beyond what would be allowed in continental legal tradition. Nevertheless, his formulation in this passage represented an attempt to apply to occupation law the ideas that had been set forth in the eighteenth and nineteenth centuries with a view to restricting the bearers of police power from interfering with life, liberty, and property, except where such activities were necessary for the preservation of public order and security.

Rousseau's formulation was less precise. Although he theoretically recognized the proposition that the occupant had the right to act only if the 'maintenance and safety' of the occupying armies were at stake, he almost abandoned that position by denying that this clause had any concrete significance. The proclamation of the principle that the guardian of public order and security is permitted to act only if public safety is endangered means, from a legal point of view, that the exercise of that power is restricted to such interference as has been made necessary by a disturbance of public order. Rousseau did not mention the 'necessity' test, and thus he denied the applicability to occupation law of legal principles that the administrative courts, both of Germany and of France, had developed during the decades preceding the First World War. About ten years after the publication of Rousseau's study, Carl Schmitt, in justifying the measures of the Papen regime against the democratic Prussian Government, was to use the same argument, that the bearer of the police power is entitled to do whatever is necessitated 'by the circumstances, by the moment.'

It is only one step from this 'law of the situation' to Tirard's theory that the occupant can do whatever is necessitated by his interests. The High Commissioner dropped the basic safeguard of the population's rights when he went beyond the position that interference was permissible only if the safety of the occupying troops was endangered. If an occupant is entitled to act whenever his interests require his interference, his power becomes absolute. This is not the place to discuss whether such an authorization is justified under the peculiar conditions of a belligerent occupation. Tirard's statements were concerned not with a belligerent but with a pacific occupation; he was the highest representative of a regime that was planned not as an occupation of expediency but as an occupation of law. A regime in which the occupant is entitled to act whenever he considers his action necessary for his own interests is the opposite of the regime that was envisaged by Noyes and finally adopted by the peace conference.

There are indications that Tirard's use of the word 'interest' was more than rhetorical. The significance of his formulation is exemplified in a highly interesting decision of the French Cour de Cassation (Dalloz, 1923, Part 1, p. 124), rendered on 10 August 1922, *in re* Florange and Chamayou.

Florange and Chamayou were French businessmen who resided in the French zone of occupation. After the sanctions period of 1921, they were tried by a French military tribunal for violating the customs ordinances that had been enacted at that time by the High Commission, in its capacity as agent of the London

Conference; in Ordinance 84 of 27 April 1921, the High Commission had vested the military courts with jurisdiction in such cases. After their conviction Florange and Chamayou appealed to the Cour de Cassation, pleading that according to the French code of military justice it was not within the jurisdiction of the military tribunal to sentence French civilians for violating customs regulations.

The court held that the High Commission had acted within its rights in declaring the military tribunal competent in such cases, and it based its decision on Article 3 of the Rhineland Agreement. In a most significant passage the court declared: 'The customs regulations were enacted in the Rhenish provinces in the interest of the Allied powers which occupy these territories, and therefore in the interest of the French state,' and 'consequently the military tribunal was competent to judge Florange and Chamayou in matters affecting French interests.' Thus the Cour de Cassation, although it referred to Article 3 of the Rhineland Agreement, justified the High Commission's action not by reference to the 'maintenance, safety and requirements of the occupying forces' but by reference to the 'interests' of France.

Marcel Nast commented on this decision in a remarkable note (Dalloz, 1923, Part 1, pp. 121-4), in which he declared:

The occupation of a foreign territory does not represent an end in itself; its end is the realization or the protection of certain public interests; it is an act of sovereignty. The occupying power makes use of its army, which is nothing else but its executive agent, in order to exercise its sovereignty and to realize and protect its interests. The grant of jurisdiction to the military tribunals, in all questions that have some bearing on the security of the occupying army, is intended to protect not only the army itself but also the state of which it is the executive agent, and that state's sovereignty and independence.

Hitherto, he continued, the function of the military tribunals had been 'primarily the protection of the mission entrusted to the occupying army, that is, the execution of the occupation and the protection of the army . . . From now on the jurisdiction of the military tribunals in military occupation of foreign territory is extended to assuring the realization of the aims of that occupation, and the protection of the interests that justify the occupation.'

The opinion of the Cour de Cassation, as interpreted by Marcel Nast, leads to the most inauspicious results. If the occupants are entitled to do whatever they consider proper in their own interests, their rule becomes that of the police state before despotism was 'enlightened' by natural law. In fact, a pacific occupation of such a character would offer the occupied territory less protection than would be afforded by a belligerent occupation that was circumscribed only by the rules contained in the Hague Convention. An occupation under martial law would be preferable to one defined by the interests of the occupying power, for even martial law, limited to the suppression of disorder and lawlessness, does not grant its bearer a blank check to do whatever he thinks useful for his own interests. The decision of the French Cour de Cassation in the Florange case revealed tendencies that were to play a powerful role throughout continental Europe during the following twenty years.

The reasoning of the Cour de Cassation was not unchallenged, even by French jurists. J. A. Roux, maintaining that the customs regulations had no connection with the maintenance, safety, and requirements of the occupying forces, declared (p. 90): 'One may even derive from this provision of the Rhineland Agreement some legal arguments against the opinion of the court. One may argue that the High Commission, when it exercised its legislative power in a field that is not provided for in the Rhineland Agreement, transgressed its jurisdiction and consequently committed an illegal act.' He maintained that jurisdiction was vested in the military tribunal not by virtue of the Rhineland Agreement but by the fact of the occupation itself: the occupying power, he said, is entitled to take at will all steps that are necessary in order to execute and to require respect for the rights and duties which it can claim from the peace treaty as well as from the occupation as a fact. Thus, while he denied the relevance of the Rhineland Agreement, he approved the result reached by the Cour de Cassation.

Roux was right in eliminating Article 3 of the Rhineland Agreement from the issue whether the military tribunal was competent in the Florange case, but his other argument is not convincing. It was based on the assumption that the Rhineland regime was still—long after the ratification of the peace treaty— a belligerent occupation, and this position is obviously untenable.

Ordinance 84, on which the jurisdiction of the military tribunal was based, had no connection with the Rhineland Agreement. In the preamble to that ordinance, the High Commission declared that it acted 'in pursuance of the decisions of 7 March 1921, of the Conference of Allied Governments held in London, and of 2 April 1921, of the Conference of Ambassadors, empowered for this purpose by the Allied Governments.' The Rhineland Agreement had nothing whatever to do with the case. The only legal problem that was relevant was whether the High Commission's jurisdiction regarding the sanctions imposed upon Germany by the London Conference was in accordance with international law. If this question is answered in the affirmative, Ordinance 84 was valid; otherwise it was void. But in either case the question whether the High Commission was entitled to vest military tribunals with jurisdiction in the sanctions cases had no connection with occupation law.

Unlike the French Cour de Cassation, the French army command in the Rhineland analyzed the legal situation very clearly, in an instruction of 13 July 1921 (quoted in Huguet, p. 177, note 108):

This ordinance [said the instruction, referring to Ordinance 84], like all other customs ordinances, was enacted by the High Commission not by virtue of a convention concluded between the Allied powers and Germany, but in execution of a unilateral decision of the said powers [the London Conference], and thus, as far as customs and export and import questions are concerned, it substituted an occupation regime of power for the regime by agreement which continues to control the relations between occupied Germany and the occupying powers in all other fields. It is therefore out of the question to base the jurisdiction of military tribunals in customs matters on the Rhineland Agreement attached to the treaty.

No word need be added to this excellent legal statement, which clearly indicates that the decision of the Cour de Cassation in the Florange case was beside the point.

It should be noted, however, that the Florange case became a precedent in French law. The Cour de Cassation applied the same reasoning to the leading cases that arose out of the Ruhr conflict—the Thyssen case, decided on 22 March 1923, and the Krupp case, decided on 9 August 1923 (Sirey, 1924, Part i, pp. 92-3). The 'interests' theory was, of course, a convenient instrument to justify the measures taken in the Ruhr valley during that conflict. The question whether the Florange precedent has 'made' law, as far as France is concerned, need not be decided here; it should be emphasized, however, that the conclusions reached in that case cannot be regarded as generally valid principles of occupation law, because they are based on a legal error.

The Florange case was but a reflection of the attitude of the French authorities toward the Rhineland problem during the first peace period. After the Anglo-American democracies had failed to fulfil their promise of military protection, France attempted an alternative provision for her security, through economic and cultural penetration of the Rhineland. If the 'interests' theory of the Cour de Cassation had been adopted by the High Commission, France would have been able to achieve by means of facts what she had not reached by means of treaties. If such an interpretation had prevailed, the occupation regime would have been converted into a despotism ruling only by force —the very contrary to the peaceful reconstruction intended in the Rhineland Agreement.

Certainly the High Commission, as an official body, never explicitly maintained that the 'safety of the occupying forces' implied a recognition and protection of whatever the occupying powers regarded as their interests. But did the Commission implicitly assume this principle in its actual use of its authority?

In considering this question it is important to bear in mind that the High Commission was not a homogeneous body. Its actions inevitably reflected the divergent loyalties and convictions of its members.

Thus on 14 October 1921, General Allen remarked in his diary (*Journal*, pp. 268-9):

This afternoon I have had very serious talks with Rolin [the Belgian High Commissioner] and Tirard concerning certain events which have taken place in the Rhineland due to the actions of French officials . . . In plain language, we were violating our own ordinances and failing to admit it, much less punish our officials when they were wrong. The Commission has no right under the Agreement to govern in the Rhineland, and we cannot usurp the administration or control of affairs unless the maintenance, security and requirements of the armies are involved.

Allen emphasized that he fully understood Tirard's difficult position; 'political conditions in France make heavy demands on Tirard which he must satisfy.' On the other hand, American public opinion reacted the other way around regarding violations of the Rhineland Agreement, which was after all an international treaty: 'If some of the communications that have been exchanged were given publication in the United States, they would be badly received.'

It was not always an easy task to come to a compromise within the High Commission on borderline cases. In the Smeets affair the French High Commissioner induced the majority to decide a legal question as if it were a political one; in the Momm affair the dismissal of a high official was justified by considerations of expediency. In both cases the 'interests' of one of the occupying powers led to a solution that was not reconcilable with the wording of the Rhineland Agreement. On the whole, however, the instances in which the High Commission exercised functions based exclusively on political considerations were the exception rather than the rule. Since several of the 'exceptional' cases have been described, it may be desirable to mention one or two of the instances in which the occupation authorities showed a careful regard for the legal limits of their jurisdiction.

On 6 October 1922, the High Commission had to decide whether the German railway administration should be permitted to carry out certain plans intended to improve the railway system. It was rather doubtful whether the planned work was particularly urgent, and the contention was advanced that execution of the plan might interfere with the payment of the German reparations debts. The High Commission decided, however (Rousseau, *La Haute Commission* . . . p. 70, note 1), that 'even if the expenses necessary for the execution of that plan are excessive, no provision of the Rhineland Agreement or of any ordinance entitles the High Commission to induce the German authorities to stop or modify their plans.' In this declaration the Commission not only denied its power to interfere with German finances; it also rejected the idea that it was entitled to enforce provisions of the peace treaty that were not explicitly placed within its jurisdiction. On this matter the legal situation would of course have been quite different if Noyes' skeleton plan had not been modified in the final document drafted by the Loucheur committee.

The High Commission's regard for the fact that its powers were restricted to occupation problems is evident also in its refusal to follow certain suggestions of the Reparation Commission dealing with the enforcement of economic provisions of the peace treaty: on 8 May 1920, it refused to participate in the transactions concerning war booty and industrial material that Germany was obliged to restore to Belgium and France, and on 10 September of that year it rejected the Reparation Commission's request that it control the shipments of coal in the occupied

territory (Rousseau, *La Haute Commission* . . . p. 69). In fact,
until it was entrusted by the London Conference with extraordinary powers regarding customs problems and questions of
foreign trade, the High Commission refrained from any interference with financial, economic, and social conditions in the
Rhineland. One of its most important decisions on such matters
has already been mentioned: its rejection of the French view that
the German foreign-trade regulations of 22 March 1920 should
be prohibited in the Rhineland because they might 'indirectly'
jeopardize the safety of the occupying forces.

The lack of any specific restrictions on the powers of the High
Commission raises certain fundamental questions regarding occupation law. In a modern constitutional state, the powers of the
government are subject to certain definite limitations—whether
by a system of checks and balances, by the requirements of natural law as incorporated in specific bills of rights, or by constitutional prohibitions. Can comparable restrictions be imposed on
a military occupation?

The question is irrelevant, of course, if the occupation is conducted under martial-law conditions. The problem arises only
if the occupation is intended to be a rule of law, but then it becomes a test of the very concept of peaceful occupation. It is
self-contradictory to repudiate martial law as the basis of occupation government and at the same time vest that government
with unlimited power.

Nevertheless, an occupation government, even if it is conducted under the rule of law, is basically different from the government of a constitutional state. In the latter, the bearers of
power are the representatives of those who are subject to that
power, and the stability of the whole system demands that there
be some degree of mutual trust, each in the other. Such a government, functioning under firm restrictions on the scope of its
authority, can accomplish its tasks only if the governed are prepared to collaborate in the maintenance of the regime, and to
grant the validity of its basic principles—only if they recognize

the will of their government as an expression of the national *volonté générale.*

An occupation regime, however, is the rule of a foreign government which does not even pretend to represent the will of the governed population. No ethnic ties, no shared traditions, no voluntary act of political confidence unite the rulers and their subjects. Indeed, each mistrusts the other. Under these conditions, limitations of power which derive from the people's participation in the government—such as those provided in a 'checks and balances' structure, in which the people are entrusted with legislative power—are out of the question.

It may be assumed that the framers of the Rhineland Agreement took it for granted that the occupation regime would be conducted in accordance with the fundamental principles of human rights. But when the governing authorities are the supervisors rather than the representatives of the people it is inevitable that the conflict between the power of rulers and the rights of the ruled will sooner or later, and in greater or lesser degree, result in infringements of the rights of the ruled—if those rights are not specifically guaranteed. When the Rhineland Agreement made it possible for the High Commission to act as the bearer of 'police power,' in the continental sense of the term, without providing the restrictions on that power which had found expression in the traditional concept of Rechtsstaat, particularly in bills of rights, it gave the Commission a position comparable to that of an absolute prince in the final phase of despotism. An occupation agreement cannot afford to leave the protection of civil liberties to the vagaries of good intentions.

Today there is a good deal of discussion on the question whether the basic rights of the individual and the idea of supremacy of law can be protected by an international bill of rights. The proponents of this idea should consider whether they are prepared to apply the principle to an occupation regime, at least after the purely military phase of the occupation has ended. Universal recognition of an international bill of rights implies that the values expressed in such a document are recognized by those who rule in the name of international law. Indeed, the application of these principles to the subjects of an occupation regime can be regarded as a test case for the general validity of such proposals. The answer to this problem will considerably affect the character of a future occupation, and may even prove of vital significance for the restoration of the rule of law in the postwar world.

IX

Judicial Review by Courts of the Occupied Country

ONE of the crucial problems of occupation law is whether and to what extent and by what authorities the actions of the occupying powers are subject to review. In an occupation, the 'constitution' or body of legal principles which in ordinary circumstances serves as the norm in the exercise of judicial review can be only the general principles of international or customary law, or specific rules of the Hague Convention, or treaty provisions regarding the occupation. But the question immediately arises what agency is entitled to determine legality under this type of law. If the occupation authorities in the Rhineland had flagrantly violated their rights as occupants, it is conceivable that Germany might have appealed to international arbitration, at least after the ratification of the peace treaty. But in the absence of incontestable and consistent violations, during the period dealt with in this study, such a procedure was neither feasible nor likely of acceptance.

During the Rhineland occupation there was never the slightest doubt that the occupying powers themselves, and their administrative agencies, were outside the jurisdiction of the German courts (see Feilchenfeld, p. 90). Neither the regular courts nor the administrative courts, which handled cases concerning infringements of law by administrative agencies, ever claimed the power to hear cases in which actions of the occupation authorities were the primary reason for adjudication. But whether the German courts had a right of review was not nearly so self-evident when the legitimacy of occupation measures was, or could be regarded as, a collateral issue in cases within their proper jurisdiction—cases involving German nationals. Judicial review of administrative actions has a centuries-old tradition in German law. And under the Weimar Constitution, as it was interpreted by the German courts (107 RGZ 377), both the regular courts, hearing criminal or civil cases between German nationals, and the administrative courts, hearing cases between German nationals and German administrative authorities, could review the constitutionality of German legislative acts if the legitimacy of such acts was a collateral issue in the case. Could the German courts, under the same conditions, review the 'constitutionality' of legislative acts of the occupation authorities? And were they entitled to review the legality of High Commission administrative actions? [1]

At the time of the Rhineland occupation, the German courts, in general, refrained from open discussion of this complicated problem; in one of the rare decisions in which it was openly dealt with—one of the first occupation decisions of the Reichsgericht—the conclusion was actually in the negative. In a considerable number of later cases, however, the Reichsgericht implicitly claimed the right of judicial review by rendering judgments supported by opinions on the legality of occupation measures. And at the end of 1926 the Reichsfinanzhof, a supreme administrative court, expressly asserted the right of review.

In these cases a decision denying legality had immediate significance, of course, only for the litigants themselves. Since the German courts had no power to overthrow an occupation meas-

---

[1] The question of judicial review had arisen a number of times during the German occupation of Belgium. See *International Law News*, 1915, pp. 55-6, for decisions of the appellate court of Liége (31 May 1915) and the appellate court of Brussels (19 July 1915); ibid. 1916, p. 136, for a decision of the Belgian Cour de Cassation (18 May 1916); *Journal du droit international*, 1917, vol. 44, p. 1813, for a decision of the appellate court of Liége (13 February 1917); *Pasicrisie belge*, 1917, I, pp. 241, 256, for a decision of the Belgian Cour de Cassation (14 June 1917). A very illuminating analysis of the latter decision may be found in De Visscher, p. 81.

ure, and the occupation authorities ignored the pronouncements of the German courts, the latter exercised only a kind of truncated judicial review. But such decisions had, in addition, a more far-reaching significance that warrants their consideration in some detail. For one thing, they had a considerable psychological effect on Germany's attitude toward the occupation, and at the same time reflected the mutations in that attitude. Much more important, however, than this historical interest is the fact that these decisions may in the future be invoked as precedents. Some of them have already been mentioned, in other contexts, but there are in addition several outstanding cases that deserve special attention for the principles that they exemplify. Whether precautions should be taken in order to render such precedents inoperative in a future occupation, and to prevent further decisions of the same character, can be most convincingly discussed by presenting the cases themselves.

Before the peace treaty was ratified no case was decided by the Reichsgericht in which problems of occupation law were either the chief or a collateral issue. This is easily understandable in view of the fact that for technical reasons alone a period of more than a year was usually necessary from the day on which events gave rise to a procedure until the highest court rendered its judgment. Thus the occupation cases that arose out of armistice conditions, which lasted about thirteen months, were decided by the Reichsgericht after the armistice had been terminated. Though the principles developed by the high court in deciding these cases were consequently even less significant to the occupation authorities than were the peacetime decisions, their possible use as precedents is not thereby affected.

The mysterious, unpublished Uhlmann decision of 25 October 1920, which was mentioned in the preceding chapter, provided the outstanding instance in which the Reichsgericht explicitly considered its right of judicial review. Uhlmann, a German resident of the occupied territory, was indicted by a German court for having exported silver from Germany between 14 and 20

January 1920, in violation of a wartime trade decree of 1917. During the armistice period, it will be remembered, such decrees were rendered ineffective by the occupation authorities, and, *de facto*, that situation still existed in January 1920.

As already mentioned, the Reichsgericht in this decision declared that the power of the occupants derived, in the armistice period, from Article 43 of the Hague Convention, and, in the peace period, from Article 3 of the Rhineland Agreement. In regard to the question of judicial review the outstanding passage of the decision was the statement (Bruns, p. 575) that if the occupying powers

transgress their jurisdiction such an action represents a violation of an international treaty; the legal consequences of such a violation must be judged in accordance with international law. The courts of the occupied territory are not in a position to examine and to decide whether the Allied powers, when exercising state power in the occupied territory, have transgressed the borderline of their authority, as for instance whether there existed in reality an absolute prevention (*empêchement absolu*) in the meaning of Article 43 which forbade the application of municipal law.

This decision was not published, however, in the official German reports, nor was it mentioned in any German law review. In Germany it is up to the Reichsgericht to decide whether a decision shall be published in the official reports, and only those are published which the members of the court consider important; many of the others are given publication in one or another law review. But the Uhlmann decision, though it was of the greatest practical and theoretical significance, was withheld not only from the German public but also from the legal profession. The French jurist Alléhaut, in 1925, was the first to give it publicity (pp. 52-3), and it was not until 1931, when the last French soldier had left Germany, that the opinion was released to the German public (the text is now available in Bruns' *Fontes juris gentium*, pp. 575-8).

Alléhaut rightly summarized this opinion in the words (p. 53):

'Thus the Leipzig court completely abandoned the idea of internal judicial review and shifted the problem to the domain of international law.' And Alléhaut, who wholeheartedly approved the Uhlmann decision, doubted whether an international body was in existence that was vested with the right to annul an act of the occupation authorities. Certainly such a review would have been practically out of the question during the period in which the Rhineland occupation represented the final phase of the war, that is, before the peace treaty was ratified.

It may be mentioned that the Uhlmann decision cropped up during the Ruhr conflict, in a most inconvenient way. When the French army entered the Ruhr, early in 1923, the German Government characterized the action as illegal and declared that its officials and citizens were not obliged to obey the French military authorities in that region. But the military commanders demanded strict obedience to their orders. In a sitting of the Reichstag on 13 February 1923, Wilhelm Kahl, member of that body and professor of law at Berlin University, pointed out that the military commanders, in justifying their demand for obedience, had referred to a German supreme court decision of 1920. Professor Kahl doubted that the Reichsgericht had ever developed a theory according to which all commands of the occupation authorities must be considered automatically binding, and asked for information (Reichstag, vol. 358, p. 9653). In his answer (ibid. p. 9659) Dr. Heinze, Minister of Justice, said that the military commanders had compelled the local papers in many parts of the occupied territory to publish a statement according to which the Reichsgericht had laid down such a principle, but he added: 'The decision of the Reichsgericht of 25 October 1920 has been overruled by several decisions of the highest court which are published in the official record, particularly in 56 RGSt 228 [sic; read 288], decided on 7 March 1922 . . . This fact remains unmentioned in the proclamation of the occupation authorities.'

The only way in which the Uhlmann decision can be recon-

ciled with the Reichsgericht's subsequent practice of reviewing
actions of the occupation authorities is by reference to the
phrase declaring that 'the courts of the occupied territory' were
prevented from exercising judicial review. This wording left the
door open for the supreme court, which had its seat in Leipzig,
in the unoccupied part of Germany, to exercise a reviewing
power which was denied to the trial courts in the occupied zones.
Such an interpretation is strained, however, and would attribute
to the Reichsgericht an attitude on judicial review that would
be even less defensible than an outright assertion of that power.
Nevertheless, it is significant that the lower courts within the
occupied territory were far less inclined than the Reichsgericht
to examine the legal basis of actions taken by the occupation
authorities.

Another aspect of the Uhlmann decision is noteworthy because of a later, contradictory opinion by the Reichsgericht. The
lower court had maintained that in the period 14-20 January
1920, when Uhlmann's exports had taken place, the peace treaty
was not yet in force in Germany, because statutes became valid
in Germany only fourteen days after they had been published
in the *Reichsgesetzblatt;* therefore, the Wiesbaden court held,
the case was to be decided on the basis of armistice conditions.
The Reichsgericht, however, based its decision on the principle
that German nationals could not be punished for violating German statutes that were *de facto* ineffective in the occupied territory, and rejected the theory that principles of German constitutional law are applicable to an international treaty.

The various principles enunciated in the Uhlmann decision
were at least consistent with one another. But as further cases
began to reach the Reichsgericht some of these principles were
applied and some were contradicted. The court, as has already
been shown, had meanwhile been impressed by Strupp's theory
of *Mischbesetzung;* and in addition, as the occupation progressed
and the events of 1918 receded farther into the background, a
more resistant attitude began to make itself felt in Germany.

Thus in an armistice case decided on 19 April 1921 (102 RGZ 106; *Annual Digest*, 1919-22, case 305, p. 440) the court pursued a line of reasoning quite different from that in the Uhlmann decision, six months earlier. During the first weeks of the armistice, the defendant had bought from the German military authorities a large quantity of nails, horseshoes, and the like, paying about 12,000 marks. Shortly afterward he sold the goods to the plaintiff, for 68,000 marks. The American military government confiscated the property, and released it only after the plaintiff had paid 56,000 marks to the occupation authorities—the difference between the price paid and the price received by the defendant. Its action was based on an armistice provision (Article 6), which declared that all military establishments should be 'delivered intact,' and on a proclamation of the American military authorities on 14 January 1919, which nullified all post-armistice sales of military goods in the occupied zone.

But the sale was held valid and the action dismissed. In regard to the violation of the armistice agreement, the Reichsgericht made the remarkable declaration that that document had not been assented to by the German legislative authorities and had not been published in the Reich's official journal of laws, and that therefore it did not have the 'force of municipal law'—a direct contradiction of its position in the Uhlmann decision. In thus denying the current legal validity of the armistice in Germany, the court conformed with Heinrich Triepel's theory that in any state the provisions of international agreements are binding only after they have been 'transformed' into municipal law. But its statement in regard to the actions that would have created such legal validity was scarcely short of impudence. The armistice was signed at a time when the November revolution had swept away both the Kaiser and the Reichstag, and therefore it is hard to see what German legislative agencies the court had in mind. And failure to publish the armistice agreement in the *Reichsgesetzblatt* can scarcely be considered important in view of the fact that the widest publicity had been given to that vital document.

In this decision the Reichsgericht established a precedent according to which the provisions of an armistice agreement become part of municipal law only after they have been explicitly enacted as municipal statutes; and if the agreement has been signed by a revolutionary government, after a military defeat, it becomes a part of municipal law only if the constitutional requirements of the old regime have been observed. It should be noted that the denial of the immediate validity of the armistice agreement in municipal law did not touch upon its validity as an instrument of international law. In this distinction the court's position accorded with its characterization of the Rhineland occupation as a *Mischbesetzung*.

Even more strained was the reasoning of the Reichsgericht in this case in regard to the American proclamation of 14 January. It was impossible, of course, to deny that this order was in accordance with the armistice agreement. Therefore the court went back to the Hague Convention in order to prove that the proclamation was *ultra vires*. By Article 43 of that convention, said the Reichsgericht,

[the American authorities] were bound to respect the German laws as far as possible. It would have been sufficient for their purpose if they had declared the purchase in question null and void, as far as the United States was concerned. There was no reason to interfere with the private law relations between the German military authorities and private purchasers, or between the latter and further purchasers.

In other words, the Reichsgericht, applying the 'rule of mildest means' (see Morstein-Marx, p. 286), held that the confiscation and fine represented an improper means for a lawful end. The result of all this reasoning was that the defendant, who had made a profit of nearly 500 per cent, was given protection, while the plaintiff was obliged to pay the purchase price twice—a particularly impressive illustration of a decision in which the interests of the parties are sacrificed to a proclamation of principles of high policy.

Only three weeks later, however, on 10 May 1921 (JW 1921, vol. 50, p. 1454), the court, deciding another armistice case, was more realistic. The plaintiff had sold to the defendant a quantity of mineral oil which was to be imported from abroad, and sued for the contract price. Defendant pleaded that the contract was void because a German statute provided that such transactions needed a special license from the Reich foreign-trade agency. Plaintiff replied that the contract was concluded in, and was to be fulfilled in, the occupied territory under the armistice conditions, and he denied the applicability of German law because under the prevailing situation German law was unenforceable. The Reichsgericht, deciding in favor of the plaintiff, pointed out that the German statutes remained valid unless nullified by the occupation authorities as contrary to the purposes of the occupation, and that in the present instance the statute had not been so nullified; but it declared that 'After the bearers of actual power in the occupied territory had permitted free imports and trade in mineral oil, and after the German authorities were in fact deprived of the power of enforcing that statute, the mere fact that the statute had not been officially repealed . . . cannot be considered significant from a practical point of view.'

In other foreign-trade cases, too, the Reichsgericht, though holding that the actions of the occupying powers were *ultra vires*, adopted a generally realistic attitude.[2] And that point of view was also evident in an armistice case decided on 2 May 1923 (107 RGZ 173; *Annual Digest*, 1923-4, case 238, p. 440), at the time of the Ruhr conflict; in that decision, however, the court applied reasoning that was apparently intended to validate the resistance in the Ruhr. This case was a suit for breach of contract. In July 1919 the defendant had bought a quantity of

[2] See the Reichsgericht decisions of 7 June 1921 (102 RGZ 255); 2 February 1922 (104 RGZ 105); 22 September 1922 (105 RGZ 179); 13 December 1922 (JW 1923, vol. 52, p. 287).

wine, for delivery in Coblenz, but when it was delivered he refused to accept it, on the ground that the contract was void because the commander of the American army of occupation had forbidden the sale of alcoholic beverages in the American zone, except beer and light wines, and because in German law no legal transaction is valid which violates a statutory order.

The Reichsgericht denied that 'ordinances of foreign occupation authorities which are intended to protect the interests of foreign powers and of their troops and agencies' could be regarded as statutory orders in the meaning of German law; such ordinances 'originate in foreign legal views and are enacted without consideration for German legal feeling and German economic conditions.' The high court also denied that the occupation authorities were entitled to enact ordinances that affected the relations dealt with in private law.

Nevertheless, the plaintiff did not recover. Although the Reichsgericht held the contract valid it acknowledged that fulfilment of the transaction would have made the defendant liable to prosecution and to possible confiscation of the merchandise and closure of his enterprise. By thus granting equitable relief the Reichsgericht practically admitted that *de facto* considerations controlled the issue. It is significant that the court declared that the American prohibition was not an 'arbitrary' order, as it was not contrary to either the armistice or Article 43 of the Hague Convention, and that therefore non-compliance 'was not required from the defendant by legal, moral or patriotic considerations.' It was in this statement that the Reichsgericht offered a legal justification for the passive German resistance during the current Ruhr conflict.

In its tendency to deny the jurisdiction of the occupying powers in matters belonging to the domain of private law—questions of contract, inheritance, family relations, possession, private property, and the like—the Reichsgericht could cite the judgment of eminent authorities in international law, including Professor Nast ('De la compétence . . .' p. 289). But the distinction between public and private law was almost meaningless in the 'planned economy' that Germany lived under even at that time. In a total war—and even World War I was such a war—private law is absorbed by administration, and at its end the occupying powers, confronted with a regulated, centralized, bureaucratized economy, cannot be expected to conduct their administration as if a non-planned economy existed.

After the statement in the Uhlmann decision on judicial review, which was later repudiated both implicitly and explicitly, the theoretical question of the German courts' right to exercise this power was not dealt with again until 1922, when Heyland published his article on the legislative power of the High Commission ('Zur Lehre . . .' pp. 44-64). Heyland based his theory on the argument that a judge is subjected only to the law, a principle enunciated in the Weimar Constitution. The judge, he maintained, is therefore obliged to examine the legal character of all legislative acts, and the High Commission, since it did not object to this provision in the Weimar Constitution, implicitly recognized the right of German judges to exercise judicial review. In the field of occupation law, he argued, judicial review means that the courts of the occupied country as well as those of the occupying powers are obliged to recognize only those measures which conform with the international treaty defining the powers of the occupation authorities.

In adapting the general theory of judicial review to the peculiar problems of occupation, Heyland followed Heinrich Triepel's 'transformation' theory. Since the Rhineland Agreement had been properly made a part of German municipal law, the High Commission was entitled, by German law, to enact ordinances within the borderlines of Article 3. But the enactment of ordinances not wholly covered by that provision constituted, from the point of view of German municipal law, a nullity, and, from the point of view of international law, an international tort. If the High Commission thus transgressed its jurisdiction, the German Government, according to Heyland, was entitled to bring suit in the Permanent Court of International Justice, but 'under the prevailing conditions it is not practically possible for the German Government to inflict reprisals on the occupying powers for the enactment of such illegal ordinances' ('Zur Lehre . . .' p. 48, note 6).

In this article Heyland held that German officials of the executive branch of government did not have the same powers as German judges with respect to ordinances that they considered *ultra vires*. These officials, he maintained, did not have the same independence as the judges, and therefore they could question a command of the occupying powers only if so ordered by their immediate superiors; in case of conflict between commands of occupation authorities and of German authorities, a German official was obliged to disregard the former (ibid. p. 63). But in his book on the Rhineland occupation, published in 1923, Heyland modified this position. There he contended that in this respect there was no distinction between judges and other officials: the right and duty of legal review was the same, he said, for judges and non-judges (*Die Rechtsstellung* . . . pp. 119-29, especially p. 125, note 2, and p. 128, note 2).

Heyland's theory has been presented here in detail because it was adopted by both the Reichsgericht and the Reichsfinanzhof (the supreme financial court). On 7 December 1926, the latter decided a case (21 RFH 68-82) [3] in which it not only exercised but explicitly affirmed a right of judicial review. This case concerned a legal tangle over the payment of coal taxes due in 1923. Of the several German statutes that were relevant to the case, some, in accordance with the general practice of the German Government during the Ruhr conflict, had not been submitted to the High Commission for approval, and some had been at

---

[3] Information on this case is available also in DJZ 1927, vol. 32, p. 232, and in JW 1927, vol. 56, p. 2330, where an elaborate note by Heyland is appended; a short extract was published in *Annual Digest*, 1925-6, case 7, pp. 9-10. For an excellent analysis of this case see Bilfinger, pp. 567-71.

least partially invalidated in the occupied territory by an administrative decision of the Commission on 9 May 1924 (*Gazette*, 1924, No. v, p. 329).

It is not necessary to describe the complicated circumstances of this case. In the present context the important point is that the Reichsfinanzhof's decision took the extreme form of an attack on the basic provisions, in Articles 7-9 of Ordinance 1, in which the High Commission declared its right to pre-examine all German laws and regulations before they became valid in the occupied territory.

Explicitly adhering to Triepel's 'transformation' theory, and refusing Kelsen's theory that the rules of international law are the basic rules of the whole legal system, the court (p. 75) contended that High Commission ordinances were to be recognized only to the extent that they were 'transformed' into German municipal law. The peace treaty and the Rhineland Agreement, having been duly published in the *Reichsgesetzblatt*, were so 'transformed.' But ordinances of the High Commission—authorized by Article 3 of the Rhineland Agreement—were valid in German law only to the extent that they conformed with the requirements laid down in Article 3.

After thus shifting the problem from international to municipal law, the court examined the question whether the German judge was entitled to review the conformance of these ordinances with the enabling statute, that is, the Rhineland Agreement.

The right of judicial review [decided the court (p. 76)] could be denied only if such a denial was laid down in generally recognized rules of international law (Article 4, Reich Constitution), or if it was explicitly provided for in the Rhineland Agreement, the latter by transformation a part of German law, or in a rule of international customary law valid in addition to the Rhineland Agreement and transformed into municipal customary law. Since none of these alternatives actually exists, the right of judicial review must be recognized as a matter of principle.

On the basis of this reasoning the court concluded (p. 76) that Articles 7-9 of Ordinance 1 were *ultra vires* and therefore void. The Reichsfinanzhof did not deny the right of the High Commission to prohibit, in the occupied territory, the enforcement of statutes that actually endangered the maintenance, safety, and requirements of the occupying forces. It maintained, however, that the Rhineland Agreement, as a matter of principle, recognized the authority of the German legislature over the occupied territory, and that therefore the obligation imposed upon the German Government to subject all German statutes to a pre-examination by the High Commission was contrary to the Rhineland Agreement.

This argument is not convincing. When the High Commission's power of annulment was acknowledged, it was scarcely possible to deny the Commission's right to subject all German statutes to an examination that would determine whether the power of annulment should be exercised. A denial of this right, if enforceable, could have meant that statutes which were highly dangerous to the safety of the occupying troops were in force in the occupied territory, at least for an intermediate period. Such a situation would obviously have been contrary to Article 3 of the Rhineland Agreement. Articles 7-9 of Ordinance 1 represented a proper means to an end that was recognized as lawful by the court. Whether the approval of the occupying powers was construed as an approval or a veto power was a mere technicality. By overstressing the technical aspects of the problem the Germans lost sight of its substance. The logic of the Reichsfinanzhof was of a kind that would permit the High Commission to cut a pound of flesh but forbid it to shed a drop of blood.

Whether Articles 7-9 of Ordinance 1 were authorized by Article 3 of the Rhineland Agreement is actually a question of 'implied powers.' It is the question raised by Chief Justice Marshall, in McCulloch *v.* Maryland (17 U.S. 316), whether there was a 'phrase in the instrument which . . . excludes incidental or implied powers; and which requires that every thing granted shall be expressly and minutely described' (p. 406). The Rhine-land Agreement described the jurisdiction of the occupying powers in a very broad way, and did not contain the slightest hint that all powers not expressly granted to the High Commission rested with the agencies of the occupied country. What Marshall said about the Constitution of the United States holds true also for the magna charta of a military occupation: 'Its nature, therefore, requires, that only its great outlines should be marked, its important objects designated and the minor ingredients which compose those objects be deduced from the nature of the objects themselves' (p. 407).

When the Reichsfinanzhof rendered its decision in this case, the German courts had had little experience in reviewing the constitutionality of the content of legislative acts (as distinguished from the legality of the enactment procedures). It was only a little more than a year before the coal-tax case was decided that the Reichsgericht had recognized for the first time the right of judicial review of German legislation. Thus no legal tradition had taught German judges that 'the government which has a right to do an act, and has imposed on it the duty of performing that act, must, according to the dictates of reason, be allowed to select the means' (ibid. pp. 409-10). No constitutional experience existed in Germany on which the judges could rely when they interpreted the term 'necessary' in Article 3 of the Rhineland Agreement. They had no understanding of the principle that 'To employ the means necessary to an end is generally understood as employing any means calculated to produce the end, and not as being confined to those single means, without which the end would be entirely unattainable' (pp. 413-14).

As a matter of fact, it was not necessary to go so far as to attack the legality of Ordinance 1, in order to challenge the High Commission's invalidation decision. The Reichsfinanzhof could have reached the same result, on a much sounder basis, by declaring the High Commission's decision contrary to Ordinance 1, on the ground that there was no plausible connection between the safety of the occupying armies and measures intended to clear up, in the field of taxation, the results of German inflation. The court would have been exercising the right of judicial review in either case, but there was a considerable practical difference between judicial review of a basic legislative act of the High Commission and judicial review of a relatively unimportant administrative act of that body. Since the High Commission, as was to be taken for granted, ignored the opinion of the Reichsfinanzhof, and continued to base its actions on the provisions that the court had declared null and void, the 'nullification' served only to reduce the prestige of legal processes in the Rhineland.

It should be mentioned that the Reichsgericht, in deciding a case devolving upon the High Commission's veto of the German *Devisen* statutes in November 1923, paid lip service to the principles developed by the Reichsfinanzhof but reached a realistic result. In its decision on this case, rendered on 9 March 1929 (JW 1929, vol. 58, p. 1594; *Annual Digest*, 1929-30, case 48, pp. 77-8) the Reichsgericht declared:

The force of circumstances prevented the coming into operation of the German Devisen legislation in the occupied territory. The prohibition of the occupying powers therefore found the tacit toleration of the authorities of the Reich. The Devisen legislation was accordingly to be regarded as having been rendered inoperative as a consequence of the ordinances of the occupation authorities.

By means of a fiction, the fictitious 'nullification' of Articles 7-9 of Ordinance 1 was ignored.

In decisions concerning the legal basis of actions taken by the occupation authorities the high courts were clearly influenced not so much by definite legal principles as by considerations of opportunism and political expediency. Though such questions of 'constitutionality' were only collateral issues in the cases that came before the courts, the collateral issue, as a rule, wholly overshadowed the conflict between the parties. It is true that in most cases of this kind the high courts allowed *de facto* considerations to shape their decisions, even though they regarded an occupation measure as invalid. But in at least two instances—the nails decision of 19 April 1921 and the coal-tax decision of 7 December 1926—the courts produced judgments that were not only arbitrary but inequitable; in both these cases the plaintiff was the victim of nationalistic self-assertion and legal doctrinairism. And in all these cases in which the courts implicitly exercised a right of judicial review, the unilateral repudiation of occupation measures, as contrary to the occupation convention, served only to diminish the prestige of the occupying powers, by introducing a dual system of justice in the Rhineland.

Such a situation is to be carefully prevented in any well-planned occupation regime. And therefore the question of judicial review of occupation measures is one that should be explicitly dealt with in the occupation agreement. But whether this power should be accorded to the courts of the occupied country is far more than a question of mere technicality. Judicial review is not a technical legal device but a protective mechanism imbued with tradition. It is based on the idea that one branch of the government exercises a check over another branch—of the same government—and that both branches 'are equally the representatives of the people'—of the same people. Since judicial review is meaningless unless the reviewing court has confidence in the intentions of the legislature, it must be used sparingly and with the utmost sense of responsibility.

If judicial review is mechanically extended from the field of constitutional law to the field of occupation law, it is transformed into something different. When the Germans exercised this right in regard to occupation measures they were animated not by confidence but by mistrust, not by wholehearted co-operation but by nationalistic assertiveness, not by a disinterested desire to examine constitutionality but by a wish to annul. And judicial review coupled with resentment undermines rather than safeguards the basic legal instrument that is interpreted by the reviewing court.

It is perhaps conceivable that in some circumstances an occupied country would not feel hostility toward the occupying power, and that its courts would interpret the occupation convention with the same objectivity that they would apply to their own constitution. But even in that situation—if it ever existed— it is highly doubtful whether the courts of the occupied country are the proper agencies to review the actions of the occupants. Considerations of reason as well as of legal philosophy suggest that this function can be properly fulfilled only by an independent international body.

X

Conclusions

THE Rhineland Agreement, which was in many respects similar to the Covenant of the League of Nations, was an idealistic model plan for an occupation statute rather than a treaty created for the solution of one of the most complicated problems of postwar Europe. If a statute does not correspond to the realities it is supposed to deal with, idealists are always encouraged by the hope that facts will be adapted to the law, realists by the belief that law will be adapted to the facts. In the occupied Rhineland the realists triumphed over the idealists.

A basic characteristic of the Rhineland Agreement was its attempt to combine a maximum of protection of the occupying forces with a minimum of interference with the occupied country. It would be a mistake to regard these two goals as essentially contradictory. But the way in which they were combined represented the expression of a particular political philosophy. The Rhineland Agreement, product of the democratic optimism of the first postwar period, reflected the confidence of its authors in the necessarily peaceful results of an undisturbed democratic process. Convinced that political and economic *laissez-faire* was the only guarantee of international and internal peace, they looked upon non-interference with German domestic politics as an essential part of the security of the occupying forces. And believing that details were best worked out in practice, they failed to provide a clear definition of powers and duties, even for the vital task of preserving public order in the interest of the security of the occupying armies; and failed to provide to the body entrusted with power an executive machinery for carrying out its laws and regulations.

But this product of American political tradition was interpreted and executed in an environment devoid of American legal and customary controls. Occupation under the rule of law must be based on a political philosophy that is reconcilable with the political tradition of the occupied country. In the Rhineland Agreement, however, American liberals, trained in Anglo-Saxon legal and political concepts, tried to transplant their own political philosophy to a government that was essentially different from their ideals and traditions. In the occupation of such a country as Germany, with a strong centralized bureaucracy, the occupying powers must be provided with an apparatus that can deal with the bureaucratic machine. The supremacy of law, in such a situation, is to be accomplished not by disallowing or weakening the executive branch but by subjecting it to clearly defined rules of jurisdiction, procedure, and substantive law.

The High Commission, faced with the necessity of working out procedures and developing an apparatus that could meet the realistic requirements of the occupation—requirements that the Rhineland Agreement left to automatic beneficence—developed powers far greater than those of a constitutional democratic executive. And just as its powers were a matter of its own interpretation, so too were the restrictions on them. Not bound by any bill of rights or specific statutory limitations, it was able, when and where it pleased, to exercise its power without regard for the individual liberties that it is the function of bills of rights to assure. The Rhineland occupation is ample evidence that conformance with due process cannot be taken for granted. The civilian character of the highest occupation authority and the restriction of martial law to exceptional cases do not in themselves provide sufficient protection from violations of the rule of law, and from violations of individual liberties.

The problem of supremacy of law under the peculiar conditions of an occupation regime cannot be solved merely by reference to general considerations of justice and democracy. The rule of law in a democratic state is based on the consent of the citizens. In an occupied territory, public power is enforced upon the residents regardless of their inner feelings. Therefore the concept of 'rule of law' has different meanings in a government based on democratic consent and a government based on military force. It was the failure to recognize this fundamental fact that constituted the greatest weakness of the Rhineland Agreement.

The outstanding attribute of that document was its fictitious character. Its framers treated a government of military occupation 'as if' it were a democratic regime. The High Commission tried to correct this misconception by enacting ordinances which, though they were supposed to be in the framework of the enabling statute, represented in fact a basic change in the nature of the regime. Consequently the occupation law too, as contained in the ordinances of the High Commission, was fictitious in character. Though far more realistic than the Rhineland Agreement, and in many respects diametrically the opposite in spirit, it was supposed to be the realization of the rule of law regime which that agreement had envisaged. Thus the basic problems of the Rhineland occupation were hidden under a twofold juristic veil.

It was not so much the harshness of the occupation methods which produced resentment and embitterment among the subjects of the occupation regime, as it was the discrepancy between the proclaimed principles and their practical application. The proclamation of an ideal occupation instrument created hopes and expectations that could not be fulfilled, even if no considerations of power politics had interfered. And the repeated violations of the Rhineland Agreement, however necessary they may have been, provided German nationalists with dangerous and efficient weapons.

In a legal sphere that is so deeply imbued with politics, unpredictable situations will occasionally necessitate the substitution of political considerations for legal arguments. But so long as the exceptional character of such political deviations from legal principles is recognized, the occupation regime need not lose its character as a legal institution. It is when the bearer of political power looks upon legal regulations merely as rules of expediency, valid only by sufferance, that the supremacy of law is replaced by the supremacy of force.

The Rhineland occupation clearly revealed that the dangers involved in a government by condominium are as great in temporary military occupation as they are in permanent political rule. Differences among the Allies—far-reaching differences in interest, outlook, and methods—produced a regime of compromise, satisfactory to none and often inconsistent with its own principles, as well as with those of the treaty that created it. And the Germans were not slow to make use of the opportunity afforded them by this disunity at the helm.

Under modern conditions no military occupation can completely eliminate the existing administrative agencies and courts. Especially a totalitarian state in dissolution cannot be run exclusively by foreign authorities. Wherever the borderline may be drawn between direct and indirect occupation administration, vast fields of administrative and judicial activities have to be entrusted to controlled local and regional agencies. And control of these agencies is possible only if they are bound by definite rules.

A future occupation of Germany, whether or not it is preceded by an internal revolution, will be confronted with the unique situation of having to deal with a country living under a rule without law. The first step to be taken by the occupying armies will be the declaration of a state of siege; and this will produce a peculiar situation. A state of siege was declared in Germany on 28 February 1933, and has never been lifted; martial law represents the constitution of the Third Reich. It is unthinkable, however, that two separate bureaucratic hierarchies exercise the powers of martial law on the same territory at the same time. Thus it is essential that the German state of siege be replaced by the martial law of the occupying powers, on the very day on which those powers declare their ultimate responsibility for the preservation of public order inside Germany. This will mean the nullification of all statutes, decrees, and orders which have entitled German agencies to act in accordance with a legally unbound discretion; the abolition of all those institutions, such as Gestapo, concentration camps and storm troops, which depend exclusively on the existence of German martial law; and the prohibition of the activities of all other party agencies and of those state agencies that are neither based on nor controlled by law. For reasons of self-protection, a future occupation of Germany will eliminate what I have elsewhere called the 'prerogative state,' and will subject the 'normative state' to intensive control.

In a recent article on 'Military Government as a Step Toward Self-Rule,' Carl J. Friedrich, in referring to this 'dual' character of the Nazi state, has remarked (p. 539) that 'the destruction of the Nazi sector will automatically revive the other, giving the latter opportunity to fill the vacuum created by the disappearance of the party.' This wholly valid conclusion should be supplemented, however, by a warning that the situation will be far from simple. Even before the outbreak of the present war, the activities of the ordinary administrative agencies were 'greatly influenced by the existence of the Prerogative State' (Fraenkel, *The Dual State*, p. 70), and this tendency has increased considerably during the war. It may be expected that the nucleus of a 'normative state' will still be in existence at the end of this war, but much political wisdom and administrative ability will be needed to free the agencies of the normative state from the remnants of the Nazi period, when they existed only by sufferance. It is worth emphasizing that Friedrich, too, contends (p. 536) that government according to law is the 'clue' to the solution of occupation problems in Europe. Though he recognizes the paradoxical nature of an attempt to establish the rule of law under conditions of military government, he believes that the difficulties can be overcome.

The rule of law in the full meaning of the term cannot be restored in Germany at the moment the occupying powers take over ultimate authority. At the beginning, one state of siege will merely be replaced by another. It is not only because martial law is an attribute of sovereignty that the occupying powers will deprive the German authorities of the right to exercise martial-law powers of their own: it is also because the establishment of German agencies that are exclusively controlled by law, in the place of Nazi agencies empowered to deal with all problems by virtue of a fraudulently created state of siege, represents one of the basic war aims of the United Nations.

This elimination of German institutions that are contrary to the idea of the Rechtsstaat must be supplemented, however, by positive steps. It cannot be expected that the German agencies will feel themselves bound by law unless the occupation government is itself based on law. An arbitrary regime can be enforced upon a conquered nation by force; a lawful regime can be built up only by the consistent application of legal methods. Therefore even in the first phase of occupation, which will have to be controlled primarily by considerations of expediency, the occupying powers must consider whether it is not possible to provide a minimum of legal control. Much will depend, of course, on the response of the German population; on whether the Germans realize that their co-operation is essential in the process of adapting the regime to the ideals of the rule of law; on whether they themselves recognize the rule of law as a basic principle of the western world.

However that may be, even the most enthusiastic adherents of that principle cannot recommend an uncritical repetition of the experiment of 1918. The Rhineland Agreement, so strongly influenced by the Wilsonian period's messianic belief in general formulas and programs, attempted to convert military occupation into a rule of law by formulating broad principles. But experience in the Rhineland proved that the problem cannot be solved by general regulations. An effective occupation statute must be enacted on the basis of the experience accumulated during the first phase of the occupation.

If the future occupation of Germany is not planned as a permanent one, the attempt must be made to give autonomous forces inside Germany a chance to rebuild organizations of their own which may serve as cells for a reconstruction of democracy. It is most unlikely that a revolution after Hitler's downfall will result in a working democratic self-government in Germany, or that general democratic elections will be possible during the first stages of post-Hitler development. Since all German groups have been radically co-ordinated into the National Socialist organization, there will be an unprecedented vacuum in the social structure after the Nazi party itself and all of its auxiliaries have been dissolved. The reconstruction of autonomous groups inside Germany, which will eventually be capable of filling this vacuum with a democratic regime, demands the granting of certain civil liberties, and a guarantee that the bearers of public power will not arbitrarily interfere with the rebuilding of religious, local, and professional bodies in the territories subjected to military occupation. If the occupying powers promote the process of rejuvenescence of autonomous groups, by preventing the municipal state machine from arbitrarily interfering with civil liberties and by granting protection to all those who are attempting to overcome the heritage of Nazi dictatorship, military occupation may prove to be a benefaction both for the victors and for the vanquished.

APPENDIX I

Text of the Rhineland Agreement [1]

ARTICLE 1

In accordance with Article 428 and the following Articles of the Treaty of even date, the armed forces of the Allied and Associated Powers will continue in occupation of German territory (as such occupation is defined by Article 5 of the Armistice Convention of the 11th November 1918, as extended by Article 7 of the Additional Convention of the 16th January 1919) as a guarantee of the execution by Germany of the Treaty.

No German troops, except prisoners of war in process of repatriation, shall be admitted to the occupied territories, even in transit; but police forces of a strength to be determined by the Allied and Associated Powers may be maintained in these territories for the purpose of ensuring order.

ARTICLE 2

There shall be constituted a civilian body styled *the Inter-Allied Rhineland High Commission,* and hereinafter called *the High Commission* which, except in so far as the Treaty may otherwise provide, shall be the supreme representative of the Allied and Associated Powers within the occupied territory. It shall consist of four members representing Belgium, France, Great Britain and the United States.

ARTICLE 3

(a) The High Commission shall have the power to issue Ordinances so far as may be necessary for securing the maintenance, safety and requirements of the Allied and Associated forces. Such ordinances shall be published under the authority of the High Commission, and copies thereof shall be sent to each of the Allied and Associated Governments and also to the German Government.

When so published they shall have the force of law and shall be recognised as such by all the Allied and Associated military authorities and by the German civil authorities.

(b) The members of the High Commission shall enjoy diplomatic privileges and immunities.

(c) The German courts shall continue to exercise civil and criminal jurisdiction subject to the exceptions contained in paragraphs (d) and (e) below.

(d) The armed forces of the Allied and Associated Powers and the

[1] *Gazette*, 1920, No. 1, pp. 5-15.

persons accompanying them, to whom the General Officers Commanding the Armies of Occupation shall have issued a revocable pass, and any persons employed by, or in the service of such troops, shall be exclusively subject to the military law and jurisdiction of such forces.

(e) Any person who commits any offence against the persons or property of the armed forces of the Allied and Associated Powers may be made amenable to the military jurisdiction of the said forces.

ARTICLE 4

The German authorities, both in the occupied and in the unoccupied territories, shall, on the demand of any duly authorised military officer of the occupying forces, arrest and hand over to the nearest commander of the Allied or Associated troops any person charged with an offence who is amenable under paragraph (d) or paragraph (e) of Article 3 above to the military jurisdiction of the Allied or Associated Forces.

ARTICLE 5

The civil administration of the provinces (Provinzen), Government departments (Regierungsbezirke), Urban Circles (Stadtkreise), Rural Circles (Landkreise), and Communes (Gemeinden), shall remain in the hands of the German authorities, and the civil administration of these areas shall continue under German law and under the authority of the Central German Government, except in so far as it may be necessary for the High Commission by Ordinance under Article 3 to adapt that administration to the needs and circumstances of military occupation. It is understood that the German authorities shall be obliged, under penalty of removal, to conform to the Ordinances issued in virtue of Article 3 above.

ARTICLE 6

The right to requisition in kind and to demand services in the manner laid down in the Hague Convention 1907, shall be exercised by the Allied and Associated Armies of Occupation.

The charges for requisitions effected in the zone of each Allied and Associated army and the estimate of damage caused by the troops of occupation shall be determined by local Commissions composed in equal representation of German civilians appointed by the German civil authorities and Allied or Associated military officers, and presided over by some person appointed by the High Commission.

The German Government shall continue to be responsible for the costs of maintenance of the troops of occupation under the conditions fixed by the Treaty. The German Government shall also be responsible for the costs and expenses of the High Commission, and for its housing. Suitable premises for the housing of the High Commission shall be selected after consultation with the German Government.

ARTICLE 7

The Allied and Associated troops shall continue undisturbed in possession of any premises at present occupied by them, subject to the provisions of Article 8 (b) below.

ARTICLE 8

(a) The German Government shall undertake, moreover, to place at the disposal of the Allied and Associated troops and to maintain in good state of repair all the military establishments required for the said troops, with the necessary furniture, heating and lighting, in accordance with the regulations concerning these matters in force in the various armies concerned. These shall include accommodation for officers and men, guard-rooms, offices, administrative, regimental and staff headquarters, work-shops, store-rooms, hospitals, laundries, regimental schools, riding schools, stables, training grounds and rifle and artillery ranges, aviation grounds, grazing grounds, warehouses for supplies and grounds for military ma-noeuvres, also theatre and cinema premises, and reasonable facilities for sport and for recreation grounds for the troops.

(b) Private soldiers and non-commissioned officers shall be accom-modated in barracks, and shall not be billeted on the inhabitants, except in cases of exceptional emergency.

In the event of the existing military establishments being insufficient or not being considered suitable, the Allied and Associated troops may take possession of any other public or private establishment with its personnel, suitable for those purposes, or, if there are no such suitable premises, they may require the construction of new barracks.

Civilians and military officers and their families may be billeted on the inhabitants in accordance with the billeting regulations in force in each army.

ARTICLE 9

No German direct taxes or duties will be payable by the High Com-mission, the Allied and Associated armies or their personnel.

Food supplies, arms, clothing, equipment and provisions of all kinds for the use of the Allied and Associated Armies, or addressed to the military authorities, or to the High Commission, or to canteens and officers' messes, shall be transported free of charge and free of all import duties of any kind.

ARTICLE 10

The personnel employed on all means of communication (railways, rail-roads and tramways of all kinds, waterways (including the Rhine), roads and rivers), shall obey any orders given by, or on behalf of, the Com-mander-in-Chief of the Allied and Associated armies for military purposes.

All the material and all the civil personnel necessary for the maintenance and working of all means of communication must be kept intact on all such means of communication in the occupied territory.

The transport on the railways of troops or individual soldiers or officers, on duty or furnished with a warrant, will be effected without payment.

ARTICLE 11

The Armies of Occupation may continue to use for military purposes all existing telegraphic and telephonic installations.

The Armies of Occupation shall also have the right to continue to install and use military telegraph and telephone lines, wireless stations and all other similar means of communication which may appear to them expedient. For this purpose, subject to the approval of the High Commission, they may enter upon and occupy any land, whether public or private.

The personnel of the public telegraph and telephone services shall continue to obey the orders of the Commander-in-Chief of the Allied and Associated Armies given for military purposes.

Telegrams and messages to or from the Allied and Associated authorities and the High Commission and of an official nature shall be entitled to priority over all other communications and shall be despatched free of charge. The Allied and Associated military authorities shall have the right to supervise the order in which such communications are transmitted.

No wireless telegraphy installations shall be allowed to be erected by the authorities or by the inhabitants of the occupied territory without previous authorisation by the Allied and Associated military authorities.

ARTICLE 12

The personnel of the postal service shall obey any orders given by or on behalf of the Commander-in-Chief of the Allied and Associated Armies for military purposes. The public postal service shall continue to be carried out by the German authorities, but this shall not in any way affect the retention of the military postal services organised by the Armies of Occupation, who shall have the right to use all existing postal routes for military requirements.

The said armies shall have the right to run postal wagons with all necessary personnel on all existing postal routes.

The German Government shall transmit free of charge and without examination letters and parcels which may be entrusted to its post-offices by or for the Armies of Occupation or by or for the High Commission; and shall be responsible for the value of any letters or parcels lost.

ARTICLE 13

The High Commission shall have the power, whenever they think it necessary, to declare a state of siege in any part of the territory or in the whole of it. Upon such declaration, the military authorities shall have the powers provided in the German Imperial Law of May 30th, 1892.

In case of emergency, where public order is disturbed or threatened in any district, the local military authorities shall have the power to take such temporary measures as may be necessary for restoring order. In such case the military authorities shall report the facts to the High Commission.

Done at Versailles, the twenty-eighth day of June, one thousand nine hundred and nineteen.

APPENDIX II

Selected Ordinances of the High Commission

ORDINANCE 1 [1]

Part I: The Ordinances of the High Commission

ARTICLE 1

The Ordinances of the High Commission shall have the force of law and on publication shall be recognised as such by the Allied Authorities and by the German Authorities.

ARTICLE 2

The Ordinances of the High Commission shall be published in an official gazette of the Inter-Allied High Commission.

ARTICLE 3

An ordinance of the High Commission shall come into effect on the day of its publication, unless it is otherwise expressly provided.

ARTICLE 4

The Inter-Allied High Commission, the Inter-Allied High Command, the Army Commands, and the competent German Authorities shall be responsible, in so far as they are severally concerned, for the execution of the Ordinances of the High Commission.

ARTICLE 5

Any German Authority disobeying any Ordinance of the High Commission may, in addition to being liable to the penalties provided for an offence against an Ordinance of the High Commission, be suspended or deprived of his office or expelled by decision of the High Commission.

Part II: Orders of the Military Authorities

ARTICLE 6

(i) It is the duty of all German Authorities and of all persons within the Occupied Territories to obey all orders, including orders of requisition, given by or on behalf of the Allied Military Authorities of the said

---

[1] *Gazette*, 1920, No. 1, pp. 19-25.

territories, in pursuance of their lawful power, subject to the provisions of the Agreement annexed to the Treaty of Peace.

(ii) Any German Authority disobeying such orders may, in addition to being liable to the penalties provided for an offence against an Ordinance of the High Commission, be suspended or deprived of his office by decision of the High Commission.

Part III: The Operation of German Laws and Regulations in the Occupied Territories

ARTICLE 7

German Imperial and State Laws or General Regulations not already actually in force throughout the Occupied Territories shall, previously to their coming into force in the Occupied Territories, be transmitted by the competent Authorities to the High Commission, who will examine them in order to ensure that no provision is contained therein of a nature likely to prejudice the maintenance, safety or requirements of the troops of occupation.

ARTICLE 8

The said Laws and Regulations shall come into force in the Occupied Territories ten days after they have been duly registered with the High Commission, provided always that no provisional or final veto has been pronounced against them by the High Commission.

The High Commission may subsequently order the suspension of any of the said Laws and Regulations.

The High Commission may, at the request of the German Government, order immediate application of any Law or Regulation so soon as it is published.

ARTICLE 9

The High Commission, when necessary, and after consultation with the competent German Authorities, shall examine the methods by which the said Laws and Regulations may be made to conform with the conditions set out in Article 7 above.

When necessary, the High Commission shall issue an Ordinance to modify, temporarily to suspend, or to prohibit the said Laws and Regulations.

Coblence, this tenth day of January 1920

ORDINANCE 2 [2]

Part I: Criminal Jurisdiction

ARTICLE 1

The armed forces of the Allies and the persons accompanying them, to whom the General Officers Commanding the Armies of Occupation shall

[2] *Gazette*, 1920, No. 1, pp. 27-51.

have issued a pass revocable at their pleasure, and any persons employed by or in the service of, such troops, shall be exclusively subject to the military law and jurisdiction of such forces.

ARTICLE 2

(1) Any person, other than those specified in Article 1, who contravenes any Ordinance of the High Commission, or commits any offence against the persons or property of the armed forces of the Allies may be made amenable to the military jurisdiction of the said forces.

(2) The High Commission reserves to itself the right to establish such Courts as may be considered necessary for the exercise of the jurisdiction given by the provisions of the Agreement annexed to the Treaty of Peace.

(3) The rules of procedure followed and the penalties awarded by the Military Courts shall be those provided by the laws of the Army concerned or by the Ordinances of the High Commission.

(4) In the case of German nationals and Allied nationals being jointly concerned in the commission of an offence, the competent tribunal shall always be that which would have been competent if the offence had been committed by Allied nationals alone.

(5) Nothing in this Ordinance contained shall be deemed to give Allied Military Courts or German Courts criminal jurisdiction over members of the High Commission or any person employed under the members of the High Commission or the families of such members or persons, unless such jurisdiction is expressly given by a specific order of the High Commission.

ARTICLE 3

The German Authorities, both in the Occupied and in Unoccupied Territories, shall, on the demand of any duly authorised military officer of the occupying forces, arrest and hand over to the nearest Commander of Allied troops any person charged with an offence, who is amenable under Article 1 or Article 2 above to the military jurisdiction of the Allied forces.

ARTICLE 4

(1) When the German Authorities have taken cognizance of the commission of an offence, or arrested an accused person, they shall immediately forward the papers in the case to the Allied Military Authorities who are competent to bring the matter before a Military Court.

If the Military Authorities decide to bring the case before a Military Court, they will inform the High Commission and will later acquaint it with the judgment pronounced.

If the Military Authorities decide to leave the case to the German judicial Authorities, they will transmit the papers in the case to them. The German Court which takes cognizance of the case must within 8 days of the notification of the return of the papers inform the Representative of the High Commission in the Kreis concerned of the judgment pronounced, or of the stage which the proceedings have reached.

A monthly return shall be made by the German judicial Authorities to the High Commission showing the stages which all current cases have reached.

(2) The Military Authorities may also leave to the German Courts the trial of offences concerning which information has been lodged by the Allied police.

(3) The High Commission reserves to itself the right to decide as to the classes of such cases which may be sent to the Allied Military Courts.

It also reserves the right at any stage of a case to make any order transferring any such case to any other court.

ARTICLE 5

It is the duty of all members of the police force, whether Allied or German, to ensure the execution of the Ordinances of the High Commission. They shall collect evidence, present charges and arrest accused persons for offences against the Ordinances of the High Commission, according to the forms and conditions prescribed by their respective laws.

ARTICLE 6

Whenever persons are caught in the act, or in cases of urgency, or when proceedings are being taken before the Allied Military Courts, the Allied police shall have the powers of arrest and of search given in conformity with the forms and conditions laid down by their respective laws.

ARTICLE 7

In cases where under Article 4 above proceedings have been left to the German Courts, German procedure shall be followed.

ARTICLE 8

Notwithstanding any provisions to the contrary contained in German law, any Allied Court may cause any administrative or other documents, the production of which it deems necessary for the purpose of any enquiry or trial before it, to be produced before it.

ARTICLE 9

Unless it is forbidden by the national laws of the Military Court concerned, the amount of the fines imposed by, and the court fees paid into, the Military Courts and the Courts established by the High Commission, shall be placed to the credit of the Reparations account and shall be deducted from the payment due by the German Government.

ARTICLE 10

The High Commission may pardon any offender who has been sentenced or commute or reduce any sentence which has been passed, by a German Court in exercise of jurisdiction conferred on it by an Ordinance of the High Commission.

ARTICLE 11

In respect of sentences which have been pronounced by a Military Court, the power of pardon, commutation or reduction shall be exercised in conformity with the laws and regulations of the nation concerned.

ARTICLE 12

All sentences of imprisonment passed by Allied Courts and all such sentences passed by German Courts for offences against the Ordinances of the High Commission shall be served in German prisons of the Occupied Territories, except as may be otherwise prescribed by the High Commission.

ARTICLE 13

The High Commission reserves to itself the right of supervision over German prisons for the purpose of ascertaining that the sentences, executed in conformity with Article 12, are being carried out in accordance with the judgment passed.

ARTICLE 14

The High Commission may, in special cases, or classes of cases, decide in which prison of the Occupied Territories the sentence shall be served.

Part II: Civil Jurisdiction

ARTICLE 15

(1) German Courts shall continue to exercise their civil jurisdiction, except over the persons mentioned in Article 1 and in clause 5 of Article 2 above.

(2) Notwithstanding anything contained in the clause (1) above, civil actions brought by or against any of the persons referred to therein in their private capacity shall be tried before the German Courts according to German law.

Provided that the High Commission may decide that any case or classes of cases covered by this clause shall, by reason of their character or the status of the persons named as parties, not be heard before the German Courts but be tried by the Courts of the High Commission mentioned below or disposed of in such other way as the High Commission may direct.

ARTICLE 16

(1) Every writ, summons or notice shall be accompanied by a certified translation in the language of the party served.

(2) Every writ shall be transmitted for service either to the High Commissioner of the nation concerned for the members of his staff or to their superior officer for members of the Allied forces for Allied officials or for the families of either, or to the authority designated on this behalf by the High Commission in the Kreis.

ARTICLE 17

Any party to a suit brought in a German Court by virtue of the jurisdiction conferred by Clause 2 of Article 15 above who contends that his case is not covered by the provisions of the said clause may by an application to the High Commission object to the jurisdiction of the German Court, and the High Commission or any authority empowered by it on its behalf may hear and pass orders on such objection and such orders shall be binding on the German Court.

On being informed that such an application has been made to the High Commission, the German Court shall suspend proceedings until orders have been passed on the application.

ARTICLE 18

(1) There shall be set up in each zone of occupation one or more civil Courts which shall be entitled "High Commission Courts." Each such Court shall be composed of three members; two shall be Allied nationals, one of whom shall be President of the Court; the third shall be a German. All shall be learned in the law.

(2) The procedure of the High Commission Courts shall be as the Court may direct, subject to revision by the High Commission. If several Courts exist in the same zone the procedure shall be the same for all such Courts.

(3) It shall be the duty of these Courts to decide any civil cases referred to them under the provisions of the proviso to clause 2 of Article 15 above. Their jurisdiction within the area of the zone in which they shall have been established shall extend to the nationals of any occupying nation.

ARTICLE 19

(1) Any person referred to in clause 2 of Article 15 above, who is a party to a civil proceeding in a German Court may, if he considers he has suffered injury from a miscarriage of justice on the part of the German Court, appeal from it to the High Commission Court specified in the immediately foregoing Article.

(2) The High Commission Court may either confirm the judgment which has been referred to it or remit the case for rehearing or pass final judgment itself.

(3) If the High Commission Court considers that the circumstances of the case justify it in so doing, it may inflict a fine not exceeding 10,000 Marks upon any party who has frivolously or improperly appealed against the decision of the German Court.

ARTICLE 20

The High Commission reserves to itself the right at any stage of proceedings to make an order to transfer any case from one Court to another notwithstanding any previous decision given, and to decide questions of conflicting jurisdiction.

ARTICLE 21

When final judgment has been given by a German Court and execution has issued against the Allied party, a certified duplicate copy of the judgment shall be transmitted for execution to the High Commissioner of the nation concerned for the members of his staff, or to the appropriate Army Commander for members of the Allied forces, Allied officials or the families of either.

Part III: Offences Relating to the Occupation

ARTICLE 22

Except as otherwise provided any person committing an offence against an Ordinance of the High Commission shall, on conviction, be liable to a fine of not more than 10,000 Marks and to imprisonment for not more than one year, or both.

ARTICLE 23

Any person, who, singly or in combination with others, shall attempt to commit, or who shall be accessory to the committing of an offence against an Ordinance of the High Commission shall, on conviction, be liable, except as may otherwise be provided, to the same penalties as the principal offender.

ARTICLE 24

Any person who:

(a) Does violence to or assaults or wilfully obstructs in the execution of his duty any of the personnel of the Allied Armies or of the High Commisson;

(b) wilfully damages, in a manner likely to prejudice the security of the troops of occupation, any building, road, railway, canal, bridge, telegraph or telephone line, water supplies or works or other work;

shall, on conviction, be liable to the same penalties as are provided for such offences under the Military Law of the several Allied Armies in their respective zones.

ARTICLE 25

(1) No person shall by word, act or gesture conduct himself in a manner insulting to the members of the High Commission or to the persons attached thereto, or to the forces of occupation or to any member of such forces, or to the Military Colours or Insignia of the Allied Powers.

(2) All Germans of the Armed Military Forces, Police, Fire Brigades, Customs and Forestry Services shall, when in uniform, salute the Colours and Officers of the Allied Powers.

ARTICLE 26

Any person who commits or abets the commission of any act calculated to promote bad feeling, dissatisfaction, indiscipline or mutiny amongst the troops of occupation shall, on conviction, be liable to imprisonment for not more than five years.

ARTICLE 27

No person may acquire, sell or be in possession of war material, equipment or stores (including any article belonging to military canteens, clothing stores and regimental institutions) or any military property whatsoever, belonging to or intended for the troops of occupation, or to a member of such troops, except such as may be shown to have been lawfully obtained by him.

The burden of proving his title to the ownership or possession shall rest upon the person in possession of the property in question.

ARTICLE 28

No person shall supply by sale, gift or otherwise any alcoholic beverage or intoxicating or stupefying drug to members of the troops of occupation in contravention of regulations issued by the Armies.

Upon a second conviction in such case the Court, in addition to the ordinary penalties provided, may order the closing of the establishment in which the offence was committed for a period of not more than three months, provided that the responsibility of the owner has been established.

ARTICLE 29

All merchants, manufacturers and retailers, and, in general, all persons trading with the public, are forbidden to sell to any member of the Allied forces or to any Allied official any commodity, merchandise or article of any sort whatsoever at a higher price than that which is usually paid by the German public.

ARTICLE 30

No person who is not a member of the Allied forces or employed under the High Commission shall wear a uniform or badge of the Allied Armies or of the High Commission or any colorable imitation thereof.

Part IV: Immunity and Continuation Provisions

ARTICLE 31

(1) No judicial proceedings shall be instituted or continued, and no punitive measures shall be taken, against any person or company in the Occupied Territories for any commercial, financial, or banking operation which he or they may have carried out during the period of the Armistice with the expressed or implied permission of the Allied Authorities. The decision of the High Commission that any operation was carried out with such expressed or implied permission shall be final and conclusive upon all parties.

(2) No judicial proceedings shall be instituted or continued, and no punitive measures shall be taken, against any Allied banking firm or company, or against any member thereof, on the ground that such banking firm or company has not obtained registration, licence or authority in accordance with German Laws and Regulations. Provided that the above shall not apply to any such person, firm or company unless it shall have carried on business in the Occupied Territories during the period of the Armistice and shall have applied for registration, licence or authority before the expiry of two months from the date of the coming into force of the Treaty of Peace.

(3) Without the consent of the High Commission no judicial proceedings shall be instituted or continued and no punitive measures shall be taken against any person in the Occupied Territories for any administrative or political act done during the period of the Armistice. The decision of the High Commission that any act was of an administrative or political nature shall be final and conclusive upon all parties.

ARTICLE 32

No person deported by the Allied Military Authorities from the Occupied Territories during the period of the Armistice shall re-enter the Occupied Territories without permission of the High Commission granted after consultation with the Military Authorities of the Power in whose name the order of deportation has been made.

ARTICLE 33

Officials suspended or dismissed from their positions during the period of the Armistice by the Allied Military Authorities may not again take up their duties in the Occupied Territories without permission of the High Commission granted after consultation with the Military Authorities of the Power in whose name the order of suspension or dismissal has been made.

ARTICLE 34

All proceedings instituted by the occupying Military Authorities before the entry into force of the Treaty of Peace and of the Agreement annexed thereto, may be continued before the Courts seized therewith, notwithstanding the entry into force of the Treaty of Peace and the Agreement.

ARTICLE 35

Judgments and Orders made by the Military Courts before the entry into force of the Treaty of Peace, or in consequence of proceedings instituted as laid down above, shall be carried out, notwithstanding the entry into force of the Treaty of Peace and the Agreement thereto annexed.

Coblence, this tenth day of January 1920

ORDINANCE 3 [8]

Part III: The Press

ARTICLE 13

All newspapers, pamphlets or publications, all printed matter, all productions obtained by mechanical or chemical methods, intended for public distribution, all pictures with or without words, all music with words or explanations, and all cinematograph films of a nature to prejudice public order or endanger the security or the dignity of the High Commission or of the troops of occupation, are forbidden, and if published may be seized by order of the High Commission, or, in case of emergency, by order of the Representative of the High Commission in the Kreis. In the case of a daily publication the Representative of the High Commission in the Kreis may order its suspension or exclusion from the Occupied Territories for three days.

The action taken will be reported immediately to the High Commission

[8] *Gazette,* 1920, No. 1, pp. 53-71.

who will pass orders on it. The High Commission may order that a journal be suspended or excluded from the Occupied Territories for a period not exceeding three months.

ARTICLE 14

In addition to such administrative action, proceedings may be taken against the authors, proprietors, editors or publishers of offending publications before the competent judicial authorities.

ARTICLE 15

No person shall sell, exhibit, hawk, or otherwise distribute forbidden publications or films. In addition to persons' so offending being liable to the penalties provided for an offence against an Ordinance of the High Commission, copies of such publications and films found in the possession of such persons shall be immediately seized and the High Commission may order the closing of any premises concerned for a period not exceeding three months.

Part IV: Meetings

ARTICLE 16

No political meeting shall be held unless the organiser or organisers thereof shall have given notice in writing forty eight hours before the day of the meeting to the Representative of the High Commission in the Kreis. The notice shall set out the object of the meeting and shall give the names of the organisers.

ARTICLE 17

(1) The Representative of the High Commission in the Kreis may be present in person or by representative.

(2) In cases where the discussion touches on subjects not in the notice submitted, or where disturbances endangering the public order may arise, the meeting may be dissolved by the Allied Representative present, and judicial proceedings may be taken against the organisers.

ARTICLE 18

The High Commission may prohibit the holding of political meetings or of any other meetings which it considers may endanger the security of the Allied Armies.

ORDINANCE 5 [4]

The Safety and Requirements of the Allied Forces in Cases of Industrial Disputes

ARTICLE 1

(1) The provisions contained in this Ordinance shall apply only to strikes of persons employed in or about any steam railways, railway workshops, telegraphic, telephonic and postal services, coal mines, navigation,

---

[4] *Gazette*, 1920, No. 1, pp. 79-83.

gas, electricity works, and water works; but the High Commission may at any time, by an order duly published, apply this Ordinance to any other undertaking which is necessary for the maintenance, safety or requirements of the Armies of Occupation.

(2) In case of doubt whether any undertaking comes within the scope of clause (1), a decision of the High Commission that it is of the nature mentioned in that clause shall be conclusive.

ARTICLE 2

(1) In the cases mentioned in the foregoing article no strike shall take place until the matter in dispute shall have been submitted for decision to the authorities prescribed by the German Law on the subject of conciliation in industrial disputes.

(2) The Award of the Court of Conciliation shall be given within a period of one week, calculated from the date on which the demand for conciliation was received by the prescribed authority, and shall be submitted to the Representative of the High Commission of the district (Bezirk) in which the dispute arose, who shall transmit it immediately to the High Commission.

(3) Any party to an award made by the German Court of Conciliation may, within one week from the date of the award, appeal to the High Commission. Every such appeal must be heard by a Board of Conciliation appointed by the High Commission, consisting of a president and two members with four Germans as assessors, two of whom will represent the employers and two the employees. The decision of this Board of Conciliation shall be given within a period not exceeding one week from the date on which the Board was fully constituted.

(4) No strike may take place after conclusion of the conciliation proceedings prescribed in clauses (1), (2), and (3) above, unless a formal written notice of the intention to strike has been given to the Representative of the High Commission mentioned in clause (2), nor until the expiry of one week from the date of the receipt of such notice by the said Representative.

ARTICLE 3

The provisions of Article 2 shall apply equally to any lockout by the employers of workmen employed in any undertaking of the nature described in Article 1.

ARTICLE 4

Where any strike has occurred in an undertaking to which this Ordinance does not apply, but to which it may be applied under the provisions of Article 1, the High Commission may forbid the continuance of such strike and direct all persons concerned to take the action prescribed in this Ordinance.

ARTICLE 5

Notwithstanding any provision of any existing German Law, no German authority within the Occupied Territories shall have the power to declare that any conciliation award given under such law shall be final.

Coblence, this tenth day of January 1920

ORDINANCE 90 [5]

Regulating the Right of the High Commission to Divest the German Authorities and Courts of Certain Cases which Concern the Allied Forces

ARTICLE 1

Whenever it shall appear to the High Commission upon reasonable cause shown that any person has been threatened or been the object of any penalty, whether administrative, disciplinary, criminal or civil, at the hands of any German Authority or Court on account of any service rendered by such person to the Allied Authorities of Occupation or on account of the relations of such person with the said Authorities, the High Commission may take cognizance of the matter and may itself adjudicate thereon and review any judgment or decision given or may refer the matter for judgment to such Tribunal as it shall appoint.

For this purpose the High Commission may order the production of all such documents as may appear necessary, either directly to it or through such other Allied Authority as it may authorise for this purpose.

On the transfer of any matter by the High Commission all proceedings shall be immediately suspended unless the High Commission shall otherwise direct.

ARTICLE 2

This Ordinance shall apply to the Kehl Bridgehead.

ARTICLE 3

This Ordinance shall become immediately operative.

Coblence, this sixteenth day of June 1921

[5] *Gazette*, 1921, No. v-vi, pp. 153-5.

BIBLIOGRAPHY

Full information on books and articles incompletely referred to in the text is given below. A score or so of additional publications, not referred to in the text, have also been included, because of their interest or importance in this field. No attempt has been made, however, to compile a complete bibliography. A German bibliography on writings dealing with the Rhineland occupation was published in 1929, compiled by Reismüller and Hofmann; this is listed below.

A. I., 'Le régime de l'occupation rhénane institué par le traité de Versailles,' in *Revue des sciences politiques*, 1921, vol. 44, pp. 245-73.

Alexander, Horace G., 'La Justice Militaire,' Letter to the Editor, in *Nation and Athenaeum*, 1927, vol. 40, pp. 655-6.

Alléhaut, Maurice, *Les libertés dans les pays rhénans pendant l'occupation* (Paris, 1925).

Allen, Henry Tureman, *My Rhineland Journal* (Boston, 1923).

——*The Rhineland Occupation* (Indianapolis, 1927).

Allgemeiner Kongress . . .—Zentralrat der sozialistischen Republik Deutschlands, Allgemeiner Kongress der Arbeiter- und Soldatenräte Deutschlands vom 16. bis 21. Dezember 1918 im Abgeordnetenhause zu Berlin, *Stenographische Berichte* (Berlin, 1919).

American Journal of International Law—Commission on the Responsibility of the Authors of the War and on Enforcement of Penalties, 'Report Presented to the Preliminary Peace Conference,' in *American Journal of International Law*, 1920, vol. 14, pp. 95-154.

Annual Digest of Public International Law Cases, ed. by H. Lauterpacht and John Fischer Williams (London, 1919-).

Apex, *The Uneasy Triangle*, Four Years of Occupation as seen by 'Apex' (London, 1931).

Armistice Agreement—Armistice Convention with Germany of November 11, 1918, and Conventions Prolonging the Armistice, in United States, *Treaties* . . . (q.v.), vol. 3, pp. 3307-29.

Aulneau, Joseph, *Le Rhin et la France* (Paris, 1921).

Baker, Ray Stannard, *Woodrow Wilson and the Peace Settlement*, 3 vols. (New York, 1922).

Bane, Suda Lorena, and Lutz, Ralph Haswell, eds., *The Blockade of Germany after the Armistice* 1918-1919, Selected Documents of the Supreme Economic Council, Superior Blockade Council, American Relief Administration and other Wartime Organizations (Stanford University, California, 1942).

Barrès, Maurice, *Les grands problèmes du Rhin* (Paris, 1930).

Baty, Thomas, 'The Relations of Invaders to Insurgents,' in *Yale Law Journal*, 1927, vol. 36, pp. 966-84.

Bayrischer Staatskommissar für die Pfalz, *Die Pfalz unter französischer Besetzung* (Munich, 1925).

Bilfinger, 'Die Geltung deutscher Gesetze im besetzten Gebiet,' in *Deutsche Juristen-Zeitung*, 1927, vol. 32, pp. 567-71.

Blondel, Georges, *La Rhénanie, son passé, son avenir* (Paris, 1921).

——'L'importance économique et financière de la question du Rhin,' in *La Rhénanie* (Conférences organisées par la Société des anciens Élèves et Élèves de l'École libre des Sciences Politiques), pp. 95-112 (Paris, 1922).

Boas, George, 'Human Relations in Military Government,' in *Public Opinion Quarterly*, 1943, vol. 7, pp. 542-54.

Boyer, Pierre, *De la législation par voie d'arrêtés et des tribunaux chargés de l'appliquer établis en Palatinat par l'armée française d'occupation, 1918-1919* (Toulouse, 1920).

Brugger, Ph., 'Besetzte Rheinische Gebiete,' in *Staatslexikon*, Im Auftrag der Görres-Gesellschaft unter Mitwirkung zahlreicher Fachleute, 5th ed., vol. 1 (1926), pp. 828-45.

Bruns, Victor, ed., *Fontes Juris Gentium*, Series A, Sectio II, Tomus I, Die Entscheidungen des Reichsgerichts in völkerrechtlichen Fragen (Berlin, 1931).

Cadoux, Gaston, 'Un Magnat de la Sarre Hermann Röchling,' in *Revue politique et parlementaire*, 1923, vol. 116, pp. 454-62.

Carles, Jacques, 'L'occupation interalliée des provinces du Rhin,' in *L'Opinion*, 1920, vol. 13, pp. 300-303, 326-8, 357.

Carr, E. H., *International Relations since the Peace Treaties* (London, 1940).

Cavaré, L., 'Quelques notions générales sur l'occupation pacifique. Étude particulière de l'occupation de Haute-Silésie,' in *Revue générale du droit international public*, 1924, vol. 31, pp. 339-71.

Colby, Elbridge, 'Occupation under the Laws of War,' in *Columbia Law Review*, 1925, vol. 25, pp. 904-22, and 1926, vol. 26, pp. 146-70.

'Coloured Troops in the Occupied Provinces,' in *New Statesman*, 1921, vol. 17, pp. 353-4.

Cornier, Claude, *Le statut de l'occupation rhénane interalliée. 11 novembre 1918-30 juin 1930* (Lyon, 1934).

Dalloz, *Jurisprudence générale*, Recueil périodique et critique de jurisprudence, de législation et de doctrine en matière civile, commerciale, criminelle, administrative et de droit public (Paris, 1825-   ).

Dariac, Adrien Louis, *The Dariac Report. Ruhr, Rhineland and Saar*, The full Text of the secret Report on the Ruhr, the Rhineland and the Saar Territory, Presented in 1922 to the French Government (Manchester, 1923).

De Jaer, B., *L'armée belge d'occupation et son droit de juridiction* (Liége, 1928).

De Pange, Jean, 'Notre politique rhénane,' in *Le correspondant*, 1921, vol. 285, pp. 193-223.

De Visscher, Charles, 'L'occupation de guerre,' in *Law Quarterly Review*, 1918, vol. 34, pp. 72-81.

Der Waffenstillstand—Deutsche Waffenstillstandskommission, *Der Waffenstillstand 1819-1919*, Das Dokumentenmaterial der Waffenstillstands-

Verhandlungen von Compiègne, Spa, Trier und Brüssel, 3 vols. (Berlin, 1928).

DJZ—*Deutsche Juristen-Zeitung* (Berlin, 1896-   ).

Dokumente . . .—See Reichsministerium für die besetzten Gebiete.

Dorten, Hans A., 'The Rhineland Movement,' in *Foreign Affairs*, 1925, vol. 3, pp. 399-410.

Feilchenfeld, Ernst H., *The International Economic Law of Belligerent Occupation*, Monograph Series of the Carnegie Endowment for International Peace, Division of International Law, No. 6 (Washington, 1942).

Feilitsch, von, 'Der Fall Nathusius,' in *Deutsche Juristen-Zeitung*, 1924, vol. 29, pp. 971-3.

Finch, George A., 'The Costs of the American Army of Occupation on the Rhine,' Editorial Comment in *American Journal of International Law*, 1923, vol. 17, pp. 513-17.

—— 'Jurisdiction of Local Courts to Try Enemy Persons for War Crimes,' Editorial Comment in *American Journal of International Law*, 1920, vol. 14, pp. 218-23.

—— 'Retribution of War Crimes,' Editorial Comment in *American Journal of International Law*, 1943, vol. 37, pp. 81-8.

Fleiner, Fritz, *Institutionen des deutschen Verwaltungsrechts*, 8th ed. (Tübingen, 1928).

Foreign Relations . . . 1922—See U. S. Department of State.

Fraenkel, Ernst, *The Dual State*, A Contribution to the Theory of Dictatorship (New York and London, 1941).

Friedrich, Carl J., 'Military Government as a Step Toward Self-Rule,' in *Public Opinion Quarterly*, 1943, vol. 7, pp. 527-41.

Gannett, Lewis S., 'Those Black Troops on the Rhine—and the White,' in New York *Nation*, 1921, vol. 112, pp. 733-4.

Garner, James Wilford, 'Contributions, Requisitions, and Compulsory Service in Occupied Territory,' in *American Journal of International Law*, 1917, vol. 11, pp. 74-112.

—— *The German War Code*, A Comparison of the German Manual of the Laws of War with those of the United States, Great Britain, France, and with the Hague Convention Respecting the Laws and Customs of War on Land (Urbana, Ill., 1918).

—— *International Law and the World War*, 2 vols. (London, 1920).

—— *Recent Developments in International Law* (Calcutta, 1925).

Gazette—See Inter-Allied Rhineland High Commission.

Gedye, G. E. R., 'La Justice Militaire,' in *Nation and Athenaeum*, 1927, vol. 40, pp. 555-6.

—— *The Revolver Republic*, France's Bid for the Rhine (London, 1930).

Gerbaulet, 'Bestrafung von Kriegsgefangenen wegen vor der Gefangennahme im Auslande begangener Straftaten?' in *Deutsche Juristen-Zeitung*, 1916, vol. 21, pp. 184-8.

Giese, Friedrich, 'Der Reichskommissar für die besetzten rheinischen Gebiete. Eine kritische Anregung,' in *Zeitschrift für Völkerrecht*, 1923, vol. 12, pp. 447-59.

Grimm, Friedrich, 'Das Gefangenenproblem und die Lüge vom schuldhaft geführten Krieg,' in *Deutsche Juristen-Zeitung*, 1925, vol. 30, pp. 58-64.

Grünfeld, Ernst, *Die deutsche Aussenhandelskontrolle (die Politik der Sperren) vom Kriegsausbruch bis zum Inkrafttreten des Friedensvertrages*, Bonner staatswissenschaftliche Untersuchungen, No. 2 (Bonn, 1922).

Hackworth, Green Haywood, *Digest of International Law*, vol. 6 (Washington, 1943).

Hague Convention—Convention Respecting the Laws and Customs of War on Land, of October 18, 1907, in United States, *Treaties . . .* (q.v.), vol. 2, pp. 2269-90.

Hamilton, Walton H., and Rodee, Carlton C., 'Police Power,' in *Encyclopaedia of the Social Sciences*, ed. by E. R. A. Seligman and Alvin Johnson, vol. 12 (New York, 1934), pp. 190-93.

Harden, Maximilian, 'Wehmütterhäublein,' in *Zukunft*, 1920, vol. 109, pp. 293-302.

Haushofer, Karl, 'Die geopolitische Tragweite der Rheinfrage,' in *Deutsche Rundschau*, 1922, vol. 48, pp. 113-19.

Heyland, Karl, 'Besetzungsrecht,' in *Handwörterbuch der Rechtswissenschaft*, ed. by Fritz Stier-Somlo and Alexander Elster, vol. 1 (Berlin and Leipzig, 1926), pp. 677-87.

—— *Die Rechtsstellung der besetzten Rheinlande nach dem Versailler Friedensvertrag und dem Rheinlandsabkommen*, zugleich ein Beitrag zur Lehre von der Besetzung fremden Staatsgebietes, Handbuch des Völkerrechts, vol. 2, sect. 7 (Stuttgart, 1923).

—— Note on coal-tax decision of December 7, 1926, in *Juristische Wochenschrift*, 1927, vol. 56, pp. 2330-35.

—— 'Occupatio bellica,' in *Wörterbuch des Völkerrechts und der Diplomatie*, ed. by Karl Strupp, vol. 2 (Berlin and Leipzig, 1925), pp. 154-71.

—— 'Zur Lehre vom Verordnungsrecht der Interallierten Rheinlandkommission,' in *Zeitschrift für Völkerrecht*, 1922, vol. 12, pp. 44-64.

Hill, David, 'The Rights of the Civil Population in Territory Occupied by a Belligerent,' Editorial Comment in *American Journal of International Law*, 1917, vol. 11, pp. 133-7.

Hippel, R. von, 'Strafverfolgung deutscher Fabrikanten in dem von Frankreich und Belgien besetzten linksrheinischen Gebiet,' in *Niemeyers Zeitschrift für internationales Recht*, 1920, vol. 28, pp. 183-206.

Hitchcock, Gilbert M., in *Congressional Record*, Sixty-Seventh Congress, Second Session, vol. 62, part 12.

Hue de Grais, *Handbuch der Verfassung und Verwaltung in Preussen und dem deutschen Reiche*, 24th ed. (Berlin, 1927).

Huguet, Pierre, *Le droit pénal de la Rhénanie occupée* (Paris, 1923).

Hunt, I. L., *American Military Government of Occupied Germany* 1918-1920, Report of the Officer in Charge of Civil Affairs, Third Army and American Forces in Germany (mimeographed ed., Coblenz, 1920; printed ed., Washington, 1943). Text references are to the mimeographed edition.

H. W. M., 'The French War on Germany,' in *Nation and Athenaeum*, 1922, vol. 31, pp. 644-6.

Inter-Allied Rhineland High Commission, *Bulletin officiel. Official Gazette*, 1920-28.
—— *Recueil des ordonnances, instructions et décisions*, 2 vols. (Mayence, 1923, 1929).
Ireton, Robert E., 'The Rhineland Commission at Work,' in *American Journal of International Law*, 1923, vol. 17, pp. 460-69.
Isambert, André, 'Les provinces du Rhin pendant l'armistice,' in *Revue des sciences politiques*, 1919, vol. 42, pp. 426-45.

Jacquot, Paul, *General Gérard und die Pfalz* (Berlin, 1920), translated from the French. Text reference is to the German edition.
JW—*Juristische Wochenschrift* (Berlin, 1872-1939).

Kahn, Ernst, *Zwischen Waffenstillstand und Frieden. Ein wirtschaftlicher Rückblick und Ausblick* (Frankfurt am Main, 1920).
Kelsen, Hans, 'Collective and Individual Responsibility in International Law, with Particular Regard to the Punishment of War Criminals,' in *California Law Review*, 1943, vol. 31, pp. 530-71.
Keynes, John Maynard, *A Revision of the Treaty* (London, 1922).
Kirchenheim, Arthur von, 'Kriegsgefangene,' in *Wörterbuch des Völkerrechts und der Diplomatie*, ed. by Karl Strupp, vol. 1, pp. 743-9 (Berlin and Leipzig, 1924).
Köhler, Ludwig von, *Die Staatsverwaltung der besetzten Gebiete*, vol. 1, Belgien, Wirtschafts- und Sozialgeschichte des Weltkrieges, Deutsche Serie, Veröffentlichung der Carnegie-Stiftung für internationalen Frieden, Abteilung für Volkswirtschaft und Geschichte (Stuttgart and New Haven, 1927).
Kraus, Herbert, and Rödiger, Gustav, *Urkunden zum Friedensvertrag von Versailles vom 28. Juni 1919*, 2 vols. (Berlin, 1920-21).

'La France sur le Rhin,' in *Revue des deux mondes:* 1. 'La leçon du passé,' 1928, année 98, vol. 48, pp. 762-97; 11. 'L'occupation,' 1929, année 99, vol. 49, pp. 112-39; 111. 'La leçon du présent,' 1929, année 99, vol. 49, pp. 372-400.
Lauterpacht, H., Review of Feilchenfeld, in *Law Quarterly Review*, 1944, vol. 60, p. 95.
Lebaud, 'Why Germany is Nationalist' (From *Progrès civique*, 6, 13, 20, and 27 February 1926), in *Living Age*, 1926, vol. 329, pp. 188-99 and 250-54.
Le Trocquer, Yves, 'Les chemins de fer en Allemagne occupée et la paix,' in *Revue des deux mondes*, 1925, année 95, vol. 27, pp. 269-88.
Liggett, Hunter, *Commanding an American Army. Recollections of the World War* (Boston, 1925).
Lloyd George, David, *Memoirs of the Peace Conference*, 2 vols. (New Haven, 1939).

Malaurie, Albert, 'Une année en Rhénanie,' in *Revue des deux mondes*, 1920, année 90, vol. 60, pp. 96-127.

Manner, George, 'The Legal Nature and Punishment of Criminal Acts of Violence Contrary to the Laws of War,' in *American Journal of International Law*, 1943, vol. 37, pp. 407-35.

Mende, Helmuth, 'Deutsche Militärrechtspflege im besetzten feindlichen Gebiet unter besonderer Berücksichtigung Belgiens,' in *Der Gerichtssaal*, 1919, vol. 86, pp. 207-28.

Mérignhac, A., 'De la sanction des infractions au droit des gens commises, au cours de la guerre européenne, par les empires du centre,' in *Revue générale de droit international public*, 1917, vol. 24, pp. 5-56.

Meurer, Christian, *Die völkerrechtliche Stellung der vom Feind besetzten Gebiete* (Tübingen, 1915).

Meyer-Anschütz—*Lehrbuch des deutschen Staatsrechts*, by Georg Meyer, 7th ed., ed. by Gerhard Anschütz, 3 vols. (Munich, 1914-19).

Miller, David Hunter, *My Diary at the Peace Conference*, 21 vols. (New York, 1924).

Moore, John Bassett, *A Digest of International Law* . . . , 8 vols. (Washington, 1906).

Mordacq, H., *La mentalité allemande. Cinq ans de commandement sur le Rhin* (Paris, 1926).

—— 'L'évacuation anticipée de la Rhénanie,' in *Revue des deux mondes*, 1929, année 99, vol. 51, pp. 761-75.

Morstein-Marx, Fritz, 'Comparative Administrative Law: Exercise of Police Power,' in *University of Pennsylvania Law Review*, 1941, vol. 90, pp. 266-91.

Nast, Marcel, 'De la compétence législative de la Haute-Commission Interalliée dans les provinces du Rhin,' in *Revue de droit international et de législation comparée*, 1922, année 49, vol. 3, series 3, pp. 273-99.

—— 'De la situation juridique en territoire allemand occupé des militaires de l'armée française du Rhin,' in *Revue de droit international privé et de droit pénal international*, 1920, vol. 16, pp. 376-407.

——'Les sanctions pénales de l'enlèvement par les Allemands du matériel industriel en territoires français et belges occupés par leurs troupes,' in *Revue générale de droit international public*, 1919, vol. 26, pp. 111-28.

—— 'L'occupation des territoires rhénans par les troupes des alliés et des États-Unis pendant l'armistice,' in *Revue générale de droit international public*, 1921, vol. 28, pp. 139-59.

—— Note on Florange-Chamayou decision of August 10, 1922, in Dalloz, *Jurisprudence générale*, 1923, Part 1, pp. 121-4.

Nationalversammlung—*Verhandlungen der verfassunggebenden Deutschen Nationalversammlung* 1919-1920, Stenographische Berichte.

Nelz, 'Die Verordnungen der Interallierten Rheinlandkommission,' in *Deutsche Juristen-Zeitung*, 1920, vol. 25, pp. 245-51.

Niboyet, J. P., 'L'occupation du Palatinat durant l'armistice,' in *Revue de droit international privé et de droit pénal international*, 1920, vol. 16, pp. 46-57.

Noyes, Pierrepont B., *While Europe Waits for Peace. Describing the Progress of Economic and Political Demoralization in Europe During the Years of American Hesitation* (New York, 1921).

Oncken, Hermann, 'Die Franzosen in der Pfalz,' in *Preussische Jahrbücher,* 1920, vol. 179, pp. 359-82.

Oppenheim, Lassa, *International Law, A Treatise,* vol. 1, 4th ed., ed. by A. McNair (London, 1928); vol. 2, 6th ed., ed. by A. Lauterpacht (New York, 1940).

Ordinances of the High Commission—*See* Inter-Allied Rhineland High Commission, *Gazette,* of relevant year.

Paris Peace Conference—*See* U. S. Department of State.

Pasicrisie belge, Recueil général de jurisprudence des cours de Belgique en matière civile, commerciale, criminelle et administrative (Brussels, 1841-).

Petersens, Ludvig af, 'In den besetzten Gebieten am Rhein und der Saar,' in *Deutsche Rundschau,* 1922, vol. 193, pp. 12-28.

Pinon, René, 'Le Rhin libre,' in *Revue des deux mondes,* 1920, année 90, vol. 55, pp. 775-810.

Preussischer Landtag—*Sitzungsberichte des Preussischen Landtags,* I.Wahlperiode, 1921-4.

Preussisches Statistisches Landesamt, *Besetzte Gebiete Deutschlands* (Berlin, 1925).

RAG (Reichsarbeitsgericht)—*Entscheidungen des Reichsarbeitsgerichts,* Herausgegeben von Mitgliedern des Gerichtshofes (Berlin, 1928-).

Rathenau, Walther, *Deutschlands Rohstoffversorgung* (Berlin, 1917).

Recueil . . .—*See* Inter-Allied Rhineland High Commission.

Reichsministerium für die besetzten Gebiete, *Dokumente zur Besetzung der Rheinlande:* Heft I, Die politischen Ordonnanzen der Interallierten Rheinlandkommission in Coblenz (über Presse, Vereine, Versammlungen usw.) und ihre Anwendung in den Jahren 1920-1924; Heft II, Eingriffe der Besatzungsbehörden in die Rechtspflege im besetzten Rheinland; Heft III, Urkunden zum Separatistenputsch im Rheinland im Herbst 1923 (Berlin, 1925).

—— *Liste der von der Interallierten Rheinlandkommission in Coblenz für das besetzte Gebiet verbotenen Bücher, Lichtbildstreifen und Zeitungen* (Berlin, 1925).

Reichstag—*Verhandlungen des Reichstags,* I.Wahlperiode, 1920-24, vols. 345, 357, 358, Stenographische Berichte; vol. 376, Anlage zu den stenographischen Berichten.

Reismüller, Georg, and Hofmann, Josef, *Zehn Jahre Rheinlandbesetzung,* Beschreibendes Verzeichnis des Schrifttums über die Westfragen mit Einschluss des Saargebietes und Eupen-Malmedies (Breslau, 1929).

Réponse de Versailles—Reply of July 29, 1919, to the German note regarding the occupation of the left bank of the Rhine, in Kraus and Rödiger (q.v.), vol. 2, pp. 1113-23.

Reynolds, B. T., *Prelude to Hitler,* A Personal Record of Ten Postwar Years in Germany (London, 1933).

RFH (Reichsfinanzhof)—*Sammlung der Entscheidungen und Gutachten des Reichsfinanzhofs*, Herausgegeben vom Reichsfinanzhof (Munich, 1920-).

RGSt (Reichsgericht Strafsachen)—*Entscheidungen des Reichsgerichts in Strafsachen*, Herausgegeben von Mitgliedern des Gerichtshofes und der Reichsanwaltschaft (Berlin, 1880-).

RGZ (Reichsgericht Zivilsachen)—*Entscheidungen des Reichsgerichts in Zivilsachen*, Herausgegeben von Mitgliedern des Gerichtshofes und der Reichsanwaltschaft (Berlin, 1880-).

Rhineland Agreement—Agreement between the United States of America, Belgium, the British Empire and France, of the one part, and Germany, of the other part, with regard to the military occupation of the territories of the Rhine, of 28th June 1919, in *Gazette* (q.v.), 1920, No. 1, pp. 5-15.

Rhodes, James Ford, *History of the United States from the Compromise in 1850*, 7 vols. (New York, 1902-7).

Robin, Raymond, *Des occupations militaires en dehors des occupations de guerre (étude d'histoire diplomatique et de droit international)* (Paris, 1913).

Rousseau, Jean, *La Haute Commission Interalliée des Territoires Rhénans, ses origines, son organisation, ses attributions*. Étude publiée sous le patronage du Haut Commissariat Français dans les provinces du Rhin (Mayence, 1923).

—— 'Le régime juridictionnel de l'occupation alliée en Rhénanie,' in *Journal du droit international*, 1923, vol. 50, pp. 805-17.

Roux, J.-A., Note on Florange-Chamayou decision of August 10, 1922, in Sirey, *Recueil général* . . . 1924, Part 1, pp. 89-91.

RWG (Reichswirtschaftsgericht)—*Entscheidungen des Reichswirtschaftsgerichts*, Herausgegeben von Mitgliedern des Gerichtshofes (Berlin, 1923-4).

Schmitt, Carl, *Die Rheinlande als Objekt internationaler Politik*, Flugschriften der Rheinischen Zentrumspartei, series 2, no. 4 (Cologne, 1925).

Schmitz, Joseph, 'Eine neue Einmischung der Rheinlandkommission in die sozialen Verhältnisse des besetzten Gebietes,' in *Rheinischer Beobachter*, 1922, pp. 312-13.

Schneidewin, Wolfgang, *The Burden of Military Occupation in the Rhineland*, Representative Cases and Statistics Compiled from the Memoranda of the German Ministry of Finance (Leipzig, 1923).

Schücking, Levin L., 'France, Germany and the Occupation of the Rhineland,' in *New Statesman*, 1922, vol. 18, pp. 467-9.

Schwarz, Arnold Richard, *Die deutsche Ausfuhrkontrolle nach dem Kriege*, Greifswalder staatswissenschaftliche Abhandlungen No. 21 (Greifswald, 1923).

Schweisguth, 'L'administration militaire des pays rhénans sous le régime de l'armistice,' in *Revue des deux mondes*, 1924, année 94, vol. 23, pp. 94-116 and 303-18.

Sevestre, Norbert, 'Une campagne de propagande allemande. "La honte noire,"' in *Revue des deux mondes*, 1921, année 91, vol. 65, pp. 417-33.

Silberschmidt, 'Über die Geltung deutscher Gesetze im besetzten rheinischen Gebiet,' in *Rheinische Zeitschrift für Zivil- und Prozessrecht,* 1923, vol. 12, pp. 211-15.

Sirey, J.-B., *Recueil général des lois et des arrêts,* Journal du palais, Pandectes françaises périodiques (Paris, 1791-   ).

Stauffenberg, 'Vertragliche Beziehungen des Okkupanten zu den Landeseinwohnern,' in *Zeitschrift für öffentliches Recht und Völkerrecht,* 1930-31, vol. 12, pp. 86-119.

StPO—*Strafprozessordnung für das deutsche Reich.*

Strobel, Rudolf, *Sanktionen und Rheinzollinie,* Eine politischwirtschaftliche Studie (Munich, 1922).

Strupp, Karl, 'Das Waffenstillstandsabkommen zwischen Deutschland und der Entente vom 11. November 1918 im Lichte des Völkerrechts,' in *Zeitschrift für Völkerrecht,* 1920, vol. 11, pp. 252-81.

—— 'Gegenwartsfragen des Völkerrechts,' in *Niemeyers Zeitschrift für internationales Recht,* 1915, vol. 25, pp. 339-82.

Tardieu, André, *The Truth about the Treaty* (Indianapolis, 1921).

Temperley, H. W. V., ed., *A History of the Peace Conference of Paris,* 6 vols., published under the auspices of the Institute of International Affairs (London, 1920-24).

Thiallet, Francis, *La Haute Commission Interalliée des Territoires Rhénans et la conciliation des conflits collectifs du travail* (Coulommiers, 1928).

Tirard, Paul, *La France sur le Rhin,* Douze années d'occupation rhénane (Paris, 1930).

Tuohy, Ferdinand, 'France's Rhineland Adventure,' in *Contemporary Review,* 1930, vol. 138, pp. 29-38.

—— *Occupied,* 1918-1930. *A Postscript to the Western Front* (London, 1931).

Tynan, Katherine, *Life in the Occupied Area* (London, 1925).

United States, *Treaties, Conventions, International Acts, Protocols and Agreements between the United States of America and other Powers* 1776-1937, 4 vols. (Washington, 1910-38).

U. S. Department of State, *Papers Relating to the Foreign Relations of the United States,* 1919-1920, *Paris Peace Conference,* 4 vols. (Washington, 1935-43).

—— *Papers Relating to the Foreign Relations of the United States,* 1922, 2 vols. (Washington, 1938).

Vanard, M. R., 'L'occupation des territoires rhénans. La juridiction civile des tribunaux allemands en territoire occupé,' in *Revue de droit international privé,* 1924, vol. 19, pp. 204-16.

Verdross, Alfred von, *Die völkerrechtswidrige Kriegshandlung und der Strafanspruch der Staaten* (Berlin, 1920).

Versailles treaty—Treaty of Peace between the Allied and Associated Powers and Germany of June 28, 1919, in United States, *Treaties . . .* (q.v.), vol. 3, pp. 3329-524.

Vogels, H., and Vogels, W., *Das Rheinlandabkommen sowie die Verord-*

nungen der Hohen Kommission in Coblenz, Dreisprachige Textausgabe (Bonn, 1920).

Vogels, Werner, *Die Bestimmungen der Interallierten Rheinlandoberkommission und der Besatzungsarmeen über Einquartierung, Requisitionen und Schäden* (Berlin, 1925).

——'Die Organe der Allierten im besetzten Rheinland,' in *Preussisches Verwaltungsblatt*, 1921, vol. 42, pp. 413-15.

Wachendorf, Karl, *Zehn Jahre Fremdherrschaft am deutschen Rhein*, Eine Geschichte der Rheinlandbesetzung von 1918-1928, Rheinische Schicksalsfragen, No. 22-24 (Berlin, 1928).

Wunderlich, Georg, *Der Belgische Justizstreik, insbesondere die deutschen Staatsanwaltschaften in Belgien* (Berlin, 1930).

Zitelmann, Ernst, 'Zwischenprivatrecht im besetzten Gebiet,' in *Festgabe für Otto Liebmann*, pp. 128-36 (Berlin, 1920).

ZPO—*Zivilprozessordnung für das Deutsche Reich.*

TABLE OF CASES

AMERICAN CASES

United States Supreme Court

McCulloch *v.* Maryland (1819) 17 U.S. 316, pp. 220-21
Coleman *v.* Tennessee (1878) 97 U.S. 509, pp. 47, 66
Dow *v.* Johnson (1879) 100 U.S. 158, pp. 49-50
Freeland *v.* Williams (1889) 131 U.S. 405, p. 50

BELGIAN CASES

Belgian Supreme Court (Cour de Cassation)

Procureur *v.* Marteaux (1916) 1916, *International Law News*, 136, p. 208 n.
Société Semal *v.* Piérard (1917) *Pasc. belge*, 1917, I, 241, p. 208 n.
In re Gebhardt (1919) *Pasc. belge*, 1920, I, 10, p. 57
In re Norz (1919) *Pasc. belge*, 1920, I, 7, pp. 57-8
In re Bockstegen (1920) *Pasc. belge*, 1920, I, 104, pp. 56-7
In re Kauhlen (1920) *Pasc. belge*, 1921, I, 100, p. 57
In re Hermann (1920) *Pasc. belge*, 1921, I, 84, p. 58

Belgian Appelate Courts

Brussels Cour d'Appel

19 July 1915—1915, *International Law News*, 55, p. 208 n.
26 January 1920—47, *Journal du droit international*, 732, pp. 192-3

Liége Cour d'Appel

31 May 1915—1915, *International Law News*, 56, p. 208 n.
13 February 1917—44, *Journal du droit international*, 1813, p. 208 n.

FRENCH CASES

French Supreme Court (Cour de Cassation)

In re Florange et Chamayou (1922) Dalloz, 1923, Part I, p. 124, pp. 197-8
In re Thyssen (1923) Sirey, 1924, Part I, p. 92, p. 201
In re Krupp (1923) Sirey, 1924, Part I, p. 93, p. 201
Conseil de Revision de l'Armée du Rhin, 10 July 1924—53, *Journal du droit international*, 649, p. 163 n.

GERMAN CASES

German Supreme Court (Reichsgericht)

26 July 1915—21 DJZ (1916) 134, p. 187
22 March 1917—46 J.W. (1917) 721, p. 187

23 February 1920—54 RGSt 139, pp. 164, 184

25 October 1920—Bruns 575-578, pp. 184-6 (Uhlmann Case)

2 November 1920—55 RGSt 109, p. 85

19 April 1921—102 RGZ 106, pp. 213-14

26 April 1921—Bruns 299, p. 155

10 May 1921—50 JW (1921) 1454, p. 215

7 June 1921—102 RGZ 255, p. 215 n.

29 September 1921—56 RGSt 194, pp. 86, 87, 186

24 October 1921—56 RGSt 196, p. 196

25 November 1921—52 JW (1923) 184, p. 23

28 November 1921—103 RGZ 231, p. 187

2 February 1922—104 RGZ 105, p. 215 n.

7 March 1922—56 RGSt 288, pp. 186, 211

7 March 1922—104 RGZ 171, p. 137

22 September 1922—105 RGZ 179, p. 215 n.

1 November 1922—105 RGZ 326, p. 63

13 December 1922—52 JW (1923) 287, p. 215 n.

15 December 1922—106 RGZ 59, p. 86

2 May 1923—107 RGZ 173, p. 215

14 November 1923—107 RGZ 282, pp. 187-8

8 December 1923—107 RGZ 377, p. 208

29 September 1924—54 JW (1925) 138, p. 188

19 December 1924—59 RGSt 9, pp. 164-5

9 March 1929—58 JW (1929) 1594, p. 222

20 February 1930—64 RGSt 15, p. 162

German Supreme Labor Court (Reichsarbeitsgericht), 28 January 1931—7 RAG 301, p. 139

German Supreme Financial Court (Reichsfinanzhof), 7 December 1926—21 RFH 68, pp. 87, 218-19 (Coal-tax decision)

German Supreme Economic Court (Reichswirtschaftsgericht), 14 October 1922—1 RWG 364, pp. 174-5

Bavarian Supreme Court (Bayerisches Oberstes Landesgericht), 29 July 1922—12 *Rheinische Zeitschrift*, 211, p. 87 n.

Bavarian Supreme Administrative Court (Bayerischer Verwaltungsgerichtshof), 5 December 1928—*Annual Digest* (1927-8), 119, p. 87 n.

INDEX

Aachen, 7
Administrative sanctions, 24, 129, 134-5
Alcohol monopoly, 100-101
Alexander, Horace G., 161
Alimony proceedings, 148, 170-71, 174
Alléhaut, Maurice, 166, 178-9, 210-11
Allen, Henry Tureman, 11, 17, 20, 40-42, 54, 75, 79, 91, 94-5, 106, 108-10, 116, 141, 153, 202
Alsace-Lorraine, 40, 187-8
Amnesty, 52-3, 144, 156
Anschuetz, Gerhard, 195
Apex, 94-5, 106-7
Appeasement policy, 4, 31
Armistice Agreement:
  Art. 5, 8, 25-6
  Art. 6, 13, 52, 213
  Art. 7, 8
  Art. 27, 15
Arrests, 118, 175, 177-9, 181-2
Assessment Commissions, 139-40, 173-4
Aulnau, Joseph, 17, 21, 40, 98-9

Baden, 6, 45
Baker, Ray Stannard, 37, 74, 97
Bane, Suda L., 13, 20
Barrès, Maurice, 34, 107, 141
Basic Order 562 CR, 7, 8, 12, 184
Baty, Thomas, 31-2
Bavaria, 6-7, 112
Belgian zone of occupation, 7
Belgium, Rhineland policy, 5, 106, 144
Belligerent occupation, 183-8, 190, 192, 197, 199-200
Bilfinger, Carl, 218 n.
Billeting, 74, 108, 174, 193-4
Birkenfeld, 6
Blockade, 13, 15, 17-18, 20-21
Blondel, George, 18-19, 99, 104

Boards of Conciliation, 42, 76, 135-40
Boas, George, 143 n.
Boelitz, Otto, 124-5
Boycott, 20, 98-9, 103, 114, 141
Boyer, Pierre, 7, 9, 21, 184
Braun, Otto, 157
Brugger, Ph., 107
Bruns, Victor, 184, 210
Brussels Food Conference, 15
Brussels Industrial Sub-Committee, 62
Bullitt report, 33
Burkhard, Dr., 165

Cadoux, Gaston, 60
Carles, Jacques, 75, 80, 98
Carr, E. H., 6, 108, 161
Cartels, 20, 38-9, 73, 76-7, 98, 105
Catholic Party, 34, 115, 190
Censorship, 92, 94
Chambers of Commerce, 7, 20, 169
Charitable Institutions, 12
Churches, 7
Civil law, 23, 145, 166-71, 172-3, 214-17
Civil liberties, 9, 92, 130, 195, 204-5, 226, 231
Civil servants:
  appointment, 27, 120-25
  deportation, 27, 126, 129-31
  disciplinary proceedings, 120, 134-5
  dismissal, 27, 44, 120-21, 125-6, 129, 132
  high officials, 114
  petty officials, 37-8
  political officials, 26-7, 128
  promotion, 120
  replacement, 28
  technical officials, 131-5
  vested rights, 27, 128
Clemenceau, George, 72, 90
Clunet, Edouard, 51
Coblence, 6, 7, 37, 82, 93

261

Colby, Elbridge, 185 n.
Collaborationists, 103, 141-8, 154, 156-7
Collective agreements, 73, 76, 135, 139
Collective fines, 24
Cologne, 6, 7, 35-6, 119
Colored soldiers, 159-61
Commercial relations, 13, 15-21, 37-40, 97-105
Commission on the Responsibility of the Authors of the War and on Enforcement of Penalties, 54
Communists, 29
Condominium, 108, 228
Confiscation, 58-63, 118
Conflict of Laws, 171
Conseil de Justice de la Haute Commission, 172
Contract claims, 167-8, 171
Control over:
    administration, 8, 10, 12, 96-8, 121-3, 126
    alcohol monopoly, 100
    banks, 21
    cartels, 73-6
    courts, 21-2, 45-6, 84, 144-5
    custom offices, 40-41, 100
    economic enterprises, 21
    foreign trade agencies, 38-40, 100
    governmental powers, 84, 93
    legislation, 86
    local authorities, 25, 94
    public utilities, 131-5
Contrôleur général, 10
Cornier, Claude, 23-4, 29, 40, 45, 114, 123
Council of Notables, 36
Courjou case, 51, 55
Courts, German, 7, 23, 42-6, 77, 152-3, 161-2, 168-71, 172
Craig, General, 37
Criminal law, 22-3, 145, 158, 166, 177
Crimes:
    occupation, 48-68
    political, 42-5, 52
    sexual, 159-61
Custom regulations, 37, 39, 97, 100, 101, 122, 125, 198, 201, 204
Cutting case, 61 n.

Dariac report, 123, 141
Darmstadt, 29, 89
Davis, John W., 28
Davis, Norman H., 97
De Jaer, B., 22-3, 56, 154, 163, 193
De Pange, Jean, 17, 40-41, 98, 101-2, 104, 105
De Visscher, Charles, 208 n.
Degoutte, General, 89, 178
Demobilization, 27-9, 30
Deportation, 24, 39, 41, 115, 129-31, 179
Derivative Jurisdiction, 152-3, 166
Diplomatic Notes:
    German Questionnaire of 12 July 1919, see Questionnaire
    Allied answer of 29 July 1919, see Réponse de Versailles
    German note of 7 August 1919, 77, 92, 133, 168, 173
    Allied answer of 14 October 1919, 77, 133-4
    German note of protest of 12 January 1920, see German note of protest
    Allied answer of 2 March 1920, see Note Millerand
Disciplinary procedures, 120, 134-5, 145-6
Dorten, Hans, 34, 117, 127, 148
Dorten Putsch, 34, 72, 75, 112
Double jeopardy, see Ne bis in idem
Drexel report, 33
Due process, 24, 122, 126, 128, 129-31, 226
Duisburg, 6, 31, 89, 100
Düsseldorf, 6, 31, 35, 89, 100

Ebert, Friedrich, 33, 157-8
Economic committee, 83, 97, 100
Economic questions, 13, 14, 83, 95, 97
Eight-hour day statute, 29, 135, 156
Empêchement absolu, 8, 188-9, 210
Employees, 138-41, 152-6
Emser Amt, 100, 102, 103, 105
England, Rhineland policy, 5-6, 106, 144
English, zone of occupation, 7
Erzberger, Mathias, 26, 52-3

Essen, 31

Exemptions from jurisdiction, 22-3, 140-41, 150, 152-6, 169-70, 171-2, 175

Extraterritoriality, 50, 51, 54, 64-7

Factory inspections, 42

Farquhar's report, 58

Fayolle, General, 29, 123

Feilchenfeld, Ernst, 185, 207

Files, 45, 123

Financial questions, 12, 13, 203

Finch, George A., 50, 53

Fleiner, Fritz, 84

Foch, Marshal, 7, 8, 9, 10, 14, 16, 22, 23, 24, 26, 36, 40, 43, 53, 62, 72, 75, 91, 132, 189

Food problems, 13-16, 28, 83

Foreign trade agencies, 16, 37-9, 97-100, 102-3, 105, 204, 215

Forgery, 193

Frankfurt, 89, 117

French Rhineland policy, 5-6, 16-17, 33, 71-2, 105-6, 144, 201

French zone of occupation, 7

Fresenius case, 90-91

Friedrich, Carl J., 229

Frisch, judge, 45

Froitzheim case, 119

Gannet, Louis, 160

Garner, James W., 58, 63, 65

Gedye, G. E. R., 34, 161

Gelsenkirchen, 31

Geneva Convention, 65-6

Gerbaulet, 51

German note of protest, 78, 92, 130, 151, 153, 155, 178, 192

German occupation of Belgium, 9, 21, 23-4, 43, 54-8, 60-63, 86

German occupation of France (1871-1873), 12, 73, 89, 112, 114-15; (1914-1918), 9, 21, 23-4, 54-5, 60-63, 187

Goebbels, Paul Joseph, 53 n.

Goering, Hermann, 160

Gottschalk, Max, 138

Grimm, Friedrich, 60

Grünfeld, Ernst, 19, 39, 40, 41

Hague Convention, 8-9, 60, 63, 65, 183-6, 188, 189, 192, 199, 207, 210, 214, 216

Harden, Maximilian, 160-61

Heinze, Dr., 211

Helmer, attorney, 51

Hesse, 6, 7, 29, 112

Hesse-Nassau, 6

Heyland, Karl, 78, 96, 150, 151, 185, 217, 218

High Commission Court, 169-70

High treason, 42-6, 117

Highways, 132, 134

Hippel, R. von, 60-63

Hirschfeld, Hans, 120

Hitchcock, Gilbert M., 160

Höchst, 7

Hoffmann, Adolf, 34

'Hole in the west,' 18-19, 21, 104, 144, 156

Hue de Grais, Robert, 119 n.

Huguet, Pierre, 200

Hunt, J. L., 11, 20, 32, 41-2, 53-4, 74, 143

Hüsgen, judge, 44

Implied powers, 193, 220-21

Independence of courts, 22, 43-5, 157-8, 166-7, 168, 217

Inflation, 18-19, 99, 110

Instruction 9, 88-9; 18, 138-40

Instructions, in general, 84, 93

Inter-Allied conflicts, 5-6, 71-2, 80, 99, 106-9, 160, 201, 228

Inter-Allied Railway Commission, 133-4

Inter-Allied Rhineland Commission, 14, 15, 16

Inter-Allied Rhineland High Commission:

American representative, 79

chairman, 82

civilian character, 77, 180

committees, 82-3

employees, 138-41

history, 15

internal organization, 81-3

jurisdiction, 189-206

and military authorities, 88-91

staff, 81-2

Interest theory, 196-203
International Bill of Rights, 205-6, 226
Ireton, Robert E., 40, 42, 85
Isambert, André, 17
Italy, 100

Jacquot, Paul, 36
Judicial review, 24, 78, 206-24
Jusserand, Ambassador, 33
Juveniles, 23, 152

Kahl, Wilhelm, 211
Kahn, Ernst, 19
Kehl, 6, 45
Kelsen, Hans, 219
Keynes, John M., 99
Kirchenheim, Arthur von, 51
Koch, Erich, 45, 130, 131, 191-2
Königswinter, 158
Korn case, 156
Kraus, Herbert, see Diplomatic Notes
Krefeld, 7

Labor conflicts, see Strikes
Labor questions, 41-2, 132-3, 135-41
Landespolizei, 118-20
Lansing, Robert, 54
Lauterpacht, H., 189
Lebaud, Colonel, 19
Leverkusen, 7
Liaison officers, 91-2, 94, 96
Lieber Instructions, 49, 66
Liggett, Hunter, 36, 37, 75, 107
Lloyd George, David, 72, 75
Local administration, see Municipalities
Local police, 118-20
Local representatives, 91-7, 122, 126, 137, 180
London Conference, 99, 100, 104, 200, 204
Looted machines, 21, 58-63, 203
Loucheur Committee, 75, 76, 131, 203
Ludendorff, Erich, 52
Ludwigshafen, 7
Lutz, Ralph H., 13, 20

Luxemburg, 10
Luxemburg Commission, 16, 17
Lynch justice, 48, 49

Mainz, 6, 20, 30
Malaurie, Albert, 98-9
Manner, George, 50
Mangin, General, 30, 75
Marshall, Chief Justice, 220-21
Martial law, 9, 24, 27, 39, 42-4, 73-5, 88-9, 114, 130, 131, 178-9, 199, 204, 226, 228-30
Meetings, 92, 94
Mende, Helmuth, 24 n.
Mérignac, A., 51, 52
Military administration, types of, 10-12
Military police, 175, 177-80
Military tribunals, 22, 56, 77, 149-54, 158-9, 161-4, 198-201
Millerand, Alexandre, see Note Millerand
Miller's Diaries, 72-3, 88
Mischbesetzung, 185, 187, 212, 214
Model Ordinances, 10
Momm case, 127-8, 202
Mordacq, General, 75, 90-91, 105-6, 107, 127
Morstein-Marx, Fritz, 214
Mülheim, 31
München-Gladbach, 7
Municipalities, 7, 35, 95, 118-19

Nast, Marcel, 23, 29, 61-2, 168, 185-6, 195-6, 198-9, 216
Nathusius von, 55
National Assembly, 28, 35
Nationalism, German, 115, 124, 146-7, 176, 223, 227, 228
Navigation, 132, 134, 136
Ne bis in idem, 56-7, 164-6
Netz, 192
Neuss, 7
Neuwied, 153
Newspapers, 92, 94
Niboyet, J. P., 23, 46
Note Millerand, 78, 151, 152, 178
Noyes, Pierrepont, 72, 74-5, 107, 120, 136 n., 197, 203

Occupatio bellica, see Belligerent occupation
Occupatio pacifica, see Pacific occupation
Occupied territory, 6-8
Oldenburg, 6, 112
Opel, 7
Oppenheim, Lassa, 50
Ordinances, in general, 82-6, 93, 113-14, 117, 120
  Ord. 1, 237-8; 78, 83, 87, 126, 129-30, 219-21
  Ord. 2, 238-45; 78, 53-84, 92, 117, 144, 149-55, 162-3, 165-6, 169, 177, 180-82
  Ord. 3, 245-6; 78, 84, 92, 150
  Ord. 4, 78
  Ord. 5, 246-7; 78, 136
  Ord. 6, 132, 134-5
  Ord. 15, 134
  Ord. 17, 134
  Ord. 29, 121-2, 126
  Ord. 33, 134
  Ord. 43, 155
  Ord. 44, 155
  Ord. 48, 117
  Ord. 49, 174
  Ord. 53, 136-7
  Ord. 54, 122-3
  Ord. 56, 162
  Ord. 59, 174
  Ord. 66, 163
  Ord. 78, 175
  Ord. 82, 102
  Ord. 84, 198, 200
  Ord. 86, 101
  Ord. 87, 103
  Ord. 88, 101
  Ord. 89, 101
  Ord. 90, 248; 103, 145, 147, 156
  Ord. 93, 84, 126
  Ord. 94, 155-6
  Ord. 98, 104
  Ord. 107, 137
  Ord. 120, 118
  Ord. 205, 123, 125
Ortspolizei, 118-20

Pacific occupation, 183, 185, 197, 199, 204

Palatinate, 6, 29, 34, 36, 46
Pardon, 166
Parliamentary representatives, 112
Perjury, 161-2
Pershing, General, 36
Petersens, Ludvig af, 108
Pillage, 51, 53, 55
Pinon, René, 112
Planned economy, 28, 38, 217
Police forces, 89, 118-20, 122, 125, 127, 176-8, 181-2, 195
Police power, 194-5, 205
Polizeipräsident, 118-19
Postal services, 101, 132, 136
Prisons, 92
Propaganda, German, 5, 18, 49, 160, 179-80
Prostitution, 143
Provost Courts, 22
Public health, 12
Public law cases, 171-5
Public order, 7-12, 191, 192, 194-6
Public utilities, 12, 76, 131-7

Questionnaire, 78, 91, 112, 121, 133, 154, 168

Railways, 101, 125, 132-6, 169-70, 203
Rathenau, Walther, 38, 109, 127
Raw materials, 15, 16, 28
Rechtsstaat, 176, 205
Reichskommissar, 92, 93, 102, 109-16, 118, 128, 145
Reine case, 165
Renault, Louis, 51
Réponse de Versailles, 78, 88, 91, 112, 113, 121, 154-5, 162-3, 168
Requisitions, 139-40, 174-5
Respondeat superior, 53-4, 59-60
Revolution, German, 4, 15, 16, 28, 214, 231
Reynolds, B. T., 3, 29
Rheinberg, 44
Rheinland province, 6, 35, 93
Rhenish industrialists, 60-62
Rhenish parliament, 141
Rhenish Republic, 37
Rhineland Agreement, 233-6
  characterization, 78, 96-7
  history, 72-6

Rhineland Agreement (Cont.)
interpretation, 192-7
ratification, 78-9
Art. 2, 77
Art. 3, 77, 85, 88, 149, 168, 175,
177, 190, 194, 198-200, 210, 217,
219, 220
Art. 4, 77, 149, 175
Art. 5, 77, 97, 116, 121, 126, 145,
166, 178
Art. 6, 77, 88, 174
Art. 7, 77
Art. 8, 77, 193-4
Art. 9, 77
Art. 10, 77, 88
Art. 11, 77, 88
Art. 12, 77, 88
Art. 13, 77, 88
Rhodes, James F., 67
Robin, Raymond, 12, 152, 181
Röchling, Hermann, Ludwig and
Robert, 59-60
Rödiger, Gustav, see Diplomatic
notes
Rolin, Belgian Commissioner, 202
Rousseau, Jean, 21, 82, 83, 94, 116,
153, 169, 171-3, 195, 197, 203, 204
Roux, J. A., 199-200
Rouzier case, 161

Saar Valley, 7
Saarbruck, 29
Sanctions, 99-100, 104, 200
Schleichhandel, 18-19
Schmitt, Carl, 108, 197
Schneidewin, Wolfgang, 80, 95
Schools, 7, 12, 83, 124-5
Schwarze Schmach, see Colored
soldiers
Schweisguth, Colonel, 30, 32, 33, 40,
95, 144
Scott, James B., 54
Sections de contrôle industriel, 20
Sections économiques, 17, 18, 20, 40,
41, 97, 104
Separation of powers, 84-5, 120, 121,
204, 205
Separatist movement, 34, 36-7, 43,
45-6, 106, 112, 123, 141-2, 156-8
Sevestre, Norbert, 160, 161

Sexual relations, 143-4
Skeleton plan, 74, 75, 80, 203
Smeets case, 156-8, 202
Social Democrats, 28, 29, 33, 115-16
Social Insurance, 140
Solingen, 7
Sollmann, Wilhelm, 109, 115
Spahn, Peter, 130, 189-90
Spartacists, see Communists
Starck, Reichskommissar von, 112,
114, 115
State of siege, see Martial law
Strikes, 34, 41-2, 76, 90, 132, 135-8
Strobel, Rudolf, 102, 142
Strupp, Karl, 185, 186, 212
Stuart, British Commissioner, 74
Supreme Economic Council, 14
Supreme War Council, 14, 72-4, 79,
104, 132
Swedish Christian Society, 159-60

Talleyrand, Prince de, 32
Telegraph services, 101, 132, 134
Telephone services, 101, 132, 134
Tesmar, 58
Thiallet, Francis, 42, 138
Tirard, Paul, 10, 13, 14, 93-5, 102,
115, 118, 141, 145, 153, 166, 169,
178, 195-6, 202
Total war, 13, 189, 217
Trade unions, 28, 34, 42, 127, 133
Trading with the Enemy Acts, 15-
17, 40
Transformation theory, 213, 219
Travel permits, 92
Triepel, Heinrich, 213, 217, 219
Tuohy, Ferdinand, 37, 102, 151 n.,
161, 163-4
Tynan, Katherine, 108

United States:
and collaborationists, 144
and German Labor, 42
and Germany, 108-9
and High Commission, 79
Rhineland policy, 5-6, 36, 37, 106
and separatists, 36-7
zone of occupation, 7

Vanard, M. R., 168-9
Verdross, Alfred, 52, 68

Versailles Treaty:
  Art. 51, 188
  Arts. 227-30, 47-56
  Art. 249, 173
  Arts. 428-32, 72
Veto power, 73, 87, 121-2, 136 n., 146, 173-4, 204, 220-21
Vogels, Werner, 78, 174 n., 181-2
Vogelsang case, 50, 55

Wachendorf, Karl, 17, 36, 102
War criminals, 46-68
War prisoners, 49, 50, 52, 54, 66-7
Weber, Max, 114

Weimar Constitution, 35, 89, 124, 208, 217, 219
Werber, state attorney, 45
Wiesbaden, 20, 23, 36, 75, 90-91, 119, 127
Wilson, Woodrow, 36, 71-2, 74-5, 97
Wilsonian principles, 4, 230
Wirz case, 67
Work councils, 133, 135, 136 n., 139
Workers' and Soldiers' Councils, 28, 29-34

Zitelmann, Ernst, 86
Zones of occupation, 6-7, 31